The Archaeology
of Mesopotamia

Ancient Mesopotamia (modern Iraq) was the original site of many of the major developments in human history, such as farming, the rise of urban literate societies and the first great empires of Akkad, Babylonia and Assyria.

The work of archaeologists is central to our understanding of Mesopotamia's past; this innovative volume evaluates the theories, methods, approaches and history of Mesopotamian archaeology from its origins in the nineteenth century up to the present day.

Dr Matthews places the discipline within its historical and social context, and explains how archaeologists conduct their research through excavation, survey and other methods. In four fundamental chapters, he uses illustrated case-stud' ' --- how archaeologists have approached central themes such a

- the shift from hunting to farming
- complex societies
- empires and imperialism
- everyday life

This is the only critical guide to the theory and method of Mesopotamian archaeology. It will be both an ideal introductory work and useful as background reading on a wide range of courses.

Roger Matthews was Director of the British Institutes of Archaeology in both Baghdad and Ankara. He has directed excavations and surveys in Iraq, Turkey and Syria, and currently lectures at the Institute of Archaeology, University College London. His recent publications include *The Early Prehistory of Mesopotamia* (2000).

Approaching the Ancient World

Epigraphic Evidence
Ancient History from Inscriptions
edited by John Bodel

Literary Texts and the Greek Historian
Christopher Pelling

Literary Texts and the Roman Historian
David S. Potter

Reading Papyri, Writing Ancient History
Roger S. Bagnall

Archaeology and the Bible
John Laughlin

Cuneiform Texts and the Writing of History
Marc Van De Mieroop

Ancient History from Coins
Christopher Howgego

The Sources of Roman Law
Problems and Methods for Ancient Historians
O. F. Robinson

The Uses of Greek Mythology
Ken Dowden

Arts, Artefacts, and Chronology in Classical Archaeology
William R. Biers

The Archaeology of Mesopotamia

Theories and approaches

Roger Matthews

LONDON AND NEW YORK

First published 2003
by Routledge
2 Park Square, Milton Park, Abingdon, Oxon, OX14 4RN

Simultaneously published in the USA and Canada
by Routledge
270 Madison Ave, New York, NY 10016

Reprinted 2003, 2004, 2006, 2007 (twice)

Routledge is an imprint of the Taylor & Francis Group, an informa business
© 2003 Roger Matthews

Typeset in Baskerville by Taylor & Francis Books Ltd
Printed and bound in Great Britain by TJ International Ltd,
Padstow, Cornwall

British Library Cataloguing in Publication Data
A catalogue record for this book is available from the British
Library

Library of Congress Cataloging in Publication Data
Matthews, Roger, Dr.
The archaeology of Mesopotamia : theories and approaches /
Roger Matthews.
(Approaching the ancient world)
Includes bibliographical references and index.
1. Iraq–Antiquities. 2. Excavations (Archaeology)–Iraq. 3.
Archaeology–Methodology. I. Title. II. Series.

DS69.5 .M37 2003
935'.001–dc21

2002068224

ISBN 978-0-415-25316-1 (hbk)
ISBN 978-0-415-25317-8 (pbk)

For Wendy
fellow traveller

Contents

List of illustrations   ix
Preface   xi
Acknowledgements   xiii

1 Defining a discipline: Mesopotamian
   archaeology in history   1
   A chequered past: origins and development 1
   Theories and approaches: culture history and anthropological
   *   archaeology 19*

2 Tools of the trade: scope and methods of
   Mesopotamian archaeology   27
   Things and ideas: approaches to archaeological research 27
   Excavating the past into the present 32
   Surveying for the past 7
   Archaeology and Assyriology 56
   Chronology of the Mesopotamian past 64

3 Tracking a transition: hunters becoming farmers   67
   Settling down 67
   Climate: something in the air 70
   Population: getting together 72
   Plants: a green revolution 74
   Animals: partners in clime 79
   People first and last 89

4 States of mind: approaching complexity   93
    The complexity of complexity 93
    Approaches to the study of social complexity 96
    Complexity in the fifth millennium BC: the Ubaid period 102
    Kings, captives and colonies: the Uruk phenomenon 108

5 Archaeologies of empire   127
    Empires in archaeology 127
    Empires in Mesopotamia and Mesopotamia in empires 132
    The imperial core 134
    Domination of peripheral polities 142
    At the edge of empires 146
    Empires in time and space: expansion, consolidation, collapse 147

6 People's pasts   155
    'Humble people who expect nothing' 155
    Cities 157
    Houses and households 169
    Town, country and nomad 182

7 Futures of the Mesopotamian past   189
    AD 2084: a vision 189
    Telling tales and painting pictures 190
    Mesopotamia in England AD 2002 193
    An uncertain future: transcending history? 198

    Bibliography   205
    Index   231

Illustrations

Tables

| 5.1 | Empires: characteristics and correlates | 129 |
| 5.2 | Mesopotamia and empires | 133 |

Figures

1.1	Map of Mesopotamia and environs	2
1.2	Borsippa, central south Iraq, mistakenly identified in the past as the Tower of Babylon	3
1.3	Telloh, south Iraq	10
1.4	Nippur, south Iraq	11
1.5	Aššur, north Iraq	13
1.6	Rescue archaeology. Excavations at Tell Mohammed ' Arab on the Tigris river	18
2.1	Excavating buildings of later-third-millennium BC date at Tell Brak	34
2.2	Building VI.A.10 at Çatalhöyük	36
2.3	Plan of surface architecture of the Neolithic period in the north area at Çatalhöyük	42
2.4	Regions where archaeological survey has been conducted in Iraq, northeast Syria and southeast Turkey	48
2.5	Intensive field-walking survey in north central Turkey, Project Paphlagonia	56
2.6	Patterns of residence through time in TA House 1 at Nippur, south Iraq	62
3.1	Plan of the early settlement at Hallan Çemi, southeast Turkey	83
3.2	Abu Hureyra, north central Syria. Large mammal bones from Trench B	85

3.3	Umm Dabaghiyah, northwest Iraq. Wall-painting depicting onagers and possible net-hooks	87
3.4	Umm Dabaghiyah, northwest Iraq. Composite plan of levels 3–4	87
4.1	Development of states through time in Mesopotamia	101
4.2	Eridu, south Iraq. Cultic building, temple VII	103
4.3	Tepe Gawra, north Iraq. Temple of level XIII	104
4.4	Uruk-Warka, south Iraq. Major structures of the fourth-millennium city	111
4.5	Najaf, central Iraq	112
4.6	Seal impressions from Uruk-Warka	113
5.1	Khorsabad, north Iraq. Plan of the city	137
5.2	Khorsabad. Plan of Sargon's palace	138
5.3	Samarra, central Iraq, imperial racecourse in cloverleaf plan	140
5.4	Tell Brak, northeast Syria. Hoard of silver, gold, lapis lazuli, carnelian and other items	151
6.1	Maškan-šapir, south Iraq. City plan	161
6.2	Abu Salabikh, south Iraq. Plan of the mounds	164
6.3	Abu Salabikh, south Iraq. Plan of Early Dynastic buildings	165
6.4	Tell Madhhur, east central Iraq. Distribution of small finds within the excavated house	171
6.5	Abu Salabikh, south Iraq. Plan of House H, Main Mound	173
6.6	Abu Salabikh, south Iraq. Adult and child burial within Early Dynastic house	177
6.7	Resources and production in terms of city/village/nomad interactions	184
7.1	Daur, central Iraq	203

Preface

Archaeologists spend much of their time attempting to capture the essence of a moment in time. In this book I intend to explore how we make our attempts by considering the theories, approaches and mechanisms that are the currency of Mesopotamian archaeology at the start of the twenty-first century AD, and through which we try our best to encapsulate the past for study in the present.

The need for a book such as this was confirmed as I read Marc Van De Mieroop's excellent study *Cuneiform Texts and the Writing of History*, in which the following sentence occurs: 'Methodological discussions of art history and archaeology with specific focus on ancient Mesopotamia are not available, but it is to be hoped that they will appear in the near future' (Van De Mieroop 1999a: 5). As a discipline, Mesopotamian and Southwest Asian archaeology has not been renowned for its critical awareness or self-reflexivity, but if this is a failing it is one that it shares with many other regional archaeologies of the world, for there are extremely few specifically methodological studies available in any field of modern archaeology.

In this volume I aim to explore the historical context of Mesopotamian archaeology, to consider its theoretical and methodological alignments, to investigate how archaeology is constructed and practised within the context of a series of major research arenas, and finally to speculate on some potential future directions of the discipline. As with all archaeology, the production of this book has been above all an exercise in sampling. Within each selected research issue, I have had to limit the coverage to a small proportion of the available subject matter, but in covering the so-called 'big issues' of the human past, for which Mesopotamian archaeology is uniquely suited, I hope to give some idea of the special nature of this wonderful discipline.

Acknowledgements

I owe thanks to several people who have helped with this volume in one way or another, but I should first stress that any faults or errors remaining are entirely my responsibility. For courteous assistance in libraries at the British Institute of Archaeology at Ankara, and the Institute of Archaeology, University College London, I am extremely grateful to, respectively, Yaprak Eran and Robert Kirby. For helpful comments and advice on several aspects I am very grateful to Bob Chapman and Wendy Matthews, both of the Department of Archaeology, University of Reading, as well as to three anonymous referees for useful suggestions. For advice and comment on sections of Chapter 7, my sincere gratitude goes to Sam Moorehead of the British Museum and to Harriet Martin. Hugh Alexander of the Public Record Office Image Library, Kew, provided invaluable assistance with regard to permissions for reproduction of aerial images held in their collections, and I thank him for that. I also thank Matthew Reynolds for his able assistance with illustrations used throughout this volume. Finally, my sincere thanks go to the staff at Routledge, particularly Richard Stoneman and Catherine Bousfield, for steering me and the book towards a productive meeting point.

Roger Matthews
London
11 June 2002

Chapter 1

Defining a discipline

Mesopotamian archaeology in history

A chequered past: origins and development

The history of Mesopotamian archaeology as a modern discipline is rooted in the entrepreneurial and colonial past of the Western powers. The story of modern Western involvement with Mesopotamia, as with other parts of the world, begins with sporadic encounters by enterprising traders and travellers pushing out their horizons and setting up initial and tentative lines of contact between vastly disparate worlds. Since the end of the Crusades in the Middle Ages, a largely disastrous engagement between the West and the East had been in abeyance, but with the widening of cultural, political and economic horizons attendant upon, initially, the Renaissance and then, more urgently, the Industrial Revolution in Western Europe and the consequent capitalist drive towards new resources and markets, a renewal of interactions became inevitable. Over the past two centuries or so, the nature of that renewed engagement has scarcely been less catastrophic than that of the Middle Ages, as is attested by at least one story a day in our newspapers, but one of the surviving waifs of that intercourse is indeed the modern study of the Mesopotamian past. In assessing the role and position of Mesopotamian archaeology within the contemporary world, however, let us try not to visit the sins of the parent upon the child, at least not without a full and fair hearing.

Where, then, in history can we assign the beginning of Mesopotamian archaeology? Does it begin with the long journey through the region in the later twelfth century of Rabbi Benjamin of Tudela, or with the Italian noble Pietro della Valle collecting a handful of bricks bearing cuneiform inscriptions from the ruins of Ur, Babylon and Borsippa, where he conducted some excavations, and returning with them in 1625 to Europe where his finds caused considerable interest (Invernizzi 2000)? Or do we see a start in the voyage of the Dane Carsten Niebuhr and

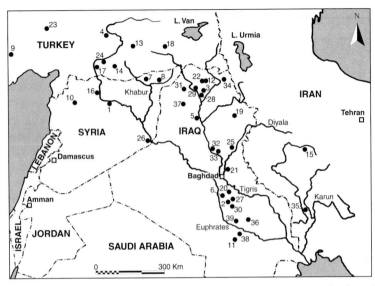

Figure 1.1 Map of Mesopotamia and environs, depicting location of selected sites mentioned in the text

Key to sites:	
1 Abu Hureyra	20 Jemdet Nasr
2 Abu Salabikh	21 Khafajah
3 Arpachiyah	22 Khorsabad
4 Arslantepe	23 Kültepe-Kaneš
5 Aššur	24 Kurban Höyük
6 Babylon	25 Madhhur
7 Beydar	26 Mari
8 Brak	27 Maškan-šapir
9 Çatalhöyük	28 Nimrud
10 Ebla	29 Nineveh
11 Eridu	30 Nippur
12 Gawra	31 Qermez Dere
13 Girikihacýyan	32 Samarra
14 Göbekli Tepe	33 Sawwan
15 Godin Tepe	34 Shanidar
16 Habuba Kabira	35 Susa
17 Hacýnebi	36 Telloh
18 Hallan Çemi	37 Umm Dabaghiyah
19 Jarmo	38 Ur
	39 Uruk-Warka

his basic mapping of Nineveh in March 1766? Does the discipline begin with Claudius Rich surveying the ruins of Babylon in December 1811 and of Nineveh in 1820 on outings from his post as Baghdad Resident of the East India Company? Or in December 1842 with Paul Emile Botta sinking the first trenches into the dusty earth of Nineveh? Or with Austen Henry Layard's discovery in November 1845 of two Assyrian palaces on his first day of digging at Nimrud? And what of early nineteenth-century attempts at the decipherment of cuneiform, such as those of Grotefend and Rawlinson on the trilingual Bisitun inscription in Iran? All these dramatic events, and many others, can be compounded as an early stage in the evolution of Mesopotamian archaeology.

Are these genuine beginnings to the discipline or are we ignoring earlier or contemporary developments outside the Eurocentric tradition? Tellingly, Seton Lloyd begins his masterful book on the history of Mesopotamian discovery, *Foundations in the Dust*, with the following sentence:

> It is a curious fact that, owing to the almost universal ignorance of Arabic literature in the West during their time, our ancestors' knowledge of the geography of Mesopotamia and Western Asia

Figure 1.2 Borsippa, central south Iraq, mistakenly identified in the past as the Tower of Babylon
Source: photo by R. Matthews.

generally was derived largely from the accounts of various
European travellers.

(Lloyd 1947: 11)

Lloyd was correct to point to the underrated (in the West) achievements of Arab intellectuals. Comparative historical narratives dealing
with ancient non-Islamic peoples and with Islamic origins, as well as with
the classical tradition of Greece and Rome, were already a feature of
ninth- and tenth-century Arab historians such as al-Tabari, al-Mas'udi,
and al-Biruni (Rosenthal 1968; Masry 1981: 222; Hourani 1991: 53–4),
while the geographical writings of Ibn Battuta in the fourteenth century
situate the world of Islam within a rich and diverse global context.

The works of the fourteenth-century historian Ibn Khaldun, above
all, are imbued with a concern to transcend particularist histories by
developing a 'science of culture' (Mahdi 1964), rooted in what we
might now see as principles of social theory, human-environment
dialectics, and ideology, an intellectual foundation upon which to
explore what Ibn Khaldun saw as the five problematic subject areas of
human existence worthy of scientific historical investigation: the transformation of primitive culture into a civilised condition, the state, the
city, economic life, and the development of the sciences. Why did
archaeology not develop out of or alongside this intellectual discourse?
In a recent article, Vincenzo Strika speculates that Islamic intellectuals
of the Middle Ages were on the verge of arriving at something that
might have become archaeology as we know it, had it not been
swamped by the European tradition of science and history from the
time of Napoleon onwards, a tradition that was too intertwined with
Western exploitative colonialism ever to be acceptable or attractive to
indigenous intelligentsia (Strika 2000).

If we look for evidence of a specifically Ottoman interest in the past
of Mesopotamia, a land ruled by the Ottomans for almost four
centuries, we are met with complete silence until after the arrival of the
European powers (Özdoğan 1998: 114), followed by the founding of
the Imperial Ottoman Museum in Istanbul in the late 1860s. In essence,
the past of Mesopotamia had reverted to dust, and its recovery and
interpretation have been largely the fruit of Western engagement. By
the time of that engagement, Mesopotamia had become 'a neglected
province of a decaying empire' (Lloyd 1947: 211), 'the system of irrigation had declined, and vast areas were under the control of pastoral
tribes and their chieftains, not only east of the Euphrates but in the
land lying between it and the Tigris' (Hourani 1991: 226–7).

But let us not forget the evidence for the practice of a kind of proto-archaeology by the ancient inhabitants of Mesopotamia themselves. Irene Winter has suggested that in the first millennium BC 'the Babylonian past was actively sought *in the field*' (Winter 2000: 1785; italics in original), by the inhabitants of Babylonia as part of a concern with royal patronage. Thus carefully executed programmes of excavation at Babylon, Sippar, Ur and Larsa of buildings a thousand or more years old were mounted by kings such as Nabonidus and Nabopolassar in the seventh and sixth centuries BC, while statues of Gudea were recovered and displayed in the palace of a Hellenistic ruler of Telloh, 2,000 years after their manufacture (Kose 2000).

The theory and practice of the modern discipline are heavily rooted in the story of Western political interest in the Middle East. At this point, it may be useful to define some of the geographical terms that will feature throughout this volume, particularly as the origin and usage of these terms cannot be separated from their political contexts in modern times (Bahrani 1998; Van De Mieroop 1997a). The term 'Mesopotamia' as used today refers to the territory largely contained within the Republic of Iraq, with much smaller areas in northeast Syria, southeast Turkey, and west Iran. Modern usage of the term 'Greater Mesopotamia' applies to the watersheds of the rivers Euphrates, Tigris and Karun (Wright and Johnson 1975: 268). In antiquity Mesopotamia was the name given to a satrapy constructed by Alexander the Great from parts of two Achaemenid satrapies, and subsequently a province of the Roman empire in what today is the region of southeast Turkey stretching from the left bank of the Euphrates at Samsat to the Tigris at Cizre (Talbert 2000: map 89). J. J. Finkelstein demonstrated some time ago that prior to the late second millennium BC, citations in Akkadian of 'Māt Bīrītim', or 'the land of Mesopotamia', referred to 'the midst of the river' rather than 'between the two rivers', and more specifically that the name Mesopotamia designated the lands contained within the three sides of the great bend of the Euphrates in Syria and Turkey, extending only as far east as the westernmost tributaries of the Habur river (Finkelstein 1962). Use of the term Mesopotamia to mean the lands between the Euphrates and Tigris rivers probably came about with the arrival of Aramaic-speaking tribes in the late second millennium BC, a usage adopted by Alexander the Great and the Romans in their definitions of Mesopotamia. Today the geographical scope of the term has greatly expanded to include all the Euphrates-Tigris lands as far downstream as the Gulf. Zainab Bahrani has argued that the application of the term 'Mesopotamia' from the mid-nineteenth century onwards serves a political end in expropriating the past of Iraq and its neighbours for the European classical tradition, at the same time dissociating the past of the region from its modern inhabitants, whose country is called Iraq, not Mesopotamia (Bahrani 1998: 165); a fair point, given that the term as originally constructed did not apply to territory south of the Habur-Euphrates confluence. Perhaps use by the Romans of the Greek word 'Mesopotamia' to designate this fiercely contested border region from the second century AD onwards served a similar political agenda in its own time.

The terms 'Middle East' and 'Near East' are also of nineteenth- and early twentieth-century origin, coined by European and North American politicians and strategists in order to define parts of what had previously been lumped together under the term 'the Orient', a catch-all phrase covering all of Asia from Constantinople to Beijing and much more besides. As Bahrani has shown, usage of the term 'Mesopotamia' to cover the pre-Islamic past of the region and of 'Middle East' to cover the modern, principally Islamic, manifestation of the region has further served to dissociate the past from the present in the eyes of the Eurocentric tradition (Bahrani 1998: 165). Increasing use of the terms 'Southwest Asia' or 'Western Asia', particularly in contemporary European academe, to denote 'the geographical region between the eastern Mediterranean and the Indus Valley and between the Black and Caspian Seas and southern Arabia' (Harris 1996: xi) is the result of an honest attempt to employ a terminology as empty as possible of political baggage. But within this still huge area we need a term to cover what most of us agree on as a specific geographical region and 'Mesopotamia' is the only term readily comprehensible by all.

The story of the early development of Mesopotamian archaeology has been related in several accounts (esp. Lloyd 1947, revised 1980; and Larsen 1996; see also Handcock 1912; Parrot 1946; Pallis 1956), and here we provide no more than a summary of some main features. The early decades of Western archaeology in Mesopotamia were at one level an episode of loot-grabbing whereby spectacular finds such as slabs of stone reliefs from great Assyrian palaces in north Iraq were sought and claimed on behalf of museums in, principally, Britain and France. Working within an intellectual framework shaped by the Bible and the classics, Western scholars and adventurers, led by Botta and Layard, uncovered enormous quantities of valuable antiquities, removed them from their original contexts and then shipped them to the Louvre or the British Museum, who encouraged them with financial inducements ranging in scope from miserly to generous. The scale of these operations was immense. At Nineveh, for example, Layard uncovered a total of 3km of wall faces with sculpted reliefs, principally using the technique of tunnelling.

What was being transported to the museums and upper-class residences of Britain and France was much more than priceless antiquities, however. An entire past was being kidnapped as part of 'building the Orientalist discourse', in Edward Said's phrase (Said 1978). In search of biblical verification and a radicalisation of the Western Graeco-Roman tradition within a region now identified as the 'cradle of civilisation', scholars sought to bring the Mesopotamian past firmly within a historical trajectory defined by the Bible, classical texts, and primitive theories on the rise of civilisation (Larsen 1989). For the Marxist prehistorian Gordon Childe, the glory of the Orient was to be viewed as an 'indispensable prelude to the true appreciation of European prehistory' (Childe 1952: 2). Their success in this expropriation may be measured by the wide acceptance of the accuracy of that trajectory from Mesopotamia through Greece and Rome to the world of the West today (Bottéro 2000; Parpola 2000). As Zainab Bahrani puts it: 'The image of Mesopotamia, upon which we still depend, was necessary for a march of progress from East to West, a concept of world cultural development that is explicitly Eurocentric and imperialist' (Bahrani 1998: 172; see also Van De Mieroop 1997a: 287–90).

While accepting the force and validity of this argument, two points may be made. First, writing as a Mesopotamian archaeologist of west European origin, I wish to bring in from the postmodern cold my colonial ancestors who, like us all, were subject to forces of history on a scale larger and subtler than they perhaps could have imagined. As Seton Lloyd has written regarding nineteenth-century excavators in Mesopotamia: 'No logic or ethics of an age which they could not foresee must be allowed to detract from the human endeavour of these great explorers' (Lloyd 1947: 212). The context of their interactions with the indigenous peoples of Iraq and adjacent lands may have been one of imperial exploitation, annexation and expropriation. In many cases, however, their intentions were noble and committed, as comes through in surviving diaries and letters, such as those of Gertrude Bell (1953) and others who learnt local languages and strove to improve the social, economic and cultural lot of the inhabitants of the region. Many of them suffered and died in pursuit of their commitments and convictions. Whatever the political context of their passion for the past, and for the present, of the lands of Mesopotamia, that passion was genuine and in some ways productive.

Second, we should not cease to appreciate on their own terms the achievements of the Eurocentric tradition in apprehending the Mesopotamian past, as much as the achievements of that past itself. There is no denying the imperialist and Eurocentric context of the creation of a place for 'Mesopotamia' within the world-view of Victorian England. In deconstructing the concept of 'Mesopotamia', however, we should not thereby reject all notion that, for example, the world of ancient Greece was heavily affected by a host of influences from the East and that these influences might indeed have been transmitted to us today, however indirectly. These influences and traditions, often subtle and inadequately studied, in fields as diverse as religion, ideology, philosophy, mathematics, music and sport, have received consideration lately in a range of stimulating publications, including Stephanie Dalley's book *The Legacy of Mesopotamia* (Dalley 1998), an article by Simo Parpola boldly entitled 'The Mesopotamian soul of Western culture' (Parpola 2000; see also George 1997), and Jean Bottéro's vision of 'the birth of the West' from Mesopotamian origins (Bottéro 1992; Bottéro *et al.* 2000). The annexation of the past of Mesopotamia by nineteenth-century travellers from Western Europe took place a century and a half ago, but the process has not stopped and the ground remains hotly contested. Above all, we need constantly to be aware of our generally implicit attitudes towards the Mesopotamian past and its part in world history: 'Perhaps the time has come that we, Middle Eastern scholars and scholars of the ancient Middle East both, dissociate ourselves from this imperial triumphal procession and look toward a redefinition of the land in between' (Bahrani 1998: 172; see also Larsen 1989). Redefining, realigning and rehabilitating the Mesopotamian past remains a major task and challenge for the decades ahead.

Moving on from the first steps in Mesopotamian archaeology, and the modern postcolonial date, we now provide a brief account of how the discipline evolved in the decades subsequent to the 1840s. Following Botta and Layard's assaults on the great Assyrian cities of the north, a mass of barely controlled investigations started up over much of Mesopotamia, with British explorers Rawlinson, Loftus and Taylor working at Borsippa, Warka, Larsa, Ur and Tell Sifr from 1849 onwards. Layard himself rather reluctantly sunk trenches into Babylon and Nippur in late 1850 without major result. French explorations at Kish and Babylon south of Baghdad in 1851 failed to find the hoped-for sculpture-clad palaces now well known in the north, and interest eventually waned. Rassam and Place continued the work of Layard and Botta at Nineveh and Khorsabad, and Rassam found time to commence digging at yet another Assyrian capital, Aššur, in 1853. A major disaster occurred in 1855 when 300 hundred packing cases full of priceless antiquities from these Assyrian capital cities, as well as material from Babylon, were sent to the bottom of the Shatt al-'Arab near Qurna by local marauders to whom the requisite protection money had not been paid by the French. On this dreadful note, European explorations of Mesopotamia came to a halt with the outbreak of the Crimean War in the same year.

From 1873 onwards European interest in Mesopotamia revived. The first sign was an expedition financed by the *Daily Telegraph* and headed by George Smith of the British Museum, sent in search of a missing fragment of the so-called 'Deluge tablet', which appeared to recount an early version of the biblical story of Noah and the Flood, in fact now known to be part of the *Epic of Gilgamesh*. Incredibly, the missing fragment was indeed found. Following Smith's death in 1876, excavations at Nineveh were continued under the direction of Rassam, previously Layard's assistant. From the Ottoman authorities Rassam obtained an extremely generous permit which allowed him to excavate anywhere within the *pashaliks* of Baghdad, Aleppo and Van, a truly vast area, and he proceeded to do exactly that in the period 1878–82, leaving gangs of workmen, with local supervisors, for weeks at a time at such widely scattered sites as Nineveh, Nimrud and Balawat in the north, and Babylon, Borsippa, Cutha, Telloh and Sippar in the south, as well as at Sheikh Hamad on the Habur in Syria, and the Urartian site of Toprakkale by Lake Van in Turkey.

The personality and career of Hormuzd Rassam are notable enough to make us pause for a moment over their consideration. Reasonably entitling Rassam 'the first Iraqi archaeologist', Julian Reade has recently attempted to rehabilitate the much-maligned Moslawi (Reade 1993), pointing out that:

> He is condemned for not recording and publishing his excavations properly, and for being a treasure-hunter rather than a seeker after truth, when such criticisms might more reasonably be directed at the people who were giving him his orders, or rather at the entire climate of opinion, concerning archaeology and Biblical antiquities, in Victorian England.
>
> (Reade 1993: 39)

Rassam, a Chaldaean Christian by birth, converted to Protestantism under the influence of European missionaries in Mosul, and thus began a life-long love affair with the religio-cultural world of the West and England in particular. Following Layard's brilliant successes at Nineveh and Nimrud, in which Rassam was heavily involved from 1846, Rassam carried on archaeological pursuits in Mesopotamia and beyond, culminating in the Aleppo-Baghdad-Van permit of 1878–82, as related above. But perhaps the main interest of his story is the way in which he attempted to cross the social bridge between the British and Ottoman empires and, above all, the reasons for his failure in this endeavour. As Reade puts it: 'Rassam in Turkey was a member of a suspect minority; in England, however hard he tried to make himself an Englishman, he seemed to many people suspiciously oriental' (Reade 1993: 50). He ended his long life neglected and largely forgotten in England.

The last quarter of the nineteenth century saw signs of the emergence of the modern discipline, at least in terms of scope if not methods. Old habits were dying hard, however. Characterised as displaying a 'total misunderstanding of stratigraphy and architecture' (Liverani 1999: 2), long-term French excavations commenced at the Sumerian city of Telloh (ancient Girsu of Lagaš state) in 1877 under Ernest de Sarzec.

Figure 1.3 Telloh, south Iraq. Large hole made by de Sarzec and Parrot
Source: photo by R. Matthews.

Exhibitions in France of Sumerian antiquities from Telloh, such as the Stela of the Vultures and diorite statues of the rulers of Lagaš, caused a national sensation and encouraged a French commitment to the site for over half a century. Our understanding of Sumerian society is still heavily influenced by the thousands of Sumerian tablets recovered from the site in these campaigns. Sadly, these years also saw the real start of extensive illicit digging in Mesopotamia and the looting of untold thousands of tablets from Telloh during de Sarzec's absence from the site. Looting of tablets from many Mesopotamian sites, especially those already under excavation, was found to be commonplace by Wallis Budge of the British Museum during his visits to Baghdad in 1888–9. It was also at this time that Hamdi Bey was appointed as first director of the Imperial Ottoman Museum in Istanbul, leading to stricter controls over foreign expeditions working in Ottoman lands. Following an initial expedition in 1884, the first American involvement in Mesopotamia came with the commencement of a long-term commitment to Nippur from 1887. Much of our knowledge of Sumerian literary compositions, in particular, stems from finds made during the campaigns directed by Hilprecht, Peters and Haynes in these early years. The American connection with Nippur has survived, with gaps, until modern times.

Figure 1.4 Nippur, south Iraq. Excavated mud-brick buildings being reclaimed by the desert

Source: photo by R. Matthews.

At the turn of the nineteenth and twentieth centuries the arrival of German scholars on the flat plains of Mesopotamia brought about a transformation in the discipline. In 1898 the German Oriental Society (Deutsche Orient-Gesellschaft) was founded, and from 1899 until the First World War the society sponsored excavations at Babylon under the direction of Robert Koldewey, who had studied architecture, archaeology and ancient history in Berlin, Munich and Vienna, and had earlier excavated at Assos and Lesbos. In 1887 at the Sumerian sites of Surghul and al-Hiba near Telloh, Koldewey first began to develop the technique of tracing and excavating mud brick, a genuine revolution in the methodology of the discipline, as until then mud-brick walls had simply been dug away without detection or recording. At Babylon Koldewey's patient and exacting work revealed great portions of the city of Hammurabi's time (eighteenth century BC) and of the era of Nebuchadrezzar (604–563 BC), including the Procession Street, the Ištar Gate and the ziggurat, as well as numerous temples, palaces and houses (Koldewey 1914). His assistants and workmen gained invaluable experience and expertise in the tracing of mud brick, thus equipping themselves for work elsewhere in Mesopotamia.

In breaks from Babylon, Koldewey excavated at Borsippa and at Fara (ancient Šuruppak) from 1901 to 1903. Most significantly, one of Koldewey's assistants at Babylon, Walter Andrae (also a talented artist: Andrae and Boehmer 1992), excavated from 1902 to 1914 at the first Assyrian capital of Aššur, exposing as at Babylon large swathes of the ancient city.

An extremely important development came in the form of Andrae's deep stratigraphic sounding through the Ištar Temple at Aššur, representing the first occasion in Mesopotamian archaeology where a chronological sequence of buildings was excavated and recorded through application of the principles of archaeological stratigraphy. A well trained cadre of local professional diggers, called 'Sherqatis' after the town of Qala'at Sherqat, the modern town by Aššur, evolved at the site and went on to serve on numerous mud-brick excavations throughout Mesopotamia in the twentieth century. These German investigations at Babylon and Aššur in the years before and just into the First World War set entirely new standards in the conduct of fieldwork in Mesopotamia, and many of their achievements remain of major significance today. In concert with the application of the principles of archaeological stratigraphy, the use of ceramic typology, as developed in Egypt by Flinders Petrie, began to enable archaeologists to arrange their pots in meaningful chronological and geographic sequences.

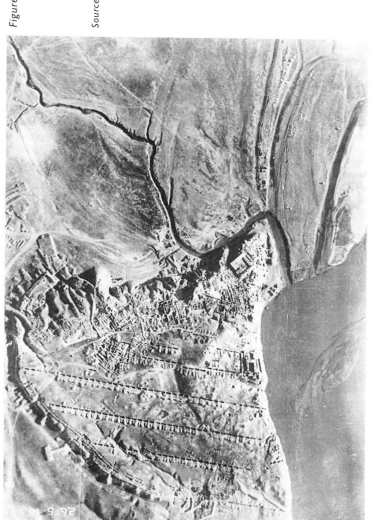

Figure 1.5 Aššur, north Iraq, photographed from 8,000 feet on 26 May 1918. Andrae's trenches clearly visible

Source: Public Record Office ref. CN 5/2 393.

While the Germans applied method and patience to their Mesopotamian investigations, others were less competent or restrained. The American Edgar Banks hacked his way through the Sumerian city of Bismaya (ancient Adab), while the French at Kish and the British at Nineveh continued largely to ignore contemporary developments in the discipline. During these years the first surveys of the Islamic remains of Mesopotamia were underway, conducted by Massignon, Preusser, Herzfeld and others. With the outbreak of war in 1914, work in Mesopotamia came to an almost complete and immediate halt.

During the First World War the political relationship between the West and the modern lands of Mesopotamia, principally Iraq, developed in dramatic ways. European engagement with the Ottoman empire took the form of rather half-hearted military campaigns, teetering on the edge of disaster (and frequently going over it), in north-west Arabia and Jordan, the Gallipoli peninsula, and Mesopotamia itself. The British capture of Baghdad in 1917 laid the foundation for the exercise of British control and influence over the newly created state of Iraq thereafter. Not surprisingly, British involvement in the archaeology of Mesopotamia took on a major new significance in the years following the end of the First World War, with the Iraqi Department of Antiquities under the guidance of Gertrude Bell, who oversaw the development of the Iraq Museum in Baghdad. Being largely artificial entities, the states created after the First World War out of the wreckage of the Ottoman empire were in need of national identities, or so believed their new imperialist occupiers, and much of the work of this time was ultimately directed towards such an end. The creation and definition of these new national identities were also seen as exercises in providing a cultural image of the past that might unite and transcend the multi-ethnic constitution of Iraq and other states.

Already in 1918 soundings at Ur and Eridu were made by Campbell Thompson, while in 1919 Hall excavated again at Ur and at nearby Tell al-Ubaid. Throughout the 1920s British and British-American campaigns were underway at several major sites, perhaps the most important of which was Ur 'of the Chaldees', excavated by Leonard Woolley from 1922 to 1932 on behalf of the British Museum and the University Museum of the University of Pennsylvania (Woolley and Moorey 1982). Woolley's discoveries, which receive scientific study to this day, threw dramatic light on the city of Ur in many of its phases. His excavation of the Sumerian royal cemetery yielded astonishing finds of jewellery, furniture and musical instruments that captured public imagination on a scale not seen since Layard's triumphs of the mid-nineteenth century, and his deep sounding at Ur provided information for the first time on the prehistoric settlement of the Lower Mesopotamian alluvium. Woolley's emphasis on the biblical connections of his work at Ur, including its claim as the birthplace of Abraham and the exposure of deposits interpreted as evidence for the Flood (Woolley 1938; see also Woolley and Moorey 1982: 8), strongly situate his work within an intellectual framework directly descended from that of the mid-nineteenth century.

Many other teams were at work in Mesopotamia during the 1920s. French archaeologists were back at Telloh. At Kish and Jemdet Nasr a British-American team from Oxford and Chicago excavated as if no advances in techniques had been made since the 1880s. As Seton Lloyd put it many years later, 'Ingharra [Kish] was badly excavated, the excavations were badly recorded and the records were correspondingly badly published' (Lloyd 1969: 48). An American expedition to Fara behaved little better. At last the Germans returned to the scene with the start of a long-term commitment to the massive site of Uruk-Warka (biblical Erech) from 1928. Here the Germans recovered plans of huge late-fourth-millennium temples and thousands of clay tablets inscribed in proto-cuneiform, as also encountered at Jemdet Nasr, now generally believed to be the earliest form of writing from anywhere in the world. Mesopotamian Palaeolithic archaeology began in the 1920s with excavations by Dorothy Garrod at the cave sites of Hazar Merd and Zarzi in the Zagros mountains. Much of the research of the 1920s and 1930s in Lower Mesopotamia was aimed, however indirectly, at addressing the issue of Sumerian origins, the so-called 'Sumerian question'. Having identified the presence in south Iraq of a pre-Akkadian, non-Semitic people, the Sumerians, archaeologists and Assyriologists were interested, within the remit of culture history, to discover their geographical origins.

The next significant development came with the large-scale deployment in Mesopotamia of teams from the Oriental Institute of the University of Chicago, starting in the late 1920s with work at Khorsabad. In the 1930s a regional approach was taken to the excavation of four sites in the Diyala region northeast of Baghdad, where many important discoveries were made. In particular, the excavations at Khafajah, Tell Asmar and Tell Agrab provided a detailed picture and chronological framework for the Early Dynastic period of Mesopotamia, which remains largely intact today. At the Diyala sites further refinements in mud-brick tracing were developed under the skilful supervision of Pinhas Delougaz (Lloyd 1963: 33–43). At the same time, work in Upper Mesopotamia continued, with Americans at the prehistoric site of Tepe Gawra and the British, under Max Mallowan, at Nineveh, Arpachiyah, Tell Brak and Chagar Bazar. Conferences in Baghdad in 1929 and Leiden in 1931 sought to make some sense of the mass of excavated material that had by then been extracted from the Mesopotamian soil. The culture historical periods, or pottery-based phases, were agreed upon in the sequence Ubaid, Uruk, Jemdet Nasr and Early Dynastic I–III. Later work in Upper Mesopotamia added Hassuna, Samarra and Halaf to the earlier end of the sequence. Slowly a pan-Mesopotamian framework was being constructed, strictly along culture historical lines. In the 1930s stricter new antiquities laws, severely restricting the amount and nature of finds which could be exported from Iraq, led to a large-scale emigration of foreign archaeologists, including Woolley, Parrot, Mallowan and the Chicago Americans, to Syria and other lands. Iraqi archaeologists continued with work at Islamic sites such as Wasit, directed by Fuad Safar, and Samarra.

Seton Lloyd had worked closely with the Chicago teams in the 1930s, and during the Second World War, as Advisor to the Iraq Government Directorate General of Antiquities, he instituted excavations at several sites, including the prehistoric mound of Hassuna near Mosul, specifically selected in order to address issues of early prehistory. In collaboration with Iraqi colleagues, in the 1940s Lloyd also excavated the late prehistoric site of Tell Uqair, south of Baghdad, Eridu in the far south, and the Kassite city of 'Aqar Quf to the west of Baghdad. The Uqair campaign was interrupted by the pro-German uprising of Rashid 'Ali in 1941 (Lloyd 1963; 1986).

Lloyd's carefully planned and executed programmes of fieldwork set the stage for the next major development in the discipline, the arrival of economic and anthropological archaeology. This step, which started in the late 1940s and blossomed fully through the 1950s and beyond, was initiated by Robert Braidwood of the University of Chicago. With the Iraq-Jarmo project as its hub, a host of innovative programmes was set in train, all sharing an interest in ancient economy and environment above all (see next section). Sites of extremely early date, such as Barda Balka, Palegawra and Karim Shahir were all explored in detail, while the work at Jarmo itself yielded an immense amount of information on Neolithic developments in the Zagros foothills (Braidwood and Howe 1960; L. S. Braidwood et al. 1983). Other Braidwood-centred prehistoric projects included excavations at the Hassuna sites of Gird Ali Agha and al-Khan, the Samarra site of Matarrah, and the Halaf site of Banahilk. In the meantime, the British under Max Mallowan had returned to

Nimrud, the Danes were digging at Shimshara, and the Americans were once more at work at Nippur. Major Palaeolithic discoveries in north-east Iraq were made in the 1950s by Ralph and Rose Solecki at Shanidar Cave, including an assemblage of Neanderthal skeletons still unparalleled in Mesopotamia and all of Southwest Asia.

Through the 1960s the pace of discovery continued to increase, with prehistoric explorations at Bouqras, Telul eth-Thalathat and Choga Mami. Large-scale research projects characterised the 1960s and 1970s, with the British still at Nimrud, Umm Dabaghiyah and many other sites, and Soviet teams working at a suite of prehistoric sites on the Jazirah west of Mosul, including Maghzaliya, Sotto and Yarim Tepe, as well as the start of long-term British investigations at the Sumerian city of Abu Salabikh, amongst many other projects too numerous to mention. These years also saw a florescence of Iraqi archaeologists, many trained at Western universities, with the prehistoric settlement of Tell es-Sawwan being excavated by Behnam Abu al-Soof, Ghanim Wahida and colleagues, as well as a host of other field projects. At the same time, the execution of coherent and extensive survey projects on the Lower Mesopotamian plains, principally by Thorkild Jacobsen and Robert Adams, generated a new and highly specific appreciation of the history of settlement in these now largely abandoned regions of Iraq.

From the late 1970s onwards a new development was an increasing emphasis on rescue or salvage archaeology, an aspect that has continued to dominate the profession in subsequent decades. As in other parts of the world, large-scale civil engineering projects have provided the driving force behind much archaeological exploration and, of course, destruction. In Liverani's words, 'archaeology has become a salvage operation, the fallout and the cultural embellishment of the extensive neo-capitalist intervention in regional planning' (Liverani 1999: 7). Within Mesopotamia such projects have taken place principally in the form of dam construction and land irrigation programmes associated with the major rivers of the region, including the Hamrin region of the Diyala river in east Iraq, the Haditha stretch of the Euphrates in west Iraq, the Tigris region to the north of Mosul, the Upper Jazirah in north Iraq, stretches of the Euphrates and Habur rivers in Syria, and much of the Tigris and Euphrates rivers, among others, in Turkey. Frequently working under tight constraints of time and funding, archaeology in these circumstances has developed to become more of a regional survey exercise with limited excavations. Thus great quantities of new sites of all periods have been located, but very few of them have been subjected to detailed, long-term excavation.

Figure 1.6 Rescue archaeology. Excavations at Tell Mohammed 'Arab on the Tigris river, north Iraq

Source: photo by R. Matthews.

The late 1980s witnessed a return to major research excavations at many sites in Iraq, including Nimrud, Nineveh, Kish, Jemdet Nasr, Hatra and Seleucia to name only a very few, while work in northeast Syria and southeast Turkey continued with an emphasis on survey and rescue. These projects employed a range of modern techniques of archaeological investigation, and many of them were planned as open-ended long-term commitments. Foreign investigations in Iran had already been halted by the revolution of 1979. Following Iraq's invasion of Kuwait in August 1990 almost all foreign, and most Iraqi, work inside Iraq came to a halt. Since that time foreign fieldwork in Iraq has been minimal, and the local antiquities authorities have been occupied principally in attempting to control the plague of illicit digging and dealing, as well as more recently running a few research operations. In field terms the discipline has been on ice for over a decade, but ongoing publication of earlier work, as well as the production of general syntheses of aspects of the Mesopotamian past, continue to demonstrate the commitment felt by many to the study of the past of this uniquely significant part of the world.

By the turn of the millennium, then, Mesopotamian archaeology had evolved over a period of some 150 years from a museum-backed antiquity-finding exercise with its roots in biblical interest to a thoroughly modern discipline utilising and generating the latest in approaches, methodologies and techniques. We can also see that the progress of the discipline has occurred in fits and starts, with frequent halts to activity brought about by political factors, as is the case today. There can be no doubt that a full return to fieldwork and research within the modern state of Iraq would rapidly repay the interest and commitment of the world-wide group of people who look forward to that time with enthusiasm and expectancy.

Theories and approaches: culture history and anthropological archaeology

Mesopotamian archaeologists are seldom explicit about theoretical stances, but in general terms there are two major theoretical contexts within which most practitioners work – culture history and anthropological archaeology, the adoption of either of which does not exclude the practice of the other. Indeed, it could plausibly be argued that the wealth of information and interpretative possibilities encapsulated within the surviving evidence from the Mesopotamian past uniquely encourages a profitable blending of the approaches of both culture history and anthropological archaeology, and that it has been the relatively successful combining of these approaches that has kept Mesopotamian archaeologists fully occupied and confident in the overall direction of their discipline, without feeling the need to engage in professional debate about the theoretical significance and meaning of what they do as archaeologists. That would be a charitable view, anyway. A starker view is: 'the bulk of the work conducted on these (and other) periods in Mesopotamia remains starkly atheoretical' (Pollock 1992: 301). Although there is much mixing of approaches, culture history is largely a European tradition while anthropological archaeology has a predominantly North American academic context.

The trajectories of a theoretical framework in Mesopotamian archaeology can be delineated only by spending a moment in consideration of the development of archaeological theory in general. Accounts of this field are readily accessible (Renfrew and Bahn 2000; Trigger 1989), and here we present only some major points. Following an early concern with the definition of cultures and cultural assemblages, the development of economic archaeology from the 1940s onwards, in which Mesopotamian archaeology was a world leader (see below), led to a concern with improved field, scientific and analytical techniques in order to recover maximum economic and environmental information.

The development of the New Archaeology of the 1960s grew out of these scientific and methodological advances, its grand aim to become a science of culture that could relate material remains to universal laws or rules of human behaviour and social processes. In reaction to these processual and universalising aspirations, there has developed from the 1980s until today a diverse school of attitudes that can broadly be grouped under the heading of interpretive or contextual archaeology, concerned with the specifics of past societies and of the contexts within which they, and their associated material cultures, are situated. There has been a move away from the search for laws or codes of human social behaviour, a willingness to accept ambiguity and polysemy in the archaeological record, an increased awareness of the embeddedness of the researcher within a specific social context, and a desire to explore the meanings and structures of social and symbolic interactions, all exemplified in the following quote from Ruth Tringham:

> Rather than shy away from these topics because they cannot be 'found' in the archaeological data, I prefer to change my strategy of archaeological investigation by celebrating the ambiguity of the archaeological record, by considering multiple interpretations of the same data, and by a more explicit use of creative imagination.
>
> (Tringham 1995: 97)

Culture history has been the dominant paradigm of European archaeology in Mesopotamia, as with many other parts of the world, since the inception of the discipline in the nineteenth century. The origins of culture history, as an intellectual approach to unfamiliar peoples and places, can be traced back to the Father of History, Herodotus (also claimed as 'the first anthropologist' – Thomas 2000: 1) and his accounts of the human societies, their mores and manners, that impinged on his direct and indirect knowledge. Today, for the majority of Mesopotamian archaeologists of European background, culture history remains the preferred approach (see Niknami 2000 for a discussion of the rule of culture history over the archaeology of Iran, Mesopotamia's neighbour to the east). There are still many senses in which we work to establish, even at quite basic levels, the chronological and spatial boundaries of cultural entities within and around Mesopotamia. For example, in the later Neolithic of north Mesopotamia and south Anatolia, in the sixth millennium BC, there exists a phenomenon widely known as 'the Halaf', by which we mean an apparently coherent assemblage of material culture attributes that we can isolate and identify, with varying degrees of confidence, across certain geographical and chronological spaces. These attributes include high-quality painted pottery, engraved stamp seals, architecture in circular forms ('tholoi'), and a distinctive settlement pattern of a bimodal nature with a few very large settlements (10 hectares and more) as against a large number of very small settlements (generally 1 hectare or less) in any given region.

Despite the best efforts of a significant number of archaeologists in the decades since the Halaf was first detected as a phenomenon, we are still some way from defining the nature of the Halaf even within the remit of culture history. What really defines a Halaf site? When and where does the Halaf begin and how does it develop from a local context? How and where does it disappear? These simple but important questions are being addressed by means of the culture history approach in the belief that more or less definitive answers can be teased out of the almost infinite available evidence. In a study of early Mesopotamian prehistory (R. Matthews 2000a), I treated the Halaf phenomenon in this way, splitting its physical manifestations into manageable geographical units and looking for signs that would enable detection of the origins, spread and demise of the culture, without making too much headway on these issues, as it now seems. Not surprisingly, there are several problems with this approach. In the first place, the cultures themselves refuse to sit still. They shift and change shape as we try to pin them down in space or time. A Halaf site in north Iraq differs in some important respects from one in north Syria or one in east Turkey, and the Halaf phenomenon at one site changes through time. What then is truly Halaf? Is the term at all valid or useful?

Other prehistoric cultural entities of Mesopotamia, such as the Hassuna, the Samarra, the Ubaid, and the Uruk are treated in much the same way, with a concern to isolate and characterise the specifics of each culture so that chronological and spatial developments might be traced and explicated. Or so the hope goes. The high point of this approach is epitomised in the brilliant survey of Mesopotamian prehistoric cultures presented in Anne Perkins' book *The Comparative Archeology of Early Mesopotamia* (Perkins 1949). By means of assembling and evaluating an enormous totality of excavated data from several decades of fieldwork all over Mesopotamia, and without conducting any fieldwork, Perkins aimed to 'provide in one work all necessary information on significant culture elements' (Perkins 1949: vii). Half a century on, Perkins' book, with its neat pottery figures and chronological tables, still stands as a highly detailed and informative guide through the maze of the painted pottery cultures of early Mesopotamia, and their chrono-logical correlation with each other, but we would not look here for discussion of ancient economics or prehistoric social structure or ritual behaviour.

In the view of the New Archaeology of the 1960s, culture history was restricted to notions of cultural influences, imprecisely caused by movements of peoples, objects or ideas across space and time, and thus totally failed to bridge the gap between stylistic archaeological traits and genuine anthropological attributes (Lyman *et al.* 1997). By stressing the importance of 'culture' as an agent of change or stability, culture history appeared to relegate the individual to a role of minor or no significance, culminating in a history peopled not by humans but by pot styles, lithic assemblages, burial practices and settlement patterns. The debate over culture history as a valid approach in modern archaeology has recently been rekindled in the work of Ian Morris (1997; 2000). Morris has shown how naive were the views on culture history held by Binford and others in the 1960s and 1970s, and how cultural history, as theorised and practised in recent years, shares many of the aims and traits of interpretive, post-processual archaeological approaches, with a concern for meaning, agency and context in accessing the past.

The application of the second major paradigm in Mesopotamian archaeology, anthropological archaeology, has been enormously influ-ential. The origins of this approach to the Mesopotamian past, rooted in North American academe, predate the early development of the New Archaeology of the 1960s, for it is during the late 1940s that we see the first appearance of anthropological archaeology in Mesopotamia. Anthropological archaeology is a very broad and diverse set of ideas and approaches, but consistent elements include a convic-tion that humans and human communities can be studied in a range of scientific ways; that hypotheses about human behaviour can be ratio-nally formulated and tested through rigorously constructed research programmes; that there are processes, structures and systems external to the human individual that can be investigated through the applica-tion of scientific methods; and that culture is above all a means by which humans adapt to their environments in the widest sense. Before we look at how interdisciplinary anthropological archaeology evolved in the Mesopotamian context, it is worth spending a moment in awed appreciation of the work of Raphael Pumpelly, who as early as 1904 led a multidisciplinary team of experts to Anau in Turkestan in order to investigate agricultural origins and other issues. During Pumpelly's excavations animal bones and plant remains were systematically retrieved according to stratigraphic position, studied and published in exemplary fashion, with full academic discussion of the results (Pumpelly 1908). It is little exaggeration to say that Pumpelly was a full half-century ahead of his time in terms of archaeological vision, planning and practice.

The fruits of the application of anthropological archaeology, or archaeologies, in Mesopotamian contexts are rich indeed, and they feature prominently in the chapters to follow (see also Hole 1995). We have already seen how culture history has attempted to grapple the Halaf phenomenon of north Mesopotamia in the late Neolithic. Let us now see how the same set of issues can be tackled from an anthropological approach. The Halaf period site of Girikihacıyan in southeast Turkey was excavated in 1968 and 1970 by two of the foremost practitioners of the paradigm of anthropological archaeology, Patty Jo Watson and Stephen LeBlanc. In their final report, published quite a long time after the excavations (Watson and LeBlanc 1990), there are some important divergences from the culture history tradition. In the first place, in the introductory chapter there is a clear exposition of the research goals of the project. Second, the nature of those research goals is distinctive, with emphasis on 'systematic recovery of botanical remains (via flotation) and of faunal remains'. Third, beyond subsistence, there is a concern to investigate the issue of Halaf society, exploring whether it might be 'egalitarian or significantly hierarchical'. Fourth, there is extensive use of statistical approaches in analysing data: an entire chapter is devoted solely to statistical analyses of recovered information, and statistical tables feature prominently throughout the volume. These elements are all very different from the culture history approach.

It is important to note, however, that much of the significance of the research at Girikihacıyan can best be appreciated when accommodated within a framework provided by the culture history approach. One of the research issues is phrased in purely culture history terminology:

> Probably the most obvious aspect of the Halaf culture is the extensive distribution of the characteristic architecture and ceramics. By what mechanism were these traits distributed? Did an original group migrate or expand over the Halafian range, or were Halafian traits adopted by previously culturally distinct groups?
>
> (Watson and LeBlanc 1990: 4)

It is no doubt significant that it is these very questions that are least satisfactorily addressed or resolved by the anthropological approaches employed in the project. But the point is that issues from both culture history and anthropology are to the fore and that, however uncomfortable and implicit the partnership may be, both approaches benefit from collaboration.

The inspiration behind the application of anthropological approaches in Mesopotamia was Robert Braidwood, whom we have met earlier in this chapter. During the course of a long and highly productive career in Near Eastern archaeology, Braidwood addressed a range of major issues in human development, including the earliest human presence, the origins and development of settled villages and of farming and herding, and the evolution of more complex societies in later prehistory. A major forum for his approaches was the Iraq-Jarmo project in northeast Iraq. In 1947, no doubt at the time that Anne Perkins was working on her volume *The Comparative Archeology of Early Mesopotamia*, the first season of fieldwork took place at Jarmo. In the final report on the first three seasons of excavations, in a chapter entitled 'The general problem', Braidwood launches the ship of anthropological archaeology with an eloquent polemic:

> Usually archeologists working in the Near East concern themselves with some particular site, such as Ur of the Chaldees or Roman Antioch, or with a particular thing, such as the tomb of Tutankhamon or the palace of the Assyrian king Sargon at Khorsabad. The expedition described here is different in that it is working toward the solution of a general problem: How are we to understand those great changes in mankind's way of life which attended the first appearance of the settled village-farming community?
>
> (Braidwood and Howe 1960: 1)

Braidwood goes on to explain how 'it takes every tool in the prehistoric archaeologist's bag, plus all the help he can get from his natural-scientist colleagues' to extract the necessary information from prehistoric sites in order to address these important issues.

He concedes, moreover, the considerable difficulties faced by the prehistoric archaeologist in attempting to apprehend what he terms 'the moral order' of past societies, and advocates a programme of close collaboration with natural scientists so that aspects of ancient environment, resource exploitation and technology might be identified and 'disengaged' from other less material aspects of past communities that would then be isolated for future study, but the process 'can go forward only with much more imaginative archeology than we have had up to now'. With a passing nod to ethnology and social anthropology, Braidwood concludes his manifesto with the visionary lines:

> We envision not the familiar old-fashioned archeology of digging royal tombs for fine-arts museums but an 'idea archeology' aimed at broad culture-historical problems, in which antiquities as such are meaningless save as tools for understanding the ways of mankind.
>
> (Braidwood and Howe 1960: 7–8)

Hereinafter seeds and bones were to be as important as crowns and chariots. The achievements of the Iraq-Jarmo project and its anthropo-scientific approaches were immense, and they can be fully enjoyed in the voluminous final publication that eventually emerged (L. S. Braidwood *et al.* 1983).

In recent years there has been an increasing emphasis on feminist or gender archaeology as a means of approaching the past. Within the Mesopotamian arena, as elsewhere, one direction has been to investigate concepts and constructions of women, sex and gender in historical and art historical terms, as most coherently and effectively essayed by Zainab Bahrani (2001). Another direction has been a concern to re-formulate the domestic household and its occupants as major active participants in the political and socio-economic contexts of their times (Pollock 1999: 24–5; Tringham 1995). There is a concern to show how the conduct of domestic activities within households both impacts on and is impacted by the socio-political world at large, even if these impacts and interactions might be difficult to trace archaeologically. The point is not necessarily to stress the role of women in past societies, but rather to demonstrate that interpretations of the past rooted in decades of masculinist approaches are seriously lacking in their appreciation of the integrity and interconnectedness of human communities at all levels, from baking the daily bread to burying the royal dead. It is not primarily a question of identifying gender-specific activities in the archaeological record, but rather an issue of correcting and transcending an existing masculine-induced bias in our ways of looking at the past, through demonstrating that activities and roles within past societies have a gender aspect to them that needs to be considered in any holistic approach.

Susan Pollock puts it thus:

> A feminist-inspired enquiry might then ask how broader political, economic, and social changes impact social reproduction and

household organization: what strategies households employ to respond to changing external demands and how these affect gendered divisions of labor. The basis of these questions is that changes in economic, social, and political spheres profoundly affect relations between men and women, adults and children, and that changes in households also contribute to larger-scale social transformations.

(Pollock 1999: 25)

It only remains to add that the obligation of all archaeologists is to strive to be aware of and to correct for the masculinist bias of the discipline that has for so long shaped the way in which we look at the past, until a state is reached where we no longer see this approach as 'feminist-inspired' but genuinely and roundedly 'humanist-inspired'.

In sum, then, both culture history and anthropological archaeology have had their successes within the arena of Mesopotamian archaeology, but it is their application in concert that is most beneficial. Without culture history we lack the spatial and chronological coordinates within which to situate the specifics of economics and society that only anthropological approaches can apprehend. For the foreseeable future it is likely that most archaeologists working in and around Mesopotamia will continue to research within an inexplicit framework built of culture history and anthropological archaeology lashed together with bindings of common sense and assorted approaches of cultural anthropology (Hole 1999) at appropriate points.

Chapter 2

Tools of the trade

Scope and methods of Mesopotamian archaeology

Things and ideas: approaches to archaeological research

In this chapter we look at how the discipline of archaeology is currently practised in the lands of Southwest Asia. We shall not restrict ourselves to Mesopotamia, much of which is out of fieldwork bounds for the time being, but will range over adjacent lands as appropriate. The overall aim is to show how archaeology in this part of the world has blossomed into a fully modern, interdisciplinary profession that can hold its head high amongst its peers. After some general comments, we look at approaches to excavation, focusing on one major, long-term project. Next we examine the case for survey, considering some of the major regional projects that have taken place in Southwest Asia, their techniques and results. Finally, the complex but stimulating question of the relationship between archaeology and text-aided history in the study of the Mesopotamian past is considered.

All archaeological research, whether it be excavation, survey, or historical enquiry of any kind, can be distilled to three essential areas of concern (after Collis 1999: 81):

(a) research agenda
(b) nature of the evidence relevant to (a)
(c) means of accessing (b)

It may seem a truism to state that all archaeological research must begin (and end) with a research agenda (for a dissenting view, see Faulkner 2001/2), but many excavations lack an explicit programme and appear to stagger from season to season without much in the way of clear strategic goals. Jean Bottéro has ruthlessly pilloried such aimless activity:

Thus I have visited many archeologists, even a certain number of philologists, and in the beginning I was amazed (later I became used to it) to see to what degree even the smartest among them could undertake their activities with some kind of psychological automatism that was extremely surprising to notice. They worked with some kind of burrowing instinct that could be compared to that of moles, by all appearances without ever in their lives having had the slightest conscious idea of the real and the final purpose of their work, of the deep sense of their research, of the place and the value of their discoveries for knowledge in general.

(Bottéro 1992: 17)

Within the UK at least, increased competition for funding and more thorough-going academic review policies have encouraged much sharper definition of research programmes in recent years. Particularly vulnerable to the charge of lack of research drive are rescue or salvage excavation projects, where sites are excavated in advance of destruction simply because they are there, and tomorrow they will not be there. For that reason some research funding bodies will not consider applications on behalf of rescue projects. But in truth it should be no more difficult to frame a research agenda for salvage projects than for non-salvage projects. All excavation should be research driven. It is just a question of how much time is available to do it in.

Having a research agenda means devising a question or, more commonly, a suite of interconnected questions, that can reasonably be asked of the archaeological record. Of course archaeological questions do not come from nowhere, and any modern research concern will be heavily intertwined with a skein of past and existing research threads, more and more so as the discipline develops. In the last chapter we saw how Robert Braidwood had a very specific and clearly articulated research agenda when he set to work in the Zagros foothills of north-east Iraq: 'How are we to understand those great changes in mankind's way of life which attended the first appearance of the settled village-farming community?' (Braidwood and Howe 1960: 1).

Braidwood's research issue here is often termed a 'big question'. It relates to a fundamental episode in the development of human societies whereby hunting and seasonal movement gradually changed to year-round farming and permanent sedentism. It is worth stressing that Mesopotamia and environs are uniquely suited to the investigation of big questions. In a recent survey, Clive Gamble identified five big questions that regularly draw archaeological attention on a major scale: the origins of hominids; the origins of modern humans; the origins of agriculture and domestic animals; the origins of urbanism and civilisation; and the origins of modernity (Gamble 2001: 157). Arguably all five of these issues could be tackled, if indirectly, in a Mesopotamian arena, and at least two of them, the origins of agriculture/domestic animals, and the origins of urbanism/civilisation, can be tackled in uniquely rich and pristine contexts within and around Mesopotamia. In the previous chapter we saw how in the fourteenth century Ibn Khaldun also defined five 'big questions' as worthy of scientific historical enquiry: the transformation of primitive culture into a civilised condition, the state, the city, economic life, and the development of the sciences. Again, the arena of the Mesopotamian past is especially suited for the investigation of these major issues.

The three simple concerns of (a), (b) and (c) noted above are of course interconnected. In the words of Henry Wright, 'Research strategy depends upon what one wishes to explain' (Wright 1978: 66). There is no validity in having a research agenda that cannot be addressed by any surviving evidence. One might as well daydream. Daydreaming *is* a part of archaeology, but ideas will be more effective, and more attractive to funding bodies, if tied to a pragmatic research strategy. Furthermore, research agendas need to take into consideration the practicalities of how the available evidence can be accessed. Time and money are precious resources, and research agendas need to be constructed on the basis of targeted tactics towards specific ends. These issues relate to the 'operationalisation' of research, whereby the mechanics of addressing a research problem are thought through, quantified, costed, and assembled in a research design. Although a project begins with a research agenda, the very generation and investigation of evidence relevant to that agenda will themselves modify the research issues as the project proceeds, although hopefully not beyond recognition. There is thus a relationship that is 'always momentary, fluid and flexible' (Hodder 1997) between question, evidence, and means of approach.

If the aim of archaeological research is the investigation of ancient societies, what exactly is it that is investigated? There are as many answers to this question as there are archaeologists, and here is not the place to provide a lengthy exposition of an already well covered subject, but a few comments are in order. The social theorist Anthony Giddens has characterised society and culture thus: 'A society's culture comprises both intangible aspects – the beliefs, ideas and values which form the content of culture – and tangible aspects – the objects, symbols or technology which represent that content' (Giddens 2001: 22). In archaeology we have a society's tangible elements, or rather we have an idiosyncratic and highly partial selection of its tangible aspects scattered through a range of physical contexts, some of which might come to be excavated. The challenge is to use those fragmentary tangible elements in order to approach intangible aspects of society, to consider the mechanisms and processes whereby 'social facts', in Durkheim's phrase, are materialised as elements of physical culture. In order to pursue this aim through interpretive or contextual archaeology, a major area of debate is therefore the question of how to connect the tangible with the intangible, how to assign and evaluate meanings and values to objects and symbols, and how to construct social relations on the basis of recovered physical remains. These fundamental concerns cannot be answered in any definitive and global sense. Rather, it is through the pursuit of defining, formulating, testing and expanding approaches to these issues that the discipline itself takes shape, regroups and moves ahead.

Archaeologists work with 'things'. An archaeological thing can vary from an entire city to a wild pig's vertebra, a multi-period landscape to a grain of barley, a queen's palace to a speck of dust on a white plaster floor. But a thing of itself has no meaning or significance until we grace it with an idea, and so archaeologists also work with ideas, either implicitly and vaguely or, better, explicitly and precisely. Where should an archaeologist look for ideas about things? The answer is all around us. Within the disciplines of sociology and social anthropology there is an increasing body of research focusing on the meanings of material culture within its social contexts. Sociologists such as Tim Dant have explored and illustrated the many social levels on which things operate:

> Things are useful in a variety of ways; they allow us to do what we need and want to do, they allow us to communicate and they enable us to express our sense of cultural togetherness as well as our individuality within that collectivity.
>
> (Dant 1999: 14)

Or, to quote the words of an archaeologist:

> Material culture becomes both the product of actions which are articulated through social relationships and, at the same time, one of the means through which social relationships are constructed, produced and transformed. Material culture ceases to be a *passive*

element in social practice and a *passive* reflection of identity and becomes an *active* intervention in the production of community and self.

(Moreland 2001: 82; italics in original)

By thinking about things that we see all around us, how they are used, shaped, emphasised, negated, transformed through what we do with them in the course of human action and interaction, we gain insights into the range of meanings and messages conveyed by things, and in so doing we can perhaps return to our archaeological things with a fresh idea or two. Here is an area of infinite research potential for archaeologists and anthropologists alike.

A further important consideration is the nature of the archaeological record itself. By no means all material remains from the past make it into that record, nor once there do they necessarily survive until excavated in modern times. Valued items and materials, such as metals and precious stones, are likely to be recycled or cherished over long time periods and may enter the archaeological record principally in the form of burial goods rather than in other contexts that might more directly inform on their significance within contemporary social relations. In addition, we are aware from textual sources, and occasional archaeological survivals, of whole ranges of organic materials that only rarely endure in the archaeological record, including textiles, carpets, garments, skin, woods, plants, mats, furniture, and numerous other items and commodities. Archaeologists working on wetland sites in other parts of the world, where organic remains do survive, often recover organic materials as 75–90 per cent, even sometimes 100 per cent, of all recovered finds (Renfrew and Bahn 2000: 68), some indication of what we are undoubtedly missing from the archaeological record of ancient Mesopotamia.

These attributes of the archaeological record – its tangibility and its incompleteness – can all too easily be viewed as drawbacks to the value of archaeology in approaching the past, especially in contrast to the surviving written record. We should not view them in this way, however. The written textual record of the Mesopotamian past, represented by thousands of cuneiform texts on clay tablets, suffers from similar and connected problems of bias, incompleteness and ambiguity. In addition, the written record hosts a potential bias that rarely distorts the archaeological record, that of deliberate falsification of the evidence. In his poem 'Archaeology', W. H. Auden characterises history, in contrast to archaeology, as being made by 'the criminal in us' (Auden 1976: 663). Indeed, there might be numerous reasons for writing a text in such a way that it distorts or reshapes reality, as every tax-form filler or politician knows, but there is no value to be had from distorting the nature of one's physical environment with an eye to remote posterity, even if one is able to do so. The archaeological record *qua* historical source, however patchy and concrete it may be, is unaffected by its makers' intentions or desires as to the nature, survivability and recoverability of that record, even if it reveals something of those intentions within their contemporary social contexts. Working together wherever possible, however, there is every prospect of archaeology and textual history arriving at fuller and more satisfying interpretations of the Mesopotamian past, as we shall see in the final section of this chapter. But archaeology must employ its own means and methods for accessing and interpreting things from the past, whether historic or not, and that is the subject of this chapter.

Excavating the past into the present

In the spring of 1936 Mortimer Wheeler made a brief tour of archaeological excavations in Egypt, Palestine, Lebanon and Syria, with the aim of expanding his first-hand knowledge of Near Eastern archaeology in advance of becoming the first director of the new Institute of Archaeology in London. He did not like what he saw, and his typically forthright comments are worthy of quotation:

> from the Sinai border to Megiddo and on to Byblos and northern Syria, I encountered such technical standards as had not been tolerated in Great Britain for a quarter of a century. With rare and partial exceptions, the methods of discovery and record were of a kind, which, at home, the Office of Works would have stopped by telegram. The scientific analysis of *stratification*, upon which modern excavation is largely based, was almost non-existent. And the work was being carried out upon a lavish and proportionately destructive scale ... the fundamental canons of the craft were simply not comprehended. I left the Near East sick at heart, ferociously determined to make my new institute in London first and foremost an effective medium for the enlargement of technical understanding. Without that, archaeology of the sort which I had witnessed was in large measure destruction.
>
> (Mortimer Wheeler 1956: 110; italics in original)

As late as 1953 André Parrot published his book *Archéologie mésopotamienne. Technique et problèmes*, in which he provided an account of how to run an excavation in Mesopotamia. Parrot's suggestion for the staff of a field project comprised the following list (Parrot 1953: 20):

1 chef de mission
1 assistant archéologue
1 architecte-dessinateur
1 photographe
1 réparateur
1 épigraphiste
1 chef de chantier
1 inspecteur

Parrot also confessed that on his excavations at Telloh in 1931 the only staff had been a director, an architect and a field director, and that they had barely been able to cope because of the demands of photography. Anyone visiting Telloh today and witnessing the immense holes made in it by Parrot, and others, will quite understand how he found it difficult to cope (see Figure 1.3). Should Wheeler ever have encountered Parrot's book it would no doubt only have confirmed his worst suspicions about archaeology in the east.

The excavation of an archaeological site is not a procedure to be undertaken lightly. I say this, for one thing, as someone who has just completed, along with a dozen collaborators, the writing and editing of a final report on three years' excavations at the multi-period site of Tell Brak in northeast Syria, one of the most important settlements of Upper Mesopotamia over a period of several millennia (R. Matthews in press).

From completion of the fieldwork to completion of the final volume took five full years. Many major excavations in Mesopotamia remain unpublished, except in scant preliminary form, several decades after their completion. Some excavators have continued digging, moving every few years from one site to another, without publishing any final reports, but those days are changing and most countries of the region now have strict provisions to ensure satisfactory progress on publication before the re-issue of fieldwork permits. Other excavators have been conscientious in the extreme about publishing swiftly and fully.

A further angle is that many authorities hold that if an archaeological site is not under threat it should not be excavated at all. Within the context of Israeli archaeology, calls have recently been made for a complete cessation to excavation in order to enable a massive publication backlog to be brought under control (Kletter and De-Groot 2001). In essence such is the view of the Turkish Directorate General of

Figure 2.1 Excavating buildings of later-third-millennium BC date at Tell Brak, northeast Syria

Source: photo by R. Matthews.

Monuments and Museums, which is directly responsible for the issue of fieldwork permits and whose current policy is not to grant permits for new research projects, while issuing them more freely for rescue excavations. A similar policy prevails in Syria. Why? Partly it is a question of staffing problems, with the local authorities being barely able to cope with the massive numbers of foreign teams coming to work in Turkey, Syria and adjacent lands, all of them needing a government representative permanently in attendance. There were over one hundred archaeological field projects in Syria in 2001, and more than twice that number in Turkey, for example. Another aspect is the growing feeling that if an archaeological site is not under threat, whether from flooding by dam construction or from illicit digging or any other cause, then it should be left in peace. In addition, some people feel that as archaeological techniques are always improving we should as far as possible leave sites alone until techniques are more advanced.

While appreciating the weight of these arguments, I am wary of such attitudes on several counts. First, it is only through the active practice of field archaeology that techniques advance at all (Lucas 2001a). If we do not dig we do not learn how better to dig. Second, I am too impatient and curious to allow all the discoveries to be the privilege of future unknown generations. Third, finite as the archaeological record is, it is nevertheless phenomenally rich and, properly managed, there is enough to go round for today and tomorrow. The complete and total excavation of a site such as Tell Brak, for example, should it ever be desired, is a task for centuries not decades. In 1857 the great cartographer Felix Jones made some interesting calculations about Nineveh in this regard. He estimated that the mound of Kuyunjik, the citadel of Nineveh, contained some 14.5 million tons, and that if 1,000 workmen excavated each day a total of 330 tons it would take 120 years completely to excavate the mound (Pallis 1956: 297). Given that current field projects employ workers in tens rather than hundreds, and that the application of increasingly refined techniques has sharply reduced the volume of earth daily removed from archaeological excavations, to kilograms rather than tons, we can increase Jones' figure of 120 years by a factor of at least fifty in a modern context and probably much more. To my knowledge, no one has yet come up with a 6,000-year plan for the total excavation of Kuyunjik, itself only a part of the entire city of Nineveh. Incidentally, 6,000 years is about how long it took for the mound of Kuyunjik to form as the archaeological entity we see today, so there is a nice symmetry of construction/destruction in these figures.

Fourth, although it is possible to generate research programmes centred on rescue and salvage contexts, there is no doubt that the really big and important projects take place as pure research exercises generally over periods of decades, timespans which are simply not available in the world of salvage archaeology. A major full-blown excavation project today requires a commitment of at least ten years and preferably much longer. Many ongoing research projects in Turkey and Syria are committed to twenty-five-year plans, and many erstwhile projects in Iraq were of similar duration or even longer. In this chapter we therefore focus our attention on one major excavation project of pure research, of long-standing duration, with the aim that it serve as a concrete exemplar of how archaeology may currently be conducted in practice in Southwest Asia.

We shall discuss the current programme of research at the site of Çatalhöyük on the Konya plain in south central Turkey (see Figure 1.1). The site belongs to the Neolithic period and is occupied from about 7,200 to 6,000 BC. Although not in Mesopotamia, the site is only a few hundred kilometres west of the Euphrates, and the approaches and field techniques applied there could as well be applied in a Mesopotamian context at contemporary sites such as Bouqras or Umm Dabaghiyah. The Çatalhöyük project is of such significance to the broader discipline that we cannot afford to ignore it. In this chapter we use Çatalhöyük as an example of how archaeologists go about their work. There is not the space here to present even a small proportion of the results that have emanated from the project, and interested readers are encouraged to follow up the references provided, especially on the project website (*http://www.catalhoyuk.com*). As a modern entity, Çatalhöyük began as a surprise, and has gone on to serve as a springboard and testing-ground for two pioneers of modern archaeology, James Mellaart and Ian Hodder. Conveying a then widely held belief, Seton Lloyd wrote in 1956 that 'the greater part of modern Turkey, and especially the region more correctly described as Anatolia, shows no sign whatever of habitation during the Neolithic period' (Lloyd 1956: 53). Only a few years later, Lloyd's colleague James Mellaart commenced his excavations at the mound of Çatalhöyük, now known to be the largest Neolithic site in Turkey and one of the most important anywhere in Southwest Asia. Excavations there in the 1960s revealed evidence for a rich and symbolically charged society, living in closely packed mud-brick houses in a community of at least several thousand.

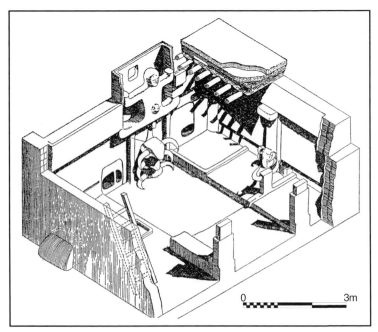

0   3m

Figure 2.2 Building VI.A.10 at Çatalhöyük, south central Turkey
Source: after Mellaart 1967: fig. 40.

James Mellaart believed he had excavated a priestly quarter, where high-status individuals lived in houses varying in their architectural fineness and decorative elaboration (Mellaart 1967). After the 1965 season Mellaart's excavations at Çatalhöyük came to a halt.

But, once stirred from its millennia-long sleep, the site was not to lie quiet for long. 'Çatal Höyük and I, we bring each other into existence. It is in our joint interaction, each dependent on the other, that we take our separate forms' (Hodder 1990: 20). With these prophetic words, a leading archaeological theorist opened an engagement with Çatalhöyük that continues to this day and that will probably continue for the remainder of his career. Ian Hodder's interest was sparked by the rich symbolism attested in the wall-paintings and relief sculptures found in many of the buildings at Çatalhöyük. Looking at Mellaart's book on the site (Mellaart 1967), Hodder confessed, 'the violence of this imagery made a vivid impression on me' (Hodder 1990: 4) and he went on to propose a system of rules underlying the representation of the art at the site, with oppositions and interactions between polarities such as male and female, inner and outer, death and life, wild and domestic. At about the same time a French archaeologist and theorist, Jean-Daniel Forest, was having his own thoughts about the art of Çatalhöyük. In a couple of highly stimulating articles, Forest took it as his premise that the location, or architectural context, as well as the content, of the Çatalhöyük art was always deliberate, never random, and proceeded to discern rules of kinship, lineages, 'an axis of life and death', and male/female tensions as structuring principles behind the art (Forest 1993; 1994).

The current programme of research at and concerning Çatalhöyük was thus from the start rooted in an environment of enquiry about the nature of symbolism and art and their significance in social terms. 'What means this art?' might be understood as the prime research question. As work has progressed since 1993, a complex web of research issues has steadily been spun, many of its strands already regular concerns in archaeology, such as ancient diet, burial practices or specific material culture studies, and others rather newer to the discipline, such as the study of the significance of Çatalhöyük to interested parties of today (local villagers and officials, foreign excavators, 'Mother Goddess' enthusiasts), or the conscious effort to develop a 'reflexive methodology' in approaching the site (Hodder 2000). In essence, Çatalhöyük has itself become a research laboratory where ideas are generated, explored, tested and discussed by means of survey, excavation, analysis and interpretation. And much of this complex and protean process can be witnessed more or less in action via the regular publications of the project or, more directly, by accessing the project's ambitious and rewarding website.

How then do archaeologists go about approaching the past at Çatal-höyük? Before examining the nature of these approaches, it is worth stressing that for Hodder, research at Çatalhöyük, like all archaeological endeavour, is not a study of the past but a study for the present. As 'the poet of the Neolithic', Hodder aims 'to erode the idea of a separate present', focusing on 'the degree to which our thoughts and actions are created through the past' (Hodder 1990: 279). 'The artifacts from the past, excavated in material contexts and ordered partly by material constraints, provide a wealth of experience through which the present can be thought about and thus changed' (Hodder 1990: 19). Ten years after these words were written their practical implications have become much clearer:

> The archaeological site at Çatalhöyük does have an impact on diverse communities in the present. It mediates between these various groups and individuals and their constructions of the past. … The archaeologist is involved in an on-going negotiation, one that penetrates into the laboratory and into the trench.
>
> (Hodder 2000: 14)

I shall never forget the excitement of that first morning at Çatalhöyük in September 1993 when, with Turkish government permit in hand, we began our new investigations of the site. Walking over the massive bulk of the great mound, a sleeping giant from the most distant past, it felt like we and the site together had the ability to generate something very powerful for the present and the future entirely out of our interaction with the evidence from the past, its interpretation, and propagation. With a site like Çatalhöyük and a research project led by Ian Hodder, that excitement has not abated in the years that have since gone by.

In this study of archaeology in action at Çatalhöyük we are going to hold up a series of lenses to the site, each lens in turn bringing succes-sively into faint focus the region, the settlement, its buildings, occupants, objects, and the smallest components of its dust and debris. As the emphasis in this book is on approaches to the past, we are as much interested in the nature and construction of the lens itself as in what we might discern as shifting shades on the far side.

The first and coarsest lens allows us to look at Çatalhöyük on the regional scale. What contemporary sites existed on the Konya plain? How did Çatalhöyük fit into the regional settlement pattern during the

Neolithic? How did that settlement pattern evolve through time? In order to address these questions a programme of regional survey is required. We shall be considering survey as a technique in the following section, so shall restrict ourselves here to a few remarks relevant to Çatalhöyük. Survey involves systematic approaches to reading landscapes in order to build up pictures of settlement history. Çatalhöyük did not exist in a void, and the more we can understand about the size and distribution of sites in the region the more we can appreciate the significance of the site itself. By driving and walking over the Konya plain, within which Çatalhöyük is located, we locate sites and date them by the material, usually pottery, lying on them (Baird 1996). Because many smaller and older settlements may be buried under recent alluvium or may have been eroded away, it is not possible to detect all sites that ever existed, nor is there time to do so over such large areas. Sampling strategies are therefore needed, and it is essential that survey is conducted in concert with geomorphological investigations of how the landscape has evolved through time, as this approach will give some idea on rates of site loss through erosion and alluviation. Using these methods a provisional picture, or series of snapshots, of settlement patterns through time has been generated. One important conclusion is that Çatalhöyük seems to have stood on the Konya plain as a site of unique importance during the Neolithic, with a few much smaller contemporary sites scattered about the plain. We thus have evidence for a bimodal settlement distribution, comprising a single very large focus of settlement, ringed by several smaller sites. On this basis we can start to consider issues such as how the two very different types of settlement interacted. Were the small sites under the control of Çatalhöyük, and were certain roles – cultic, economic, social – uniquely fulfilled by the existence of Çatalhöyük on the Konya plain?

Another lens is that of geoarchaeology, the study of past settlements and human systems within their landscape and environment contexts (Dincauze 2000). The techniques of geoarchaeology centre on the recovery of data pertaining to the ancient environment, such as coring through sediments either on land or at the base of lakes. The survival of pollen within lake-bed deposits can yield highly detailed information on past plant regimes and therefore on climate and environment. Dating of recovered sediments can be achieved by a range of means, including luminescence dating and radiocarbon dating. Using these approaches it has been established that the settlement at Çatalhöyük was founded on an alluvial plain evolving from a large lake that gradually dried up after the start of the Holocene in 10,000 BC (Roberts *et al.* 1996). A river flowed by the settlement, which may have been prone to flooding. There would thus have been good incentive to build the settlement higher and higher, steadily producing the large mound that survives today. With a wide variety of accessible ecological niches, including river, marsh, plain, hills and mountains, the inhabitants of Neolithic Çatalhöyük would have been able to exploit, for food and other purposes, a great assemblage of plant and animal species. Geoarchaeological approaches have also established that the immediate environs of the site are covered by 2–3m of post-occupation alluvium, demonstrating that the original settlement was even bigger than it appears today.

From now on our lenses focus on the site itself. We will begin by considering the overall structure of occupation at the settlement. Like many thousands of archaeological settlements in Southwest Asia, Central Asia and Southeast Europe, Çatalhöyük takes the form of a mound, *höyük* in Turkish, *tell* in Arabic. Such mounds, some of which reach enormous dimensions, are formed by the accumulation of building materials and occupation debris over periods of time that can range from decades to millennia (Lloyd 1963: 13–21). Mud-brick buildings, constructed of locally available materials, last perhaps for a generation or two before being dismantled, levelled, and built upon. Through time, this process leads to the formation of an elevated mound, itself an attractive feature as providing a degree of defensible security and a clear field of view over an often flat landscape.

When Mellaart excavated in one small part of the mound in the 1960s, he concluded that the often spectacular buildings found there must represent a special quarter, perhaps belonging to priests (Mellaart 1967: 80). Could this idea be tested somehow? That is, to what extent were the buildings excavated by Mellaart representative of the entire settlement? Was Çatalhöyük really a town, with all the diversity of function and activity implied in that designation, or rather a very large village with little spatial differentiation of activity? Were there any large buildings where special activities took place? Was all the settlement occupied at the same time? How many people lived at Çatalhöyük at any one time? These kinds of questions encourage a broad approach to the site as a whole. But excavating at the broad scale can take a very long time if, for example, a single building takes two or three annual seasons to excavate. We need approaches that allow large-scale coverage of the settlement. These approaches involve non-invasive techniques such as surface collection, surface planning, and a range of methods of investigating the nature of deposits immediately underlying the surface of the site. In brief, systematic collection of surface artefacts can reveal the distribution of different periods of occupation across the site (R. Matthews 1996a). A focus of Romano-Byzantine occupation at the south end of the mound at Çatalhöyük was localised in this way. In evaluating the significance of surface-collected material, we have to be aware of the complex range of factors that have worked to modify the surface of the mound since its final abandonment, including animal burrowing, erosion by wind and rain, and the effects of vegetation growing on the mound.

A surface technique used extensively at Çatalhöyük and other sites is that of surface planning. In this method a thin crust of surface earth is removed, the newly exposed surface is immaculately cleaned, and the resulting features photographed and planned. This technique does not yield detailed contextual information but its strength is in rapidly uncovering wide spreads of architecture and features that can give some ideas on community structure. In the north area at Çatalhöyük, for example, an area of 1,900m^2 was planned over a matter of a few weeks, containing the plans of over thirty Neolithic buildings (R. Matthews 1996b).

The layout and internal structure of these mud-brick buildings, and others found at several points on the mound's surface, begin to provide some provisional answers to the questions posed above. The buildings are exactly like those excavated by Mellaart in the 1960s, and there is no evidence for large buildings of special significance. Of course, the greater proportion of the site covered, the higher the confidence in the validity of the results. Other non-invasive surface techniques include those of remote sensing, such as ground-penetrating radar, electrical resistivity, and magnetometer survey (Roskams 2001: 51–4). The limited application of these techniques at Çatalhöyük has not met with great success, probably due to the physical nature of the deposits (Shell 1996), but at other sites substantial proportions of town plans have been recovered.

And so at last we arrive at excavation, our next lens. We have learnt about the regional context of the site, its relationship to the landscape, the processes that have shaped the mound we see today, and the periodisation and general make-up of occupation on the current surface of the site. This prelude to the discussion of excavation has at least served to emphasise the importance of getting to know a site and its setting before ever sticking a shovel in the ground. But it is now time to dig. The decision on exactly where to excavate within a site will be determined by a range of factors. If good surface plans have been made, as

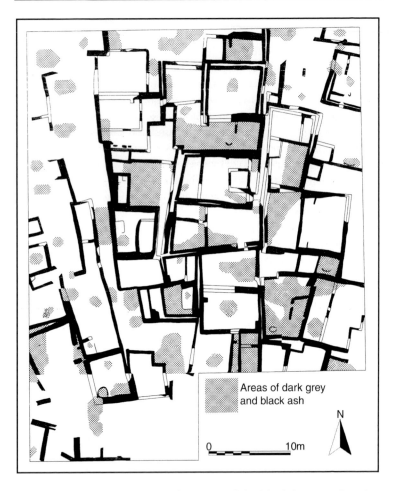

Figure 2.3 Plan of surface architecture of the Neolithic period in the
        north area at Çatalhöyük, south central Turkey

Source: after R. Matthews 1996b: fig. 7.5.

at Çatalhöyük, then a decision will at least be based on solid information. Some excavators in Southwest Asia fail to conduct adequate
surface investigations prior to digging and end up wasting considerable
amounts of time and money excavating material not of the intended
period or type.

As this volume is not intended to serve as an excavation manual,
there is no intention here to give a detailed account of contemporary

excavation practices (Roskams 2001). Instead we shall focus on some key concerns. Excavation entails the systematic dismantling of the material deposits of the past, preferably in reverse order to the sequence of their deposition, the latest deposits being removed first. Excavation is a one-off act of dismantling of the archaeological record, and so must be accompanied by meticulous recording, which will include photography, drawing, detailed description, and sampling of deposits. Types of sampling may include soil samples for flotation through water in order to recover carbonised plant remains, samples for sieving through mesh of varying sizes to recover minute artefacts and environmental evidence such as fish-bones, snail shells, and mineralised organic remains such as coprolites, and removal of intact blocks of deposits for microscopic analysis. The standard method of excavation is that of single context planning, whereby a discrete archaeological context, once identified, is recorded and removed in its entirety. Then, the next context is identified, recorded and removed, and so on. A conceptual reconstruction of the relationship between all removed deposits is constructed in the form of a matrix, usually of the type known as a Harris matrix (Roskams 2001: 156–9).

The single context planning system evolved within the practice of urban archaeology in Western Europe and, while generally suitable, needs some modification for the excavation of mud-brick sites in Southwest Asia. In particular, the failure of this system to employ sections in a systematic manner, that is to maintain portions of exca-vated deposits intact for inspection and recording as earth is removed, means that the relationship between sequences of deposits can be lost or misunderstood. Such sequences can be critical for understanding how tightly packed layers of floor plasters and occupation deposits relate to burials cut through the floors, or how deposits in adjacent rooms, connected by a crawl-hole, relate to each other. Decisions on where to distribute meaningful field sections through, for example, sequences of floors and on-floor occupation deposits will need to be arrived at through planning and consultation with interested parties in advance of removal of deposits. Location of sections will vary according to the internal layout of each excavated building, taking account of features such as platforms, hearths, doorways, and so on.

A major issue at sites such as Çatalhöyük is cleanliness in the field. Due to colour, texture and tone variations in archaeological deposits, with mud-brick sites there is an astonishing wealth of information to be read in most field situations where freshly revealed deposits are cleaned on first exposure and then kept clean as description and analysis proceeds, both in plan and in section. Even footwear is relevant here. While chunky, deep-tread boots may be suitable for excavation of a medieval waterfront on the Thames in London, on soft plaster floors at Çatalhöyük they are destructive of fragile and irreplaceable evidence. Bare feet are equally unsuitable, and unsafe. The best option is to wear light shoes with flat and featureless soles, if walking on Neolithic floors cannot be avoided at all. In fact such shoes should be worn at all times when excavating inside mud-brick buildings, whether or not a floor is exposed.

To some extent we can still agree with Seton Lloyd's assertion that the excavation of mounds in Southwest Asia 'is a specialised form of archaeology, which requires specialised training' (Lloyd 1963: 11). In my experience, British excavators are happy to learn about correct tools and techniques if the benefits of doing so are demonstrated at first hand. It is hardly surprising that excavators are unfamiliar with the correct tools to be used on mud-brick excavations. When cleaning large areas in plan, as a means of identifying walls, pits and other features prior to excavation, the most efficient and rewarding method is to use a sharp, wide-bladed hoe, with short handle so that sufficient pressure can be applied to the head, to cut the surface crust and thus expose fresh deposits. The hoe must be kept clean and sharp and can also be used to clear away loose earth once the crust has been cut. On a mud-brick site a single good hoe-person can do the work of ten trowellers and produce better results every time. Suitable hoes were not available in the Konya region when we started work, so I had some specially made by a local blacksmith. In excavation, British diggers employ the unsuitable technique of stabbing at and smearing deposits with blunt trowels rather than lightly picking them with a sharp hand-pick and cleaning with sharp trowels. Use of sharp palette knives, of a variety of types depending on soil toughness, to clean sections is also far superior to use of blunt trowels. Use of the hand-pick, in particular, is unknown amongst British diggers and is the single biggest gap in their field armoury. No tool is more effective or versatile than the hand-pick, use of which can range from full-armed strokes in removal of thick layers of destruction debris to feather-light tapping, controlled solely by wrist movement, to detach the final millimetres of earth from a plastered wall face. Short, smart strokes of the hand-pick also do minimal damage to items contained within the deposit matrix. Carbonised plant remains and unbaked clay objects, for example, get smeared, shattered, and scattered through trowelling, but will stay intact under the pick and therefore recoverable either by hand or by later screening as appropriate. A hand-pick would be my one desert island luxury.

The question of to what extent excavators should be academically motivated in their employment is another issue, particularly germane in the context of the Çatalhöyük project. Is it more worthwhile, all round, to have an experienced professional digger who knows and cares little about the Neolithic of central Anatolia, or a not so experienced amateur who is passionate about the past? To some extent an answer to this poser has eventuated through practice at Çatalhöyük, with novice diggers from Britain developing an academic interest in the site and its regional context through the experience of being there and working there. Others, by contrast, work there and develop no interest.

From within the removed deposits a host of material remains will be recovered. First there is the earth itself. If the deposit in question is a mud-brick wall, for example, then the type of earth used can tell us something about preferences for building materials. Occupation deposits, and especially refuse, often yield evidence for a range of activities, which might include animal bones and plant remains from cooking and eating, that shed light on ancient diet and environment, sherds of pottery from broken vessels, tools, and debris of obsidian and flint, fragments of clay objects that may have been a child's plaything or an adult's idol, and numerous other scattered pieces of material culture. A relatively new technique which is especially well showcased at Çatalhöyük is that of micromorphology, which involves the removal of intact blocks of deposits, such as sequences of floor plasters and associated occupation layers, which are then impregnated in the laboratory with a resin that hardens and enables large-format thin sections to be cut and mounted. These thin sections can be examined under varying degrees and types of microscopic magnification. This method is the finest of our methodological lenses widely in use at the site. Using this technique, especially in concert with other chemical and physical analyses of deposits, it is possible to identify minute fragments of evidence for activities that are otherwise not detectable, such as traces of food preparation, trampling of plaster floors, burning, and a range of domestic and other pursuits (W. Matthews *et al.* 1997).

In time an entire building is exposed, with its original plastered floors and wall surfaces, perhaps painted, now clear of later deposits. In your smooth-soled shoes you tread gently over the white plaster floor, where no-one has trodden for over eight thousand years. You try to picture what it was like to live in such a structure, but it is difficult. For one thing the roof does not survive and so the building seems more open than would originally have been the case. But you can imagine the darkness, the closeness of the walls, the smoky atmosphere, the smell of lentils cooking in a pot, the shadows of a plastered bull's head dancing over the red-painted designs on the wall as the fire flares up at the addition of a dung cake, the sound of a woman stepping lightly over the roof beams and descending the wooden ladder to the floor. You turn to welcome her. She has come from the fields or from a hunt or from a trading expedition to obtain obsidian to make tools. She smiles in greeting, opens her mouth and …

At this point, on the verge of answering the Indo-European question once and for all, you wake and your modern archaeologist's eye recommences its work. You notice slight dips or discoloration in the plaster where human burials lie awaiting excavation under the floor. It is time to meet the original householders. Unfortunately they cannot speak, at least not in tongues, but they can tell us a lot. The practice of burying one's dead only a few centimetres below the plaster floor of the living room was widespread at Çatalhöyük. By studying the distribution of the burials within the house, their ages and sexes, we detect patterns in the way the dead were treated. In Building 1 at Çatalhöyük, a total of sixty-seven individuals was buried beneath the floors of one room, less than $30m^2$ in area. In the northwest corner of the room almost all the burials are of infants and juveniles, while in the east side only adults are buried. In an area in between there are burials of adults with very small infants, probably mothers with stillborn babies. What might the significance of this pattern be? As we have mentioned above, in his stimulating articles Forest (1993; 1994) had already discerned some structuring principles at work in the layout of the art and symbolism within the Çatalhöyük houses, including a male-female axis and a death-life axis, and it is possible to situate the burial patterns of Building 1 within the general framework posited by Forest, with the burials distributed by age and sex along these same axes, which also relate to the location and content of the wall paintings and relief sculptures.

So we have ended where we started, with the art, and we have come some way to address our original question of 'what means this art?'. But along the way we have appreciated something of the workings of a modern interdisciplinary research project in Southwest Asia. Before leaving Çatalhöyük, we shall cover a more theoretical issue of the nature of the investigations at Çatalhöyük. Ian Hodder portrays the project as innovative in the development and employment of a methodology that is 'reflexive', by which is meant 'the examination of the effects of archaeological assumptions and actions on the various communities involved in an archaeological process, including other archaeologists and non-archaeological communities' (Hodder 2000: 9), with emphases on contextuality, interactivity and multi-vocality (Hodder 1997). Hodder's desire is to define and implement a methodology that moves beyond those employed by the so-called New or Processual Archaeology. It has been pointed out by others, however, that the field techniques employed in the investigations at Çatalhöyük were developed over the past few decades within the context of the New Archaeology, and that the methods and mechanics of Hodder's approach cannot reasonably be distinguished from those of the processual school (Hassan 1997: 1025; Gamble 2001; see also Lucas 2001b: 2; and Hodder 1998 for response to Hassan 1997).

The implication is that the concepts and philosophy of post-processual or contextual archaeology have had little significant impact on methodological approaches to investigating the site, which are still rooted in an anthropo-scientific concern with recording data in objective ways as a basis for the act of interpretation. This dilemma may stem from an implicit recognition of the paramount importance, and irreplaceability, of the archaeological record. Most archaeologists would see it as not acceptable to impose methodologies that, according to contemporary standards, do not adequately record information before it is lost forever. We detect therefore a tension at the heart of a statement such as 'At Çatalhöyük teams from different parts of the world are encouraged to excavate their own parts of the site. Equivalent recording and data systems are used, but each team uses its own traditional techniques of excavation and analysis' (Hodder 1999: 193). But the act of imposing equivalent recording and data systems on all teams dictates parameters within which those 'traditional' techniques of excavation and analysis are implemented, aligning them within a Western twenty-first century scientific paradigm and strictly channelling multi-vocality before it has been given voice. There is no way around this dilemma short of allowing portions of the site to be excavated in ways that might arouse the ghost of Wheeler, or accepting that multi-vocality in terms of excavation exists principally as a gloss on a Western scientific paradigm perforce adopted by all participants.

Surveying for the past

The technique of survey is a relatively recent addition to the methods of Mesopotamian archaeology. By survey we mean the systematic investigation of selected landscapes in order to map and record archaeological sites and land use evidence, dating them by the artefacts, principally pottery, recovered from their surfaces and, if possible, classifying them

according to size and nature of surface features, such as canals, enclosure walls, and debris from craft activity. By these means, and others
outlined below, the aim of multi-period survey, or settlement archaeology, is to build up a series of connected pictures of the landscape at
sequential stages in its history, and thereby to discern and bring into the
forum of debate trends and patterns in human/landscape interactions
over time periods that may vary from the short to the very long-term.
The sorts of issues that can be addressed by systematic survey include
diachronic settlement patterns, ancient land use and communications,
demography, and urban/rural flux and interaction (Wilkinson 2000).

In addition, 'to be maximally informative, the statistical data generated by these surveys must be related to their geological and modern
ethnographic and historical contexts' (Hole 1995: 2720). A uniformi-
tarian assumption in surveying for settlement patterns has been well

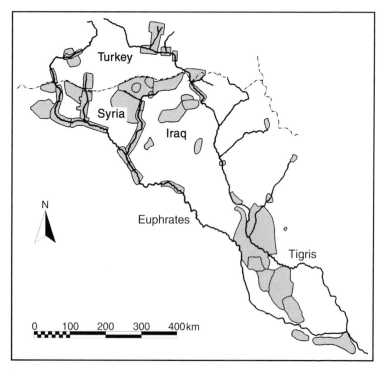

Figure 2.4 Map to show regions where archaeological survey has been
conducted in Iraq, northeast Syria and southeast Turkey

Source: after Wilkinson 2000: fig. 1.

expressed by Hans Nissen; 'the settlement systems of the ancient Near East conformed to the same laws as do the systems we find in the modern world, on the basis of which the methods of settlement geography were developed' (Nissen 1988: 9).

The origins of survey in Mesopotamia as a deliberate and self-contained process of investigation, rather than as a more or less random act of searching for profitable sites to excavate, can be ascribed to the mid-1930s when several archaeologists simultaneously apprehended the potential value of archaeological survey. In late 1934 Max Mallowan conducted a wide-ranging survey of the Habur region of northeast Syria, whereby 'a careful surface examination was made of each mound, and everywhere we collected and made drawings of the potsherds that litter the slopes of every ancient site' with the aim of obtaining 'a more exact and extended knowledge of the main periods of occupation from prehistoric times down to the Assyrian and later periods' (Mallowan 1936: 2, fig. 1). In spring 1938 a more formally structured survey was carried out in the Sinjar region of northwest Iraq by Seton Lloyd who, in his prompt publication, presented not only an interpretation of the principal results but also a catalogue of discovered sites and, most significantly, illustrations of diagnostic pottery employed to date sites to specific periods (Lloyd 1938). This last advance enabled others to build on and test his results in their own subsequent surveys of the region and beyond. Approximately simultaneous with these developments, a young Robert Braidwood was conducting archaeological survey of the plain of Antioch/Amuq to the west of Aleppo (Braidwood 1937).

A major development came in 1936–7, when Thorkild Jacobsen determined to explore the landscape of the Diyala region to the northeast of Baghdad:

> Our procedure was to visit systematically every tell in the region, section by section, locate each one on the map, pace it off for size, and date it from pottery left on the surface. We then plotted the tells of each period on period maps and saw to our great delight that they made a pattern; they ranged themselves in lines which clearly stood for the rivers and canals on which the ancient towns and villages they covered had lain and on which they had depended for their existence.
>
> (Jacobsen 1995: 2746–7)

The methods and results of Jacobsen's innovative survey were not to see the light of day till their publication in 1965 within the context of a wider-ranging survey of the Diyala region conducted by Robert Adams (Adams 1965). Indeed, following Jacobsen's pioneering work of the 1930s the approach of archaeological survey lay dormant in Southwest Asia for twenty years, until Adams took up the challenge in the later 1950s. Adams' contribution to this aspect of archaeological research in Mesopotamia is peerless, in terms not only of methodology but also of interpretative rigour and imagination. In the words of a colleague, 'Adams's research emanates from arduous fieldwork and the synthesis of disparate fields of expertise whose breadth no one since has been able to match or, it seems, even imagine' (Yoffee 1999: 808).

Adams' first experience of survey in Mesopotamia came in 1956–7 when, with Vaughn Crawford, he surveyed the Akkad area of north Babylonia, later published as an appendix in Gibson's book on Kish (Gibson 1972). But the major breakthrough came with the 1957–8 survey in the Diyala region northeast of Baghdad, building on the earlier work of Jacobsen referred to above. The motivation behind these new field surveys lay in the Iraqi government's desire to investigate the issue of whether or not previously cultivable land, now abandoned and saline, could be brought back to a state of agricultural productivity, an early example of archaeology in the service of the host state. Jacobsen was selected by the Iraqis to explore this concern and he, newly wed to an ex-wife of Seton Lloyd, in turn handed on the project to the young Robert Adams.

In his publication of these researches Adams included a detailed explication of the methods employed in topographic archaeology, as he called it (Adams 1965: 119–25). Working over a total area of some 8,000 km^2, Adams enhanced the techniques employed by Jacobsen, Lloyd and Mallowan in the 1930s by introducing the new element of aerial photographs used in concert with 1:50,000 scale maps and soil survey sheets. By these means he was able to identify tracks of ancient canals, as well as many of the ancient settlements themselves, before entering the field. Once in the field, operating by vehicle and on foot, all suspected sites were visited and a systematic collection made of potsherds and other materials from all identified periods. The sites were mainly in the form of mounds, that is accumulations of architectural remains, levelling fill, and the debris and rubbish associated with living in a largely mud-brick environment, which stood proud of their immediate surroundings, although some smaller flat sites were also detected. In all, 867 sites were identified using these methods, and their assignment to one or more of the sixteen historical periods defined by Adams for the Diyala region was done on the basis of 'index fossils', namely specific sherds distinctive enough by virtue of their shape, fabric or surface treatment to be used as chronological markers. Following Lloyd's lead in the publication of his Sinjar survey, Adams included illustrations of the ceramic index fossils as part of the publication of his project, as well as a catalogue giving brief details on all detected sites.

From the start Adams addressed an area of methodological concern: how to identify and quantify specific periods of occupation on sites that were occupied for more than one of the sixteen archaeo-historical phases, as indeed most of them were. Presumably the latest phase of occupation would be the easiest to discern, represented by spreads of sherds over the surface of the mound, but what about the evidence for earlier periods? Adams' solution was to spend time at each multi-period settlement, carefully collecting all diagnostic surface material, exploring the hypothesis that there could be considerable upward movement of pottery from earlier levels to the ever-changing surface of the settlement. Such movement, familiar to all who have excavated on Mesopotamian mounds, might be caused on the small scale by such activities as digging into the mound for brick-making material, burial of the dead, wells, or on the large scale by terracing, levelling and foundation work attendant upon the construction of later buildings. Adams' contention was that these complex post-depositional processes, coupled with careful collection of diagnostic material from the mound's surface, made it 'generally possible to find traces not only of the latest or most widespread levels in a site but of its whole span of occupation' (Adams 1965: 122). Brinkman has pointed out that the time-depth of survey periods, generally of the order of 300–400 years, is of minimal use when considering specifically historical issues (Brinkman 1984: 172), but Adams has been careful to clarify that his interpretations are of the broad-brush type.

At a higher epistemological level, a fundamental issue that taxed Adams throughout his work on Mesopotamian settlement patterns, and that continues to tax all who have followed, is that of the problem of estimating population sizes and extent of land use in antiquity on the basis of the surviving evidence. Clearly, if one is going to discuss issues of settlement, demography and land exploitation through time, there is a need for some acceptable means of estimating ancient population sizes. Adams started with the assumption that on average population sizes would be proportionate to sizes of settlements of specific periods. The most difficult issue is agreeing on a figure for population density, that is the number of people per fixed area of settlement, and there have been wide divergences in approaches to this problem. Fixing on an approximate figure of 200 persons per hectare of settlement, Adams pointed out further problem areas, such as the massive deposition of modern alluvium over parts of the previously settled landscape, leading to the complete burial of small or low sites or the partial burial of higher sites, and the fact that at any given time significant portions of any large settlement might be given over to open areas, public buildings, streets, and spreads of rubbish that would skew the population esti-mates. A further concern was that of how to estimate the occupied area of multi-period sites during each of the periods of occupation. For the latest period, the extent of the surface evidence would be taken as indicative, but for earlier periods the correlation between extent of surface evidence and extent of original occupation could not be so direct. Adams' typically pragmatic solution was to assume, explicitly, that earlier periods of occupation were the same in maximum extent as that attested by the surface evidence for the latest period of occupation at that site, unless there was clear evidence to the contrary. In other words, early periods were assumed to be as extensive as the latest period and any bias towards overestimate of area of earlier periods would thus compensate, in trend if not in detail, for the invisibility of earlier sites through the alluviation already mentioned.

On the strength of the methodological and interpretative framework outlined above, Adams' work in the Diyala region entailed the execu-tion and publication of a superb piece of topographic and demographic research (Adams 1965), paralleled solely by his own work in later years. This is not the place for an account, which could only be a feeble paraphrase, of the sweep through 6,000 years of Diyala history reconstructed by Adams in his publication, but we can start by pointing to his integrated employment of geomorphological, ethnographic and historical data in support of archaeological interpretation. The field results were presented in a series of maps, divided by period, with symbols denoting area of each site and tracks of reconstructed water-courses (Adams 1965: figs 2–9). Adams identified distinctive elements of settlement in the Diyala region, with a lesser emphasis on massive urbanisation than attested on the south Mesopotamian plains. Seeing this pattern as a 'dialect' of the paradigm of urban settlement in Lower Mesopotamia, Adams demonstrated that the maximum levels of settle-ment and land exploitation were reached during the Sasanian period (AD 226–637), when the entire Diyala region appeared to be under cultivation. It thus seemed that the political entities of the earlier Mesopotamian past had managed to live in relative stability with their environments, and that it was only with the advent of more centralised administration from the first millennium AD onwards that exploitation of the landscape exceeded the ability of that landscape to cope, leading ultimately to collapse and virtual abandonment of the region. Interpretations and ideas such as these were major and highly stimulating products of the sophisticated research agenda that Adams had devised, executed, and published in the course of a few years.

Ten years after his fieldwork in the Diyala region, Adams applied his battery of methods and approaches to a Lower Mesopotamian context, the environs of the great city of Uruk-Warka (Adams and Nissen 1972). The major focus of this research agenda was the process of urbanisation in a vital stretch of the Lower Mesopotamian plains at the very origins and rise of literate, urban civilisation: 'Here once, in a brief but heroic age, the need, the means, and the will converged to shape the first urban society. One can share with Gilgamesh the pride he felt in Uruk's ramparts, of which the epic sings' (Adams and Nissen 1972: 94). In collaboration with Hans Nissen, Adams further refined the techniques of survey that had worked so well in the Diyala region, now facing increased post-occupational concerns in the form of alluviation, wind erosion and shifting belts of sand dunes. In defence of his extensive and expansive approach to large tracts of the landscape, Adams wrote:

> The conscious choice in this survey was to cover a larger, historically more significant area, even though this made it necessary to rely on summarily recorded, rarely quantified assessments of sherd collections, and not to attempt absolute uniformity of coverage. In short, the decision here was to forego the employment of more intensive and sophisticated methods in order to provide a first approximation that would speak more comprehensively to major historical and anthropological problems.
>
> (Adams and Nissen 1972: 8)

In his Uruk work, Adams turned for the first time to new approaches in locational geography, especially nearest neighbour analysis, for added insight into his results. In substantive terms, Adams detected a major shift in the nature of settlement in the middle of the fourth millennium, culminating in the Early Dynastic I period with the maximum expansion of the site of Uruk-Warka itself to possibly 40,000 inhabitants. Most notably Adams' study demonstrated that the rapid growth of the city of Uruk-Warka was at the expense of rural depopulation and, furthermore, that processes of urban development differed in separate sections of the survey area according to quite local factors. As in the Diyala work, a forceful strength of the Uruk survey project was Adams' detailed consideration of the impact and lessons of recent history as part of long-term trends.

The work of Robert Adams in Mesopotamia culminated in his brilliant overarching survey of the central floodplain of the Euphrates river, based on fieldwork conducted in the late 1960s and early 1970s (Adams 1981). In this knotty and complex work Adams turned increasingly to methods of geographical analysis, including rank-size analysis and settlement hierarchy. New methodological developments included the use of LANDSAT satellite images for mapping ancient levees, and basic steps in the quantification of ceramics recovered from sites. Expanding on his Uruk countryside work, Adams devoted much of his efforts to elucidation of the issue of the origins and early development of complex urban society on the Lower Mesopotamian plains around 3,000 BC, packing a dense network of evidence, ideas and discussion into a single chapter entitled 'Urban origins', culminating in a key question:

> Was it [the urban explosion of Early Dynastic I times], in short, a social 'invention' with enhanced adaptive potential under certain specified conditions for those who adopted it, or was it the more gradually emerging outgrowth of smoothly evolving productive forces and institutional forms?
>
> (Adams 1981: 94)

Adams always appreciated that much of the value of his extensive studies on the Mesopotamian plains would be in the stimulus they provided to others to expand on his researches, and such has been the case. Fieldwork and publications by researchers working in Lower and Upper Mesopotamia and southwest Iran (Gibson 1972; Johnson 1975; Wright 1981; Wilkinson 1999) have taken their cue from Adams' initiative and added their own insights. Refinements to the interpretive framework of extensive survey in the Mesopotamian context have come in the form of new analytical ways of exploring the large masses of data generated by the work of Adams and others. In particular, issues of sampling, demography, contemporaneity of sites, duration of occupation, and patterns of settlement hierarchy, site abandonment and foundation have been formulated and discussed by a range of scholars (Ammerman 1981; Dewar 1991; Johnson 1972; Kohlmeyer 1981; Niknami 2000; Weiss 1977; Wilkinson 1999), often enabling insightful reinterpretations of Adams' original settlement distribution patterns

(Pollock 1999: 63–77; 2001: 210–15; Postgate 1986). A further issue worth careful investigation in the field is that of to what extent villages and smaller settlements may be expected to share the material culture of contemporary cities and larger settlements. It is conceivable that small sites may lack major features of material culture routinely found on large sites, such as high-status pot types or architectural decorative elements. There may also be greater variety and flexibility in adherence to artefact manufacturing processes and techniques in villages as opposed to cities. These and many other related questions will hopefully one day be addressed within a programme of integrated survey and targeted excavation of multiple sites within a specific region of Mesopotamia, such as has not hitherto proved possible.

In a typically practical and valuable suggestion, Frank Hole proposed some time ago (Hole 1980: 40) that the mass of survey data for Southwest Asia obtained over the previous fifty years should now be consolidated in the form of a systematic inventory of published reports, details of collections of survey materials (pottery, lithics, etc.), catalogues of relevant aerial and satellite imagery, and catalogues of relevant maps (topographic, geological, geographical, pedological), all as a basis for developing a regional-scale approach to the archaeology of Southwest Asia. So far this excellent suggestion has not been pursued, to the best of my knowledge. In conclusion, the value of field survey of Mesopotamian landscapes has been superbly demonstrated by the work of Adams and colleagues over the past few decades, building on a base constructed in the 1930s by Mallowan, Lloyd, Jacobsen and Braidwood. Future developments are likely to include the application of increasingly sophisticated analytical frameworks, including GIS (Geographical Information Systems) applications, alongside the implementation of ever more intensive field programmes in conjunction with use of satellite imagery (Verhoeven and Daels 1994; Wilkinson 2000: 221). Integrated use of backhoe sectioning across ancient canals and irrigation features, along with highly targeted excavation of sites in order to retrieve dating, environmental and economic evidence, are also likely to make a major contribution to the next generation of large-scale survey projects (Redman 1982). In addition, the sorts of high-intensity, rigorously structured and tightly focused surveys that are now routinely conducted across landscapes of Mediterranean countries such as Italy, Greece and Turkey may come to be applied within Mesopotamian contexts, although the special problems of high alluviation and fierce erosion will closely condition the planning, conduct and interpretation of any such work.

Figure 2.5 Intensive field-walking survey in north central Turkey, Project Paphlagonia

Source: photo by R. Matthews.

Archaeology and Assyriology

The archaeological record that is our inheritance from the past of Mesopotamia is an exceptionally rich and varied resource. Included within it are entire palaces clad with their powerful wall reliefs, neighbourhoods of private housing with manifold traces of ways of life, stratified sequences of temples and houses of priests, cemeteries of the dead, and vast overlapping landscapes of activity and abandonment. And beyond what we know of there is unquestionably still so much more to locate, recover and study. As the discipline has evolved, and as the quantities and types of material evidence to be studied have increased, so there has quite naturally come to be a heightened degree of professional specialisation within the study of the Mesopotamian past, as elsewhere in the world of archaeology. We have already seen how a modern long-term excavation project is conducted, its team comprising excavators, surveyors and specialists in fields such as animal bones, plants, sediments, pottery, figurines and numerous other elements.

One of the principal specialisations within the study of the Mesopotamian past is that of epigraphy, the study of surviving written documents, generally called Assyriology within the Mesopotamian context, and proudly defended as 'a useless science' in Jean Bottéro's apology (Bottéro 1992: 15–25). This branch is as old as the study of the non-literate remains of Mesopotamia, as we saw in Chapter 1, and has its own rich history and armoury of theories, approaches and methods.

In recent years there has been an increasing openness and critical awareness concerning the theory and practice of Assyriology as a means of
approaching Mesopotamian history. Rooted in an acceptance that there
is still much to learn about the structure and details of the Mesopotamian
past, as textually attested, there is a concern that Assyriologists should
explicate their principles of analysis and move on from 'assembling bits
of data from all … sources and sequencing them in chronological order,
like beads of information on threads of time, as if optimal exploitation of
sufficiently full sources might yield an unbroken necklace of historical
narrative' (von Dassow 1999: 228–9). Rather than lamenting the lack of
ancient historical narratives from the Mesopotamian past as a serious
failing in the evidence, the absence of a Mesopotamian Herodotus or
even Thucydides should be optimised as an opportunity for modern
Assyriologists to construct their own Mesopotamian histories, not necessarily as narratives, on the basis of the wealth of surviving 'primary,
unmediated sources', in Dominique Charpin's apt phrase (Charpin
1995: 807).

Several Assyriologists have indeed relished this opportunity,
displaying 'an increased delicacy as regards the document' in the words
of Mario Liverani (1973: 179). In particular, the work of Liverani and
Marc Van De Mieroop demonstrates a keen awareness of the nature of
the evidence, its pitfalls and, above all, its potentialities, as demonstrated
throughout Liverani's superb general survey of the ancient Near East
(Liverani 1988). Critically evaluating the role and status of Assyriology
in the modern world, Van De Mieroop (1997a; 1999a) has stressed the
need for Assyriologists to consider the historical context of their discipline, the nature and value of history as narrative, the social contexts of
the origin and development of documentary sources, and the value of
approaches to socio-economic history that transcend the specifics of
time and space. These healthy developments within Assyriology are
helping to shift the burden of the discipline away from its traditional
position as a warm-up act for the history of the Bible and of the classical world (see Chapter 1). It could be argued that Mesopotamian
archaeology, as distinct from Assyriology, has to a large extent already
made this shift to intellectual independence from the biblical and classical worlds, perhaps largely due to the major input from North
America of anthropological approaches to the past from the 1940s
onwards. As we have seen in Chapter 1, the introduction of anthropological archaeology in Mesopotamia led to new approaches to processes
of settlement, subsistence and society that have attempted to apprehend
ancient communities on their own terms.

An unfortunate tendency in Mesopotamian archaeology has been towards the belief that in periods and places where written texts are available, the range and purpose of non-textual archaeology may be correspondingly diminished. This attitude has in the past encouraged many archaeologists working in textually attested periods to focus their activities on areas such as art and monumental architecture, in the belief that these fields might satisfactorily complement epigraphic enquiries into fields such as economy, administration and religion (Nissen 1988: 3). It is this view, prevalent through much of the twentieth century in the archaeology of Southwest Asia, that has skewed approaches to, and understanding of, the archaeological record, so that for atextual periods ambitious anthropological, economic and ecological approaches have dominated, while for textual periods archaeology has frequently assumed an inadequate and unsatisfying role as support act for (textual) history. The unsuitability and wastefulness of this hand-maiden role for archaeology have been stressed in the work of John Moreland (Moreland 2001), who both roundly criticises textual specialists who lightly dismiss, on the basis of misunderstandings of its nature, the potential of archaeology to approach meaning in the past and, at the same time, chastises those archaeologists who have implicitly accepted their subordinate status by assigning primacy to the written word as a guide to how, where and when archaeology should be practised (see also Britton 1997). The idea that archaeology conducted within historical eras can somehow serve as a 'text-controlled laboratory' in which archaeological hypotheses based on soft, yielding data are assayed against the hard, unmoving 'reality' of documentary sources, undervalues both the worth of archaeology and the subtlety and polysemy of the textual record. Objects and texts are both shaped by social elements, are both subject to multiple readings, in the past as well as in the present, and are both agents of change and social interaction within the context(s) of their own pasts (Andrén 1998). They should be approached in fundamentally the same spirit.

Part of the problem is undoubtedly the belief amongst epigraphists in the supremacy of the written word as testimony to the past, a belief to which many archaeologists have also subscribed by virtue of their actions, if not their explicit strategies, in letting the text have the last word, so to speak. As Brinkman says, 'The testimony of cuneiform documents tends to be regarded as sacrosanct – especially by those who cannot or do not read them' (Brinkman 1984: 179). This view can manifest itself in quite subtle ways, as we see if we consider a statement by one of the most thoughtful and committed Mesopotamian archaeologists, Gil Stein; 'in prehistoric or nonliterate societies, the relationship between systems of meaning such as political ideologies and their material culture correlates is problematical and subject to serious interpretive ambiguities' (Stein 2001: 270). But these ambiguities and the problems of associating material culture correlates with political ideologies are every bit as complex, polysemous and hard to interpret in historic as in ahistoric societies, and there should therefore be no fundamental distinction in approach to the archaeological record of either.

Less subtly, a belief in the power of the written word is much to the fore in the writings of Jean Bottéro, who likes to contrast the 'hazy and uncertain outline of the past' visible to archaeologists and prehistorians with the 'precise, detailed, and analytical' knowledge of the past attainable through written documents (Bottéro 1992: 28), the 'speechless and intellectually vague' world of archaeology with the 'irreplaceable eloquence' of philology (Bottéro 1992: 43), and the 'often ambiguous and uncertain' answers of archaeology, 'absolutely unsuitable for ever responding to the great essential questions that deal with the mind and heart of mankind, much less the vicissitudes of people's behavior and lives', with the pellucid reality of written documents, 'the surest, the most complete, the most indispensable sources for our rediscovery of the past' (Bottéro 2000: 6–7). These views, manifest in milder form in the writings of A. L. Oppenheim (1977: 10–11), can be sharply contrasted with those of Marc Van De Mieroop, who recognises explicitly the unique and specific value of archaeology in approaching the Mesopotamian past (Van De Mieroop 1999a: 5). Bottéro's views on the worth and nature of both archaeology and epigraphy are a matter of some concern, and a major aim in this volume is to assert and illustrate the fact that archaeology has its own means and methods of approaching the past, which of course differ in many respects, although not in spirit, from those ideally belonging to the field of Assyriology, but which can nevertheless be employed with intellectual rigour to recover and reconstruct a tremendously detailed wealth of understandings about the past.

And if archaeology in Mesopotamia has so far failed on this account, then perhaps it is because we have been too modest in our ambitions and strategies, too willing to let the written text assume its supremacy, and too reluctant to construct and implement specifically archaeological strategies that accept epigraphy as only one element in a holistic, interdisciplinary raft of approaches to the past. Perhaps we have also let Assyriology, the power of the Word over that of the Dirt (Vermeule 1996), get away with too much for too long, for the views of Bottéro betray a misunderstanding not only of archaeology but also of his own discipline. Few historians today would accept that written texts 'teach us things distinctly and frankly and respond in plain language to our inquiries concerning the stages in life, the thought and the civilization of those times' (Bottéro 2000: 7). Indeed, one does not need to read Bottéro's own work for long before encountering admissions of bafflement when confronted with a text: 'in other words, the code that would enable us to decipher and understand these divine writings in large measure escapes us' (Bottéro 2000: 46), or of the inadequacy felt in the face of partial evidence: 'vast reaches of space and time are not documented by the least bit of information, and about numerous sectors of life … we know practically nothing' (Bottéro 1992: 52).

Without advocating an assumption of postmodernist relativism (Gellner 1992), I contend that every 'frank and distinct' statement made by Bottéro about the Mesopotamian past based on his reading of written documents is itself open to reinterpretation, expansion, revision and even refutation by any other epigraphist who might approach those same documents and/or by the recovery of new evidence in the years ahead. The suggestion is not that there is no solid ground of reality contained in the message of the texts, only that every so-called 'fact' of the past, whether drawn from an object or a document, is only a contextualised meaning read into it by the scholar who has chosen, usually implicitly, to focus on a limited number of aspects of the total available pool of evidence. Again, a contrasting point of view is well stated by Van De Mieroop, whose

> book is written with the conviction that the scholar's own historical condition determines the account that is being written, that objectivity is an elusive ideal, and that the questions asked and models and interpretative frameworks employed are determined by the scholar's contemporary concerns rather than by the sources investigated.
>
> (Van De Mieroop 1999a: 1)

Or, to quote an archaeologist who has allied himself with the 'new cultural history': 'both categories of evidence [artefacts and written texts] are generated by actors manipulating shared but contested cultural expectations in the process of living their lives' (Morris 1997: 8–9).

In the final part of this chapter we underline how profitable it can be when archaeology and epigraphy go hand-in-hand in their approach to specific problems of the past. One of the great strengths of the archaeological record of Mesopotamia is the potential it allows for combining the approaches of epigraphy and archaeology, some form of literacy being a basic element in many of the societies that trod its stage from the late fourth millennium onwards. The fundamental tenet of the archaeo-historical approach is that written documents are themselves archaeological artefacts with meaningful physical and social contexts, and that therefore value can be had from studying them as one would any other recovered artefact, over and above the undoubtedly special value to be had from written documents in terms of their substantive content.

Of course, an integrated approach relies on the discovery and adequate contextual recording of written documents as elements of a controlled excavation programme, as well as on a meaningful dialogue between archaeologist and epigraphist whereby 'after the initial courtesies, both the archaeologist and the philologist will soon acknowledge that the house has a story to tell about the tablets and the tablets about the house' (Janssen 1996: 237). It is one of the mild yet frustrating ironies of Mesopotamian archaeology that so much of the known textual material comes from unprovenanced or inadequately provenanced sources, and is therefore of restricted value, while from highly controlled excavations in modern times the finds of textual material have generally been sparse or from less informative secondary contexts. This condition holds especially true for texts of so-called proto-cuneiform type, that is of late fourth and early third millennia date, where a combination of unsuitable excavation methods and the ancient practice of throwing unwanted tablets into rubbish deposits means that contextual and archival information is minimal (Englund 1998). Even where intact archives appear to have been located and excavated, as in the large building at Jemdet Nasr, completely inadequate excavation and recording practices, even by the standards of the time, have forever destroyed the priceless contextual information that could have transformed our understanding of the very earliest writing procedures (R. Matthews 2002). Another famous lost opportunity is that of Old Babylonian Ur, where Woolley's careful excavation of a neighbourhood of housing lost much of its potential significance because of the lack of contextual information concerning many of the cuneiform tablets found within the houses. The tablets had been well excavated and documented as to exact provenance, but vital information as to context was lost during the baking of the tablets after excavation before catalogue numbers had been inked on them (Woolley and Mallowan 1976: xviii).

In her 1981 article, Elizabeth Stone expertly melds the study of

architecture and associated written documents using a glue of ethnographic analogy to produce highly detailed insights into Old
Babylonian residence patterns at Nippur.

Ground-plan areas of roofed rooms within excavated buildings
match closely with areas given in cuneiform property texts found within

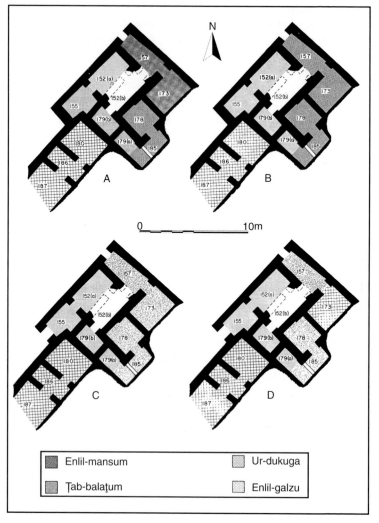

Figure 2.6 Patterns of residence through time in TA House I at Nippur,
south Iraq

Source: after Stone 1981: fig. 2.

those same buildings, so that Stone is able to assign specific rooms to individuals named within the texts, and to correlate architectural modifications of the buildings, archaeologically attested, with sequences of property transactions recorded in the texts. Bringing in analogy from modern ethnographic studies, Stone characterises Old Babylonian residential patterns at Nippur thus:

> Virilocal extended family residence was apparently practised when possible, although nuclear family residence was not uncommon. Extended families tended to occupy large, square houses with rooms on all four sides of a courtyard, while nuclear families occupied smaller, linear houses with rooms on two or three sides of a courtyard.
>
> (Stone 1981: 32)

These and the many other stimulating conclusions and hypotheses reached by Stone in her Nippur work (see also Stone 1987; and critique by Postgate 1990a) are the product of a truly interdisciplinary approach, and could not have been arrived at by study of the architecture or texts in isolation.

In another interdisciplinary study, also at Nippur, Richard Zettler uses texts and archaeological evidence to shed highly focused light on the administration of the Ur III temple of Inanna (Zettler 1987; 1992; see also Zettler 1996 for another Nippur study). The recovery of collections of sealed pieces of clay as well as inscribed cuneiform tablets at specific locations within the temple enables Zettler to provide an integrated analysis of the workings of the Ur III temple, despite the fact that later Parthian builders had seriously disturbed the integrity of the main temple archive. Analysis of the texts shows the temple's involvement in management of property and animals under the tight control of chief administrators over a duration of five successive generations. A major strength of Zettler's analysis is his ability to situate these precise and highly regulated administrative activities within their original architectural context. By studying the plan of the temple and the location of recovered artefacts we are able to walk in the steps of the chief administrator, to follow him as he goes about his duties around the great temple, to understand the import and practice of many of those duties, to appreciate the building as, amongst other things, the physical context of his high status within the Nippur community, and finally to follow him at night to his private apartments where he might enjoy a meal in room 124 before retiring to bed in room 14 where, being an administrator, he might count sheep before falling asleep.

There are all too few further examples of these highly specific and profitable integrated approaches to the Mesopotamian past, but as exemplars they demonstrate how worthwhile a study can be when founded on a willingness to regard documentary and non-textual archaeological evidence as pieces of the same past, conveyors of information and meaning about the past that are approachable in essentially the same integrated, contextual and nuanced way. The best of these approaches transcend the alleged dichotomy between written and non-written evidence from the past, frequently alluded to in the work of Bottéro, as we have seen, and maximise with great effect the totality of the often meagre residue of the past that we have at our disposal (see also Gates 1988 for detailed instances of textual and archaeological integration). As Zettler has stressed, such interdisciplinary studies are not adequate ends in themselves, but simply building blocks with which to construct larger-scale insights into, and ideas about, issues of political, social and economic process (Zettler 1996: 96).

At the wider scale, in the previous section we have seen how the work of Robert Adams uniquely enmeshes the approaches of archaeology, history and ethnography to generate long-term trajectories of human settlement patterns and landscape interactions in the Mesopotamian context. The agenda for the future is set out by Dan Potts in his book *Mesopotamian Civilization: the Material Foundations*:

> The study of ancient Mesopotamia can move forward rapidly when archaeologists, Assyriologists and natural scientists cooperate. Lateral thinking and a desire to solve problems and explore domains for which no ready synthesis exists, can lead to an entirely new brand of study in which archaeology, philology and the natural sciences combine forces to elucidate problems which no one of these disciplines can, in isolation, ever solve.
>
> (Potts 1997: 307)

Chronology of the Mesopotamian past

We shall close this chapter with a brief consideration of a fundamental task undertaken by the archaeologist: the construction of a chronology (Nissen 1988: 4–8). In the early days of the discipline this objective assumed great significance, but developments since the mid-twentieth century in scientific dating methods have partly freed archaeologists to consider more stimulating social, economic and ideological issues. These issues, nevertheless, take much of their significance from our ability to pinpoint them with some precision within a fixed chronological framework and thereby to relate them in time to each other and to other events and processes within Mesopotamia and beyond. How do we construct such a chronological framework?

There are two types of chronology: relative and absolute. In relative chronology we establish chronological relationships between sites and/or aspects of material culture assemblages that allow us to say which sites are older and which more recent, for example, or which type of pottery pre-dates which other types of pottery. These frameworks are built up using two key approaches, stratification and typology, frequently both employed together. We have seen in the above section on excavation that careful analysis of stratigraphy is fundamental in modern fieldwork. The basic field principle of removal of later deposits before earlier deposits, in reverse sequence to their historical deposition, allows the construction of a stratigraphic sequence within which relationships between associated deposits can be established. On multi-period sites it will then prove possible to establish a relative chronology that includes relationships between material culture assemblages. Thus at Ur, for example, excavations long ago established that materials of Ur III type preceded those of Old Babylonian type but succeeded those of Early Dynastic and Akkadian types in turn. Much of the basic ordering of Mesopotamian cultural assemblages has been completed at least in a general sense, although there remains a great deal of fine-tuning to be carried out.

Associated with stratification, the study of typology of recovered artefacts, such as pottery, lithics, seals, and so on, enables developmental sequences in the histories of these objects to be constructed, often using concepts and approaches borrowed from art history. When such artefacts are encountered in non-excavation contexts, reasonable estimates about their relative dating can be postulated on the basis of excavated assemblages. This assumption underlies the survey work of Adams and other practitioners, as outlined in the previous section.

Mesopotamian chronology is based partly on excavations at certain key sites, many of which have given their name to chronological episodes, such as Hassuna, Samarra, Halaf, Ubaid, Uruk, Jemdet Nasr, and so on, even where the period itself has come to be better known from materials excavated at other sites. For example, we know more about the Halaf period from Arpachiyah than we do from Halaf, but material of this type was first identified at Tell Halaf. Likewise, we know much more about the Samarra period from excavations at Tell es-Sawwan than at Samarra itself. A good example of how a detailed chronology can be constructed by employing stratification and typology in concert is the study by Michael Roaf and Robert Killick, wittily constructed in the style of an Agatha Christie thriller, of the Ninevite 5 period of Upper Mesopotamia (Roaf and Killick 1987). By meticulous analysis of the changing frequencies of types of decorated pot types through excavated levels of the site of Mohammed 'Arab, on the Tigris north of Mosul, and other sites of the early third millennium BC, Roaf and Killick demonstrate clearly for the first time how the various pottery styles chronologically relate to each other. Apart from being a rare instance of an entertaining article on the subject of prehistoric pottery, Roaf and Killick's analysis graphically shows how statistics and stratigraphy together can make a powerful case in relative chronology.

Different types of object, pottery as against seals for example, are likely to change in their stylistic and functional attributes at rates that do not coincide, a fact that can make it difficult or impossible to draw sharp dividing lines between chronological periods for all items of material culture. As Hans Nissen has put it, 'It is therefore clear that it is not possible to have one universally valid chronological scheme, but only systems that fit specific criteria in given situations and show certain inadequacies in others' (Nissen 1988: 7).

Absolute chronology has only become a real option with the development of scientific methods of dating of materials from the past, developed in the past fifty years or so (Renfrew and Bahn 2000: 128–55). Of special significance for the periods featured in this book is the development of radiocarbon dating, based on measurement of amounts of radiocarbon surviving in dead organic materials. Teething problems with field recovery and laboratory procedures have led to considerable confusion and unreliability associated with radiocarbon dating in Southwest Asia, but a more settled position is steadily being achieved. Focused research on specific periods and episodes of the Mesopotamian past is resulting in generally agreed absolute and relative chronologies, as for example with the Uruk period of Mesopotamia and adjacent regions (Wright and Rupley 2001), although as ever there remains a great deal of work to do.

Chapter 3

Tracking a transition
Hunters becoming farmers

In the next four chapters we are going to examine specific issues, or groups of connected issues, from the human past where the contribution from Mesopotamian archaeology is especially significant. They are in effect case studies selected from an almost infinite range of research areas. Even within the four chosen topics we have to be highly selective in the treatment of specific angles and elements of the fields of study, as there is an overwhelming amount of material to choose from. Topics have been chosen on the basis of their overall significance, bearing in mind the unique role the Mesopotamian past can play in addressing what many people call the 'big questions' of human development (see Chapter 2). The emphasis throughout these chapters is on explication of the theories, approaches and techniques of Mesopotamian archaeology in attempting to apprehend these issues as much as on the nature of the results themselves, but insofar as theories, methods and interpretations feed into each other in an interaction of experiment, experience and exposition, we shall no doubt include much substantive discussion as we proceed. Above all, the aim is to demonstrate the richness of Mesopotamian and Southwest Asian archaeology in terms of research agendas, the nature of the evidence available, and the ways in which that evidence can be approached. Again we underline the liberality in use of the term 'Mesopotamian'. Much of what is covered in this chapter, especially, relates to developments in adjacent regions of Southwest Asia, particularly the Levant and southeast Anatolia.

Settling down

Our first issue is not so much big as momentous, as a few quotations will serve to show. It has been called 'the most fateful change in the human career' (Harris 1996: ix), 'among the great turning points in human history' (Cauvin 2000a: xv), 'one of the most significant developments in the existence of the genus *Homo*' (Bogucki 1999: 839), 'perhaps the most remarkable event in the entire course of human prehistory' (Price and Gebauer 1995: 3), and 'the most crucial revolution of humankind after 2.5 million years of cultural evolution' (Bar-Yosef 2001: 117), amongst many other things. It has also been hailed as 'the single most dramatic (and ultimately the most catastrophic) set of changes that human society has experienced since the mastery of fire' (Hillman and Davies 1999: 70). We are going to study archaeological approaches to the issue of how human communities changed over a period of several millennia from mobile hunting and gathering to sedentary agriculture and animal husbandry. From the Mesopotamian and Southwest Asian points of view there is a vast amount of information and interpretation bearing on the wide range of issues subsumed under this rubric, and we can do no more than sample them. But in the process we hope to be able to provide a good idea of how such complex and significant issues can be approached in multidisciplinary and integrated ways.

For tens of thousands of years since their first appearance around 100,000 years ago, anatomically modern humans lived an essentially mobile life. Earlier hominid forms, including Neandertals (partly contemporary with truly modern humans, at least in Southwest Asia) and *Homo erectus*, had spent hundreds of thousands of years following essentially stable and mobile lifestyles. As Anthony Giddens has nicely phrased it: 'If we were to think of the entire span of human existence thus far as a day, agriculture would have come into existence at 11.56 p.m. and civilizations at 11.57' (Giddens 2001: 40). On the basis of these immense time spans it has been calculated that 90 per cent of all humans ever to have lived were hunter-gatherers (Roberts 1998: 81). Human groups, subsisting exclusively on hunted and gathered resources, were attached in territorial terms to large-scale landscapes over which they moved according to seasonal rhythms in pursuit of animal prey and shifting vegetational regimes, with a few regular halting points where small communities settled down for a period of weeks or months, living in shelters constructed of stones, brush, and hides. Such long-term camp-sites have been identified and excavated in Southwest Asia and within Mesopotamia, including Barda Balka in northeast Iraq, where hominids of unknown type hunted wild cattle, sheep, goat and equids, and ate shells and turtles, some 100–150,000 years ago. This site is of special note in that it provides the only evidence in Mesopotamian prehistory for the hunting, or scavenging, of Indian elephant and rhinoceros (Braidwood and Howe 1960; R. Matthews 2000a: 14).

Other more specialised hunting and gathering camps or shelters, such as Zarzi and Palegawra in the Iraqi Zagros mountains (R. Matthews 2000a: 26–8), date to the very end of the Palaeolithic period (sometimes called the Epipalaeolithic), around 13,000 BC, when there is an increased emphasis on plant processing and exploitation of a growing range of foodstuffs, the so-called 'broad spectrum revolution' (Flannery 1969; but see also Edwards 1989). From around 12,000 BC the last Ice Age ended and the epoch known as the Holocene succeeded the Pleistocene. Thereafter human communities underwent a series of major transformations so that within a period of a few thousand years they had changed from mobile hunter-gathering to fully sedentary farming and animal-rearing, a process called the 'Neolithic revolution' by the Australian prehistorian Gordon Childe (1936). How did these dramatic changes come about, and how can we study them?

A striking aspect of Palaeolithic lifeways, as they appear in the available evidence, is the astonishing continuity and stability of material culture over immense spans of time (Shennan 2001). Accustomed as we are to change as a fundamental ingredient and stimulant of human society, it is hard to envision how communities of human beings, either fully modern like us or closely related like Neandertals or *Homo erectus*, could carry on living in the same ways for tens of thousands of years with no notable changes in their material culture. Traditional views of Palaeolithic hunter-gatherer society stressed the harshness of their existence and accepted as axiomatic that a change to farming and sedentism would be to the good, and would be recognised as such by hunter-gatherers as soon as the choice was available to them. In recent decades the emphasis has shifted to a realisation that hunter-gatherer communities, through their enjoyment of intimate and thoroughly integrated relationships with their surroundings, had much to lose by switching to farming (Cohen 1977: 27–40). The stresses of farming life, perhaps especially in its initial stages, are severe and will have contrasted sharply with hunting-gathering ways (Cohen 1989). It is therefore no longer adequate to attempt to explain the origins of farming by demonstrating the co-existence of all the necessary ingredients – people, climate, plants, animals – at the right time in the right place, although that demonstration may itself be part of the explanation. There must also be a factor, or range of factors, that drives communities into farming apparently against their better judgement.

A common and often effective way to investigate a complex subject is to divide it into discrete components that can be analysed both sequentially in isolation and in terms of their connections with each other. Once that is done the pieces are reassembled and a coherent and integrated overview can be assayed. Looked at in this way, we see that the principal components to the topic under discussion can be characterised as follows: climate, population, plants, and animals. Once we have looked at these elements in turn, we can consider them as a totality within the context of human society.

Climate: something in the air

There is an entire field of study devoted to past climates, employing sophisticated theories, approaches and techniques of its own (Crowley and North 1991; Dincauze 2000), which we can merely sample here. The prominence of climate in studies of the Neolithic revolution can be ascribed to the fact that the shift to farming occurred apparently in smooth sequence with major climate changes at the transition from the Pleistocene to the Holocene from about 13,000 BC onwards (Butzer 1995). The one seems to set the stage for the other, 'a powerful coincidence' indeed (Moore *et al.* 2000: 16). An extreme hypothesis based on this coincidence is that agriculture was impossible during the Pleistocene but inevitable during the Holocene, as proposed in a recent study (Richardson *et al.* 2001).

Childe's theory, partly based on earlier work by Rafael Pumpelly, was that as Southwest Asia dried up in the early centuries of the Holocene, limited water resources came to be increasingly restricted in 'oasis' locations where human communities and animals were obliged to interact in novel and evermore intensive ways, rapidly leading to domestication (Childe 1936). This interpretation is called the oasis or propinquity theory of the origins of farming. A modified version of the propinquity theory, but without the stress on environmental change, underlay Braidwood's research programme in the 1950s on the 'hilly flanks' of the Fertile Crescent, the Iraqi Zagros mountains, with the 'nuclear zone' notion that the physical proximity of human communities and the wild ancestors of domesticated plants and animals would in due course lead to farming (Braidwood and Howe 1960: 3).

One way of testing Childe's theory is by analysis of sediment cores from lake deposits, an approach based on the fact that pollen grains and spores will find their way onto nearby lakes, marshes, or peat bogs where they sink to the bottom to be incorporated in sediments. Pollen from the past, its study known as palynology, is best preserved in anaerobic, or oxygen-free, environments such as exist in sediments submerged under water. Ancient pollen can be recovered today by coring of sediments and the deposits can be dated using radiocarbon methods. The issues of pollen dispersal, survival, and its representativeness of past plant regimes are all complex (Roberts 1998: 29–36; Renfrew and Bahn 2000: 239–42), but the main point here is that pollen can be used to reconstruct at least some aspects of ancient climate and environment, such as the prevalence of types of trees or bushes through time, and therefore changes in rainfall and temperature patterns. Study of pollen in sediment cores from Lake Zeribar in west Iran suggests that Southwest Asia did not dry up as the Ice Age ended, but that there was instead an increase in rainfall following the start of the Holocene, the reverse of the scenario conceived by Childe (van Zeist and Bottema 1977).

Furthermore, pollen evidence from Zeribar and Lake Huleh in the Levant, taken in concert with excavated evidence from the site of Abu Hureyra on the river Euphrates in Syria, provides the basis for an alternative theory, proposed by Moore and Hillman (1992) and elaborated by Bar-Yosef and Meadow (1995; see also Goring-Morris and Belfer-Cohen 1997) within a Levantine context. Attested increases in temperature and rainfall in the very late Pleistocene and early Holocene may have encouraged the spread of wild cereals and associated animals from an originally restricted homeland in the south Levant into other regions of the so-called Fertile Crescent, where expanding human communities made increasing use of them on a hunting and gathering basis. Then, around 10,000 BC, during an episode known as the Younger Dryas, there was a severe deterioration in climate with a return to much colder and drier weather, lasting for up to 1,000 years and attested on a global scale. According to this theory, the temporary return to glacial climate induced a dramatic decrease in the availability of resources, forcing now populous human communities to engage in more intensive methods of exploitation of their natural environment, thus giving rise to domestication and agriculture. A subsequent return to a fully Holocene climate at the end of the Younger Dryas then encouraged the consolidation and spread of the new suite of human/environment relationships that had originated under conditions of climatic stress.

A related climatic theory, proposed by McCorriston and Hole (1991) and H. E. Wright (1993), holds that during the Younger Dryas an increased degree of climatic seasonality, especially marked in the south Levant, and featuring warmer, drier summers, favoured the spread of cereal grains into the orbit of the newly settled peoples of the region, who rapidly domesticated them:

> The environmental and cultural history of the Near East involved the inception of the mediterranean climate and its associated flora of domesticable plants at approximately the same time as cultural evolution reached the level of sedentary communities, which themselves changed the relations of the people to their environment. Such a favorable combination for plant domestication may have been unique in human history.
>
> (H. E. Wright 1993: 468)

Roger Byrne had earlier stressed the significance of increased seasonality at the Pleistocene-Holocene boundary, showing how early agriculture developed in regions with marked seasonality and with domesticable species already adapted to seasonal rainfall regimes (Byrne 1987). Byrne demonstrates how the present pattern of seasonal rainfall and temperature in Southwest Asia originated during the late Pleistocene to early Holocene, thus providing a changed environment for the stimulation of new interrelationships between species, including animals, plants and humans, in those millennia. Byrne sees a trend towards warm dry summers and cool wet winters in Southwest Asia beginning around 22,000 BC, leading in time to increased human reliance on wild plant foods as the first step en route to full agriculture.

In their basic mechanisms, though not in chronology or location, the Younger Dryas and seasonal stress theories resemble the oasis theory of Pumpelly and Childe insofar as the prime stimulus for domestication is external to human communities and to some degree deterministic. They are so-called 'push' theories (Bogucki 1999: 847) where emphasis is on a single factor, usually, as the major drive towards change. Other theories, of the 'pull' kind, are rooted more in the notion of the opportunism and social aptitude of human communities during the early Holocene, as we shall see.

Population: getting together

Another area of research with dominant 'push' theories has been the issue of increasing human population numbers in the transition to agriculture. In an influential paper published in 1968, Lewis Binford envisioned a process of demographic fission in post-Pleistocene Southwest Asia, whereby splinter groups would be forced to develop new subsistence strategies as they occupied increasingly marginal zones, 'where less sedentary populations are being moved in on by daughter groups from more sedentary populations' (Binford 1968: 334), an idea expanded on by Kent Flannery in his study of the 'broad spectrum revolution' in west Iran (Flannery 1969). The force of population pressure as a 'prime mover' was also argued in the case of the shift to agriculture in the central west Zagros region (Smith and Young 1983).

The fullest treatment of population pressure theory came with Mark Cohen's book *The Food Crisis in Prehistory* (Cohen 1977; *contra*, see Cowgill 1975), in which Cohen argues that, as human populations naturally tend to increase in number, with the colonisation by humans of all available land surfaces by 15,000 BC changes in subsistence were bound to happen. Initial developments in the last centuries of the Pleistocene included a shift to a broader food-base, with consumption of such items as snails, birds, shells, and ever more plant types, in addition to the familiar large game species. Once this adaptation had run its course, the next stage was the intensification of means of subsistence through domestication of plants and animals.

More recent studies emphasise the lack of evidence for the active participation of population growth, in terms of pressure or stress, in the shift to agriculture (Henry 1989: 20–4; Price and Gebauer 1995: 7), although it is still cited as one possible factor amongst many (Bar-Yosef and Meadow 1995: 49, 69). Brian Hayden has argued that the archaeological evidence fails to support any of the predictions, or necessary concomitants, of the population pressure theory, such as signs of economic stress prior to domestication or the commencement of domestication in marginal zones (Hayden 1992). Cauvin makes the point that population growth within human communities is more likely to be restricted by social convention than by availability of food resources (Cauvin 2000a: 64), although high infant mortality rates and disease would also have a major effect (Groube 1996).

One factor is the difficulty of arriving at agreed absolute figures for population sizes in early prehistory. Cohen posits a world population of approximately 15 million persons at the start of the Holocene (Cohen 1977: 54), which can be contrasted with Groube's 'a few millions' (Groube 1996: 102). Recent genetic studies indicate tightly confined 'bottlenecks' in Palaeolithic populations, with humans facing almost complete extinction at a time of severe climatic conditions around 70–60,000 years ago, with subsequent population growth seen as a major factor in late Palaeolithic human cultural development (Shennan 2001). A novel theory on the origins of agriculture holds that human communities made the shift to sedentism and farming as a means of improving their reproductive efficiency in a constant battle against disease, increasingly on the rampage since the start of the Holocene as a concomitant of climatic warming: 'This micropredatorial pressure sustained the impetus of intensification, diversification and subsequent developments in productivity that resulted in agriculture and pastoralism. Perhaps we owe more to bugs than we dare admit' (Groube 1996: 125). Groube's theory elegantly upends the conventional population argument by positing the deliberate adoption of sedentism and agriculture as a means of increasing population rather than as a forced response to preceding population growth.

Plants: a green revolution

We now turn our attention to the plants that came to have such major significance within the new subsistence strategies of settled human communities of the Neolithic period and beyond. An initial point is that we are mistaken if we view plants as a constant and largely static resource-bank to be mined or exploited by human communities as and when they saw fit. Every bit as much as humans, plants too were undergoing processes of dramatic change and adaptation in the centuries of the early Holocene. With the increase in temperature and precipitation that characterised the end of the Ice Age, plant distributions and regimes changed rapidly. One might say that, as physical conditions changed, plants were amenable to the possibility of new relationships just as human communities were (Ingold 1996). The work of David Rindos (1980) in particular, stresses the importance of the co-evolution and symbiosis of plants and humans in the history of early agriculture. From the plant point of view, domestication is what happened to human communities in the early Holocene, and plants were not slow to take advantage of the new opportunities afforded by the settling down of human groups through those centuries. Furthermore, the point in time where we are able to identify domestication of plants in the archaeological record certainly comes after a lengthy period of experimentation and interaction between plants and people:

> the discovery of domesticates defines only the end point of a process that might have taken hundreds or even thousands of years. ... Agriculturally based societies did not spring up overnight as the result of an idea proposed by some prehistoric genius.
>
> (Cowan and Watson 1992: 4)

Nevertheless, the actual switch to full-blown farming of domesticated plant species may itself have been relatively swift and dramatic, 'an event(s) as much as a process' (Blumler 1996: 38), and the evidence from Abu Hureyra (see below) may be adduced in support of such a notion.

In fact there is a wide spectrum of possible interactions between plants and people, ranging from low-intensity gathering of purely wild species, through the use of fire and other means to encourage the growth of wild plants, the intentional planting of wild plants (cultivation), and the complete domestication of species involving morphological change in attributes of the species in question, culminating in their inability to reproduce without human curation (Miller 1992: 39). In the context of Southwest Asia in the Neolithic period, particular significance lies in the exploitation and domestication of cereals such as wheat and barley from naturally occurring wild ancestors that were clearly used as food for a very long time before their morphological domestication. In addition, other plant food sources such as pea and lentil were domesticated from wild ancestors at about the same time and in at least approximately the same regions.

How do we know about ancient plants and their interactions with people? The discipline of palaeoethnobotany, of relatively recent development, has been defined as 'the cross-cultural study of the interrelationships between prehistoric plant and human populations' (Cowan and Watson 1992: 3). Methods have developed in recent decades from incidental recovery of charred plant remains during excavations to systematic programmes of sampling and processing of excavated deposits in order to retrieve statistically significant assemblages of plant remains of all shapes and sizes (Renfrew and Bahn 2000: 244–7). The principal recovery method is that of flotation, involving the submersion of deposits in water leading to the separation of light charred plant remains from the soil matrix. Using reference collections and published assemblages, the palaeoethnobotanist can identify by eye or microscope a great range of species and, using quantitative methods, can build up a picture of the relative importance of plant species within set social contexts. The construction of this picture is not a straightforward matter, as the issue of how plant remains come to be contained within specific archaeological contexts is often highly complex. Plant remains may arrive on site as residues of food processing activities, themselves complex, but may also get there through ingestion by herbivores and inclusion in animal dung used as fuel for ovens or hearths, for example (Miller and Smart 1984). Thus plant remains found in ash next to an oven may be traces of cooked human food but may also represent uncooked animal fodder burnt through use as fuel. The most valuable studies of plant remains are those supported by excellent contextual information on the one hand and by statistically valid sample sizes on the other.

In addition to charred plant remains we should not underestimate the importance of plant silica remains, or phytoliths, that survive the decomposition of organic parts of plants, and that can also attest the domestication of certain plant species (Renfrew and Bahn 2000: 242–3). Such remains can be especially profitably studied through recovery of intact sections of deposits in large-format micromorphological thin sections.

Ancient plant evidence can be used to address several broad areas, including diet, climate/environment, and practices of agriculture and animal husbandry. The first serious attempt to investigate the transition to agriculture in Southwest Asia through surviving plant remains took place within the remit of Braidwood's Jarmo project, led by the botanist Hans Helbaek (1960). Subsequent important archaeobotanical research occurred within the Deh Luran project in west Iran (Helbaek 1969), Çayönü in southeast Turkey (van Zeist and de Roller 1991–2), and Abu Hureyra on the Euphrates in Syria (Hillman and de Moulins 2000; see below), amongst many others (see summary in Miller 1992).

Based on the past few decades of systematic, but still sporadic, research into the origins and early development of domesticated plants, a coherent and generally accepted picture of plant domestication in Southwest Asia has been arrived at (Zohary and Hopf 1993; Zohary 1999). Present-day distributions of wild ancestors of early domesticated cereals and pulses give some idea of the locales of potential domestication, corresponding closely to the area known as the Fertile Crescent, which arcs from the south Levant through west Syria, southeast Turkey, northeast Iraq and central west Iran (Zohary 1989; Zohary and Hopf 1993). The plants of greatest significance to Neolithic farming communities of Southwest Asia were the cereals emmer wheat (*Triticum turgidum* subsp. *dicoccum*), barley (*Hordeum vulgare*), einkorn wheat (*Triticum monococcum*), and rye (*Secale cereale* subsp. *cereale*), as well as lentil (*Lens culinaris*), pea (*Pisum sativum*), flax (*Linum usitatissimum*), chickpea (*Cicer arietinum*), and bitter vetch (*Vicia ervilia*), a suite of plants that in varying arrangements formed the basis of human vegetal subsistence throughout the region for the Neolithic period and beyond (Zohary 1999). Domesticated varieties of cereals can be identified by the form of the rachis, which in wild species is brittle and allows natural dispersal of the spikelets containing the seed. In domesticated forms this rachis has toughened so that the spikelets only detach under impact of threshing by humans. The evidence suggests that domestication of each crop species occurred only once, or at most on a few closely related occasions, followed by rapid spread from its locus of domestication, a so-called monophyletic origin (Zohary 1999).

Interdisciplinary research directed by Andrew Moore at Abu Hureyra on the Euphrates river in Syria has been especially informative on the issue of early plant exploitation and domestication, amongst many other issues. A superb recent publication has done full justice to this uniquely significant site (Moore *et al.* 2000). Of particular value is our ability to contrast the chronological episodes of occupation at the site, commencing in the Epipalaeolithic (Abu Hureyra I: *c.*10,750–9,150 BC) and, after a short gap, continuing into the Neolithic, of both late pre-pottery and early pottery periods (Abu Hureyra II: *c.*8,400–6,000 BC). Detailed study of the plant remains shows very distinctive developments. During the earliest occupation only wild forms of einkorn and rye were exploited, and the admixture of seeds from other wild plants associated with these forms indicates that the cereals were not deliberately cultivated but were collected from purely wild stands. Furthermore, a great range of plants, totalling some 150, was exploited by the Epipalaeolithic inhabitants of Abu Hureyra and on the basis of this plant evidence it has been convincingly argued that the site was occupied on a year-round basis rather than as a seasonal camp. A detailed reconstruction of the season-by-season economic life of the early occupants of Abu Hureyra has been essayed on the basis of recovered plant and animal remains. The impact of the arid Younger Dryas episode (see above) led to a reduction in the availability of plants and a shift to deliberate cultivation and domestication of a limited range of species, with an emphasis on rye. This evidence for the adoption of farming, securely dated to *c.*10,000 BC, is the earliest from anywhere in the world. The suitability of rye for cooking as a gruel usable in weaning infants may have made a major contribution to increasing population size at the settlement.

The subsequent Neolithic picture at Abu Hureyra is very different. By then fully domesticated forms of five cereal species (rye, einkorn, emmer, bread wheat, barley) and at least three pulses (lentil, pea, vetch) are found and there is a massive decline in the range of exploited wild plant species. The success of these new and intensive agricultural modes of subsistence can be appreciated in light of the fact that the Neolithic settlement at Abu Hureyra thrived over a period of some two and a half millennia, ending in an abandonment perhaps caused by environmental degradation and overworking of the landscape by the substantial population of the settlement that covered some 11.5 hectares during its Neolithic occupation.

Analysis of the skeletal remains of some one hundred of the Neolithic occupants of Abu Hureyra, many of them buried under the floors of houses, has been uniquely enlightening (Molleson 2000). Wear patterns on human teeth show the toughness of the early agricultural diet in the Neolithic period, gradually evolving to softer, better cooked foods with the use of pottery vessels for food preparation. A major interpretation is that the females of the population bore the brunt of the physical stresses of the shift to an intensive agricultural regime, in particular through the daily practice of grinding grain. Theya Molleson shows how repeated and extended spells of grinding cause alterations to bones in the back, toes and knees of individuals, and that these features are found on female skeletons. We can thus postulate a clear gender division of labour by the Neolithic, which may originate in the Epipalaeolithic period, whereby men hunted and made tools, at least, while women processed food and attended their ever-increasing broods of children. For women, the Neolithic revolution meant a steady increase in labour, in both the work and child-bearing senses.

Other ways of approaching the issue of plant exploitation include the study of ground stone and chipped stone tools, many of which were used in plant processing, from harvesting to grinding. Patricia Anderson has studied microscopic traces of use-wear on edges of stone tools, as well as surviving chemical traces and phytoliths adhering in minute quantities to tool edges (Anderson 1999). Part of her work has involved experimental replications of plant processing activities using Neolithic-style tools, and on the basis of these experiments and her analyses she detects evidence for harvesting and grinding using stone tools in the Neolithic. Complementary approaches involve the study of existing human societies who employ traditional agricultural practices, in search of insights into practices of the past (Ataman 1999).

Undoubtedly a significant factor in the intensified exploitation and domestication of plants was the settling down of human communities. Without sedentism it is clear that these complex interactions could not have occurred in the same degree or form. The settling of even a small population in one locale may rapidly deplete local stands of wild cereals and generate a demand for increased cultivation and plant management. The broad range of social changes and possible increases in population growth rates attendant upon sedentism will also have maintained a need for intensified plant exploitation. Once the shift to total domestication of a suite of plant species was complete by the end of the

Neolithic period, there was no turning back for the human communities of Southwest Asia, now largely reliant on the increased returns of agricultural means of production as the vehicle for regenerating their own newly sophisticated social structures. Just as certain plant species had come to rely on human communities for their ability to reproduce, so certain human communities could only reproduce themselves through ever-increasing dependence on those very plants, truly a symbiotic relationship of mutual and ongoing domestication.

Animals: partners in clime

The discipline of zooarchaeology has developed along lines similar to those of palaeoethnobotany, blossoming from the economic and anthropological approaches applied in archaeology from the 1940s onwards. In broad terms, this branch of archaeology is concerned to investigate the multi-stranded relationships that exist between human communities and the animals of all kinds that share their environments. Such interactions might range from distant coexistence through occasional hunting to systematic husbandry, with many possibilities in between. As with plants, animals were undergoing changes in their geographical distributions and in many other ways, through the centuries that followed the end of the Ice Age, leading in some cases to drastic redefinitions of their relationships with each other and with human communities. For a few species their new condition by the full Neolithic period was one of complete domestication and control by humans. But again, it is vital to stress the mutualistic nature of these new Neolithic relationships. In evolutionary terms animals, like plants, were to benefit from relationships, including full domestication, with the newly sedentary human communities of Southwest Asia. Freed from predation by wild carnivores, provided with fodder year-round, and aided in their fertilising, birthing and upbringing by their human overseers, the only disadvantage for domesticated animals was that humans now had absolute say in the manner and timing of their death. Domesticated animals have been labelled a 'walking larder'. From the animal point of view we might see settled human communities as a 'sedentary provider'. The success of this relationship is perhaps best illustrated by the first domesticate of human society, the dog: 'As a wild species the wolf has lost the evolutionary fight as a competitive predator, but as the domesticated dog its biological success must be counted as high as that of the human species' (Clutton-Brock 1999: 214).

The methods and approaches of zooarchaeology have increased in scope and sophistication over recent decades, and there are excellent manuals on the subject (Meadow and Zeder 1978; Davis 1987; Reitz and Wing 1999). In brief, contemporary concerns include the complex processes by which assemblages of animal bones enter and stay in the archaeological record, the representativeness of bones in terms of original animal populations, and methods of recovery, analysis and interpretation of animal bone data. Situated within these concerns, zooarchaeologists address such specific issues as animal bones as indicators of past environments and of seasonality, and the age and sex profiles of ancient animal communities. The significance of zooarchaeology in the broad topic of the origins and early development of farming is of course immense, and our coverage here will be restricted to a couple of important case studies that highlight the role of the discipline in this arena. Following some general points on animal domestication, we shall look first at the pigs of Hallan Çemi in southeast Turkey, second at the gazelles and sheep/goat of Abu Hureyra in Syria, and finally at the onagers of Umm Dabaghiyah in west Iraq.

What happens when an animal is domesticated? A major factor is the usurpation by humans of control over breeding and rearing in conjunction with separation of the domesticated stock from their wild forebears (for excellent surveys of domestication, see Davis 1987: 126–68; Clutton-Brock 1999; Reitz and Wing 1999: 279–305). It seems unlikely that the process of animal domestication, unlike that of plant domestication, can happen by accident, as wild mammals will not tolerate the company of humans unless deliberately reared by humans to do so. But Hans-Peter Uerpmann, discussing his 'niche concept' of the domestication of sheep and goats, has argued:

> In summary, the first domestication of herbivorous animals can be explained as a natural process that resulted from a rare constellation of environmental, biological and social factors that occurred together only in a very restricted area of the world, namely western Southwest Asia, during a short span of geological time, namely the beginning of the present interglacial period. Conscious human action was not required, only reaction and transformation when the process was already well under way.
>
> (Uerpmann 1996: 235)

The chronological sequence of animal domestication in Southwest Asia is broadly agreed as being first dog, then sheep, goat, pig, and cattle, although there are uncertainties, as we shall see (for selected studies of animal domestication in Southwest Asia, see Bar-Yosef and

Meadow 1995: 82–90; Garrard *et al.* 1996; Hole 1996; Legge 1996; Uerpmann 1996). Initial exploitation was probably principally for so-called primary products such as meat and skins, with secondary products like milk, wool, dung and traction gaining in importance as domestication intensified. In total, surprisingly low numbers of animal species have signed the contract of domestication with humans. Domestication appears to be feasible solely in the case of animals with an hierarchical social nature that enables humans to act as surrogate dominant males, and with lengthy juvenile status that allows humans to supplant the role of mother with respect to young animals.

As with plants, the presence of the wild forebears of domesticated animals such as pig, goat, sheep and cattle in much of Southwest Asia was clearly a *sine qua non* for their domestication in that part of the world. Separate domestications of suites of animal species occurred in other regions, principally East Asia and the Americas. As to identification in the archaeological record of the domestication of a species, there are several areas of concern. One element may be morphological change in the animal's physique leading to detectable differences in the shape of animal horns, for example. Another factor is that domesticated animals tend to be smaller than their wild forebears, perhaps as a result of human selection in favour of more manageable beasts, but this criterion does not always apply. Changes in climate, for example, can also lead to size change in purely wild populations. Another way of approaching domestication comprises study of the age and sex profiles of animal bone assemblages from excavated sites, with high proportions of bones from juvenile and male animals suggesting close human control over a species. Other approaches may include analysis of changes in species abundance within specific regions, or the introduction of new species to regions (Legge 1996: 239).

But why did humans domesticate animals in the first place? Answering this question for animals is no easier than it is for plants, and many of the same arguments and hypotheses apply. As with plants, there is likely to have been a wide spectrum of interactions between humans and animals ranging from opportunistic hunting through herd-following to full domestication. One idea, the 'crop robbers' theory of Frederik Zeuner (1963; see also Clutton-Brock 1999: 212–13), is that once cereals had been domesticated there would be a need for humans to protect their crops from wild animals that in course led to the domestication of those animals. Surpluses of grain and plant stuffs would provide the necessary fodder for maintaining the newly domesticated animals through the year. A related idea, put forward by Melinda Zeder

(1999), is that as the Pleistocene ended both humans and certain animal species began to exploit the wealth of new plant foods that accompanied the ameliorating climate, and in doing so were brought into close contact with each other. This contact may initially have taken the form of increasingly intense hunting and herding strategies, perhaps enduring for millennia, before full domestication took place. The animals involved in these early Holocene encounters varied from zone to zone – goats in the mountains of the Zagros, sheep in the foothills, pigs in the oak forests of southeast Anatolia, and gazelle in the grasslands of the Levant, this last example not leading to domestication by virtue of the social nature of gazelle. We have already discussed Pumpelly and Childe's oasis theory for the origins of agriculture, based on the notion of climate change in the early Holocene leading to a need for intensified use of resources. Another factor may have been steadily increasing human populations during these millennia, the population theory of Cohen (1977) and others discussed above. Again, these are 'push' theories that see domestication as a response or adaptation to a crisis or series of crises. As we shall see in the final section of this chapter, another way of looking at this issue is in 'pull' terms, with human societies internally generating a drive towards change.

We shall now consider some specific instances of human/animal interactions from the Neolithic past, chosen partly for their intrinsic interest and partly for the light they shed on the theories and practices of zooarchaeology within a range of Mesopotamian contexts. We shall begin with the Hallan Çemi pigs. Hallan Çemi is one of the most intriguing early Neolithic sites of Southwest Asia, located just beyond the northern fringes of the Mesopotamian plains (Rosenberg 1999). Dated to about 10,000 BC, the site represents the oldest fully settled village in southeast Anatolia, although not as old as the early settlement at Abu Hureyra in Syria to the south. The settlement comprises a series of circular stone structures arranged around a large open area that contains evidence suggestive of public feasting on animals.

Although fully sedentary, the occupants of Hallan Çemi were engaged principally in hunting and gathering of wild animals and plants, but what concerns us here is the proposition that pigs were subject to a form of 'primitive animal husbandry' or 'incipient domestication' (Rosenberg 1999: 31; Rosenberg et al. 1995: 5; 1998: 33–4).

Four strands of evidence underlie this claim. First, by using the recovered bones to calculate the age at death of the Hallan Çemi pigs it is possible to produce a survivorship curve that indicates that only 31 per cent of the animals survived to an age of thirty-six months, a

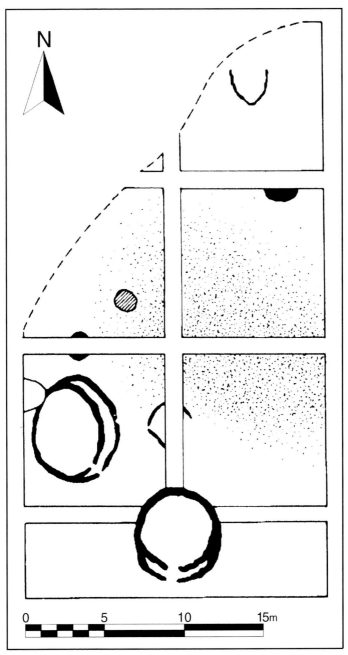

Figure 3.1 Plan of the early settlement at Hallan Çemi, southeast Turkey

Source: after Rosenberg and Redding 2000: fig. 1.

pattern of consumption associated with domesticated populations. This pattern can be contrasted with the sheep/goat bones from the site, which show survival of 66 per cent to an age of forty-two months, consistent with the hunting of wild populations. Second, measurements of the pigs' teeth from the site fall within or close to the range of tooth sizes established for domesticated pig. Third, more males than females are found in the pig assemblage, at a ratio of 11:4, perhaps because females were being retained for breeding. Finally, by examining the different body parts attested by the bones, the suggestion arises that many of the pigs were being butchered at the site itself rather than at a distance, perhaps because the animals were being kept at the site before butchery. In all, these lines of approach suggest to the excavators that pigs were in train of domestication at Hallan Çemi at a time before the domestication of sheep and goat, conventionally seen as the first food animal domesticates. Given the characteristics of pigs, including high birth rate, fast growth rate and suitability of the young for taming, their early domestication might not seem surprising.

The implications of this interpretation, however, are major. As Michael Rosenberg puts it:

> the early domestication of pigs demonstrates that the shift to food production is not simply an outgrowth of the ever more intensive exploitation of a given plant or animal species. Rather, it indicates that at the earliest stages of the process produced resources were not staples, but supplements.
>
> (Rosenberg 1999: 31)

It also presents a picture of economic variability within the earliest settled communities of Southwest Asia, and calls for revision of ideas that see cereal domestication as a prerequisite for animal domestication. The implication is that the drive for domestication of pigs was not solely or principally economic but may have been situated within a social context involving feasting and other community interactions.

Claims for pig domestication at Hallan Çemi have not met with universal acceptance, however. Peters and others have recently argued that Rosenberg's zooarchaeological premises do not stand up to close examination (Peters *et al.* 1999). In particular, Peters *et al.* aver that none of the tooth sizes fall outside the acceptable range for wild pigs, that the survivorship curve and male bias can be matched by evidence from sites in Europe where hunting alone was taking place, and that the presence of certain body parts on site at Hallan Çemi need not indicate maintenance of the animals close by but may show the proximity of suitable pig environments, such as oak forest. There is unlikely to be a resolution of this issue in the near future, and for now the relatively secure assignation of pigs to wild or domestic categories rests principally on sizes of molar teeth.

Let us move south to examine the case of gazelles and sheep/goat at Abu Hureyra where we have already looked at the issue of cereal cultivation and domestication. Once more, evidence from this important early settlement is uniquely significant in addressing issues of early agricultural practices during the transition to a fully Neolithic society (Legge and Rowley-Conwy 2000). During Abu Hureyra 1 (*c*.10,750–9,150 BC) the faunal remains show a predominance of gazelle, steadily decreasing amounts of onager (wild equid), hare and fox, as well as wild cattle, sheep and goat. In the earliest levels of Abu Hureyra 2 (*c*.8,400–6,000 BC) there is some increase in sheep and goat quantities, but gazelle are still common. Later levels of Abu Hureyra 2 show a massive increase in dependence on sheep, goat and cattle with a commensurate decline in the significance of gazelle. This emphatic reversal in the relative importance of caprines (sheep and goat) as against gazelles appears to have been 'remarkably rapid and took place in about 50 years, in other words, within a human lifetime' (Legge and Rowley-Conwy 2000: 434).

Legge and Rowley-Conwy provide a highly detailed study of gazelle and onager hunting at Abu Hureyra. Analysis of gazelle tooth measurements

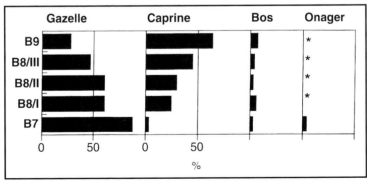

Figure 3.2 Abu Hureyra, north central Syria. Large mammal bones from Trench B, showing shift from gazelle in lower levels to caprine (sheep/goat) in upper levels

Source: after Legge and Rowley-Conwy 2000: fig. 13.10.

suggests seasonal hunting of these animals at the time of birthing in early summer. Furthermore, the presence in the bone assemblage of all age classes of both onagers and gazelles indicates 'catastrophic mortality in which whole herds are exterminated', almost certainly during annual migration (Legge and Rowley-Conwy 2000: 439). The use of so-called 'desert kites', or walled enclosures, as traps for large-scale slaughter of gazelle and onager is posited in this connection by Legge and Rowley-Conwy, with anything between fifty and 500 animals being taken at a time and much of the meat dried for year-round use.

Legge and Rowley-Conwy suggest that from the start of Abu Hureyra 2 there is a new emphasis on domesticated sheep and goat in the economy of the settlement, growing rapidly in importance in later levels. In level 2A, goat outnumber sheep by about five to one but thereafter sheep steadily gain in importance till they predominate over goat. On the basis of bone measurements, it is argued that both sheep and goat were domesticated by the time of the 2A settlement at Abu Hureyra. During phase 2A, large-scale hunting of wild protein resources, principally gazelle, continued in concert with use of domesticated sheep and goat, but from phase 2B onwards, as the settlement expands in size, gazelle and onager may have been seriously over-hunted, leading to a new emphasis on high-intensity exploitation of herds of domesticated sheep and goat.

Our third case study is that of the onagers of Umm Dabaghiyah. The low mound of Umm Dabaghiyah lies on the desert plains of Iraq between the Euphrates and Tigris rivers, some 90km south of the Sinjar mountains (Kirkbride 1982). A special significance of the site, which dates to the early seventh millennium BC, is the evidence it provides for the continued importance of hunting well into the Neolithic period. In antiquity a large area of marsh and brackish lake provided an attraction for herds of steppe animals, upon whom the inhabitants of Umm Dabaghiyah preyed. Unusually, the evidence comes not only in the form of animal bones but also as wall paintings depicting equids entering a ring of large hooks that are perhaps designed to secure a net.

Architecture includes substantial blocks of square store-rooms, rooms with large plastered basins and drains, and domestic dwellings. One store-room contained over 2,400 baked clay sling missiles. Plant remains indicate use of emmer, einkorn and barley at the site, either through farming *in situ* or through transport of the grain to the site.

The faunal remains from Umm Dabaghiyah are distinctive (Bökönyi 1986). A total of 18,683 identifiable bones was recovered. Domesticated

Figure 3.3 Umm Dabaghiyah, northwest Iraq. Wall-painting depicting onagers and possible net-hooks

Source: after Kirkbride 1982: fig. 8.

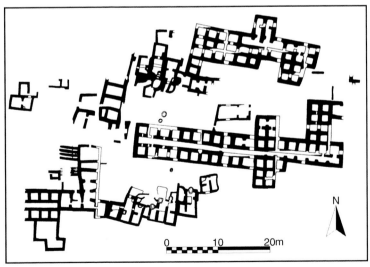

Figure 3.4 Umm Dabaghiyah, northwest Iraq. Composite plan of levels 3–4

Source: after Kirkbride 1982: fig. 2.

species, including sheep, goat, cattle, pig and dog, make up only 10 per cent of the total bone assemblage. Bones of wild species are far commoner (89 per cent in total), particularly those of onager, at 70 per cent of identifiable bones, with gazelle at 16 per cent of the total. The onager is a form of wild equid, *Equus hemionus*, that used to roam the Upper Mesopotamian steppe in great numbers. Analysis of the onager bones reveals a minimum number of individuals of at least 370, with limited variation in morphology and size suggesting origin from a closed population. The lack of complete skulls or limb extremities indicates that the remains come from kitchen refuse rather than on-site butchery. Study of the kill-off ages of the onagers and gazelles shows a classic hunting pattern with emphasis on adult animals, in contrast to the kill-off patterns for domesticated species at the site. Lack of variation in size and the kill-off patterns do not suggest domestication of the onager at Umm Dabaghiyah.

Evidence from Umm Dabaghiyah clearly points to the site's role as a base for hunting of wild animals, principally onager but also gazelle. The stone tools are mainly for cutting and scraping, as in butchery of captured animals and treatment of hides. The large storage blocks can be seen as stores for processed items such as skins, but also for hunting equipment such as nets and wooden hooks. The plastered basins with drains may have been used in curing of animal skins in brine. There is also evidence of deliberate blocking of windows prior to episodic abandonment of the buildings, strongly suggesting that the site was used for hunting on a seasonal basis, no doubt in pursuit of seasonal movements of large herds of onagers and gazelle. The evidence from Umm Dabaghiyah thus gives us a detailed and vivid picture of the nature and extent of hunting within a Mesopotamian context, long after the adoption of agricultural practices by communities of the region. It is significant that despite the great amounts of nourishment represented by the onagers and gazelle, the inhabitants were at the same time still making use of a full range of domesticated animals and cereals as elements of their diet.

These three examples clearly show how separate early Neolithic communities of Southwest Asia adopted differing strategies in dealing with the particularities of their environment, in the widest sense, with idiosyncratic mixes of hunting and herding elements in their relationships with animals. These strategies were clearly structured in opportunistic ways in response to ever-changing circumstances, and above all demonstrate the flexibility and fluidity of early sedentary human communities in approaching problems of subsistence and diet.

They also serve to illustrate how the zooarchaeologist can approach these concerns from the perspective of modern archaeology.

People first and last

The origins and early development of the Neolithic revolution are shrouded in mystery, and undoubtedly the most intriguing issue is why it happened at all. There is a general acceptance today that the hunting-gathering lifestyle was not nasty, brutish and short, as used to be assumed, but rather fulfilling, wholesome and successful. To have lasted so long as the sole *modus operandi* of modern humans and their closest relatives, it can only be classed as hugely successful. Why, then, did the system change? We have looked at the various elements – climate, population, plants and animals – in turn, and it is time now to put them back together in order to consider an integrated approach to this most basic issue, as increasingly adopted by researchers in this arena.

Clearly a major factor in the story of the Neolithic revolution was the adoption of sedentary modes of living prior to the development of agriculture. Groube has cogently argued that sedentism, whether permanent or not, was adopted by human communities as a strategy for increased female productivity in a ceaseless battle against expanding populations of dangerous bugs and their attendant diseases, particularly malaria, schistosomiasis, and hook-worm: 'each new micropredator would add incrementally to the mother's burden and the pressure for a more sedentary way of life' (Groube 1996: 124). In Groube's nightmare spiral of disease and doom, the adoption of increasingly sedentary modes of living itself leads to greater vulnerability of human communities to attack by the growing range of parasites expanding in the warmer air of the immediately post-Pleistocene centuries, in turn necessitating the intensification of modes of settlement and food production by those communities. Thus was set in train what Groube calls an 'escalator of intensification' carrying humans from simple hunting and gathering through sedentism to agriculture and on to the eventual rise of cities and states.

Whatever the stimulus, the existence of pre-agricultural sedentism is well established (Belfer-Cohen and Bar-Yosef 2000). Across large swathes of Southwest Asia human communities were settling down for increasing proportions of their lives in the centuries prior to the Younger Dryas. Within the Upper Mesopotamian context, sites such as Zawi Chemi Shanidar, M'lefaat, Qermez Dere, Nemrik and Hallan

Çemi all fit within this picture of early Holocene pre-agricultural sedentism (Cauvin 2000a: 171–4; R. Matthews 2000a: 32–9). Increased
sedentism necessitates and stimulates the development of new modes of
social interaction, particularly concerning issues of conflict resolution
and community integration. If a group of people settle down in a small
cluster of houses within long-term earshot of each other, then a failure
to resolve inter-group disputes may rapidly lead to terminal fragmentation. Barbara Bender's pioneering article stresses the importance of
these elements of social interaction and dispute adjudication as a means
of 'pulling' human communities into surplus food production in order
to maintain ever more complex social relations through public feasting
and gift-giving (Bender 1978).

Another socially cohesive and regenerative element in the earliest
sedentary societies of Southwest Asia will have been that of cult and
ritual, and it should perhaps not come as a surprise that evidence for
cult in these earliest settlements is increasingly to the fore. Of especial
note in this regard is the ongoing programme of research focused on
the impressive site of Göbekli Tepe, located near the modern town of
Şanlıurfa in southeast Turkey along the northern fringes of Upper
Mesopotamia (Hauptmann 1999). The site dates to 9,000 BC and
earlier, with purely wild forms of hunted animals and gathered plants
attested. Architecture at Göbekli Tepe appears to comprise exclusively
megalithic forms, with massive T-shaped pillars frequently decorated
with animals carved in relief. The apparent role of these buildings is
neatly summarised by the excavator:

> the function of these buildings can only be characterized as associ-
> ated with ritual purposes, and no serious claim for domestic use is
> tenable. It is clear that Göbekli Tepe was not an early Neolithic
> settlement with some ritual buildings, but that the whole site served
> a mainly ritual function. It was a mountain sanctuary.
>
> (K. Schmidt 2000: 46)

Schmidt has argued that, as some of the megaliths used in construction weigh up to fifty tons, there must have been regional assemblies of
hunter-gatherer communities from a wide area around Göbekli Tepe in
order to provide the necessary labour, and that prolonged occupation of
communities at the site, during periods of construction and use of the
buildings, may have stimulated incipient cultivation of the locally available wild cereals. Here we have a vivid example of how sedentism,

social practice and elaborate ritual may have been the 'pulling' factors within the early development of agriculture.

As Brian Hayden has articulately summarised, there is an emerging consensus in many approaches to the Neolithic revolution (Hayden 1995). For the revolution to happen at all, specific elements had to be in the right place at the right time, including at least partially sedentary societies, the use of storage facilities, population densities of a certain critical mass, high resource diversity, technology for processing and harvesting plants and, finally, plants and animals with the potential for domestication (Hayden 1995: 277–8). Hayden's own model for understanding domestication is very much of the 'pull' type, seeing socio-economic competition between hunter-gatherer individuals as the driving force. This competition, Hayden argues, was manifest as the deployment of labour-intensive foodstuffs in feasting and public interaction, such as trade and gift-giving, by individuals within complex hunter-gatherer communities. Thus Hayden sees social hierarchy as preceding and stimulating agricultural production rather than vice-versa (Hayden 1992; 1995: 289). Evidence for feasting at the early site of Hallan Çemi (Rosenberg and Redding 2000) and for large-scale social cooperation at sites such as Göbekli Tepe can be mustered in support of such a view.

Based on study of early Neolithic art and symbolism, the French archaeologist Jacques Cauvin draws on 'a transformation of the mind' involving 'the birth of the gods' as stimulating early Holocene communities into novel relations and interactions with the world about them (Cauvin 2000a; 2000b; 2001). 'Becoming Neolithic may have been much more a spiritual conversion than a matter of changing diets', as Alasdair Whittle has put it (Whittle 1996: 8). In contrast to economic and ecological explanations of the origins of agriculture, Cauvin highlights changes in human cognition and attendant social developments as the driving force behind the Neolithic revolution. To some extent, these two theoretical stances can be viewed as direct descendants of the economic theories of Karl Marx, on the one hand, and those of spiritually driven change of Max Weber, on the other. As Ian Hodder has pointed out, however, Cauvin's failure to address the key issue of the root cause underlying the shift in human cognition at this point in history leaves his argument open to the charge of relying ultimately on 'some inexorable internal logic' (Hodder 2001: 110). In his own innovative study of early agricultural Southwest Asia and Europe, Hodder (1990) also lays stress on transformations in 'symbolic structure' as underlying the shift from hunting and gathering to farming, a process whereby 'the natural (wild) is made cultural (domesticated, agri-cultured)' (Hodder 1990: 18). Hodder agrees with Cauvin in seeing fundamental changes in social and symbolic human culture before the adoption of agriculture, centred on newly sedentary lifestyles and the 'domus' or house as a focus of social relations and symbolic develop-ment: 'the "origins" of agriculture thus reside in the conjunction between processes which have a long duration in the Palaeolithic and particular climatic and social events at the end of the last glaciation' (Hodder 1990: 294).

In conclusion, the consensus today in approaches to the issue of the origins of farming in Mesopotamia and Southwest Asia is in favour of multivariate and often locale-specific interpretations rooted in broad interdisciplinary programmes of research (Watson 1991). In addition, there is an increasing concern to delineate and explore asymmetries of power, resource control, and deployment of iconography within the arena of social development in the early Neolithic period as mecha-nisms of social change and manipulation, as vividly attested at such early sites as Hallan Çemi, Göbekli, and Nevalı Çori. With the contin-uing involvement of specialists in areas such as climate, demography, disease, animals and plants, as well as in field methodology and social theory, our understanding and appreciation of this highly important and complex episode in human history is set to continue to improve and expand in the decades ahead.

Chapter 4

States of mind
Approaching complexity

The complexity of complexity

On the subject of the origin of primary states, in 1977 Henry Wright wrote: 'It is a fundamental problem which, though it cannot have an ultimate solution, serves as a measure against which to evaluate the effectiveness of new perspectives and new methods' (Wright 1977: 379). Within the arena of ancient Mesopotamia there is an unrivalled diachronic wealth of archaeological material with which to address issues pertaining to the development of complex societies. As with the previous chapter's topic, the subject of complexity in ancient Mesopotamia is such a large and diverse field that we can do no more than sample some of the major issues here. Through the millennia of later prehistory and all recorded history, and within the limits of the available, often patchy evidence, we can witness the rise, flux and fall of society after society. Attestations of some degree of complexity appear very early on in the archaeological record of Mesopotamia. As we have seen in the previous chapter, there are credible indications of social and cultic complexity of some sophistication even as early as the first sedentary settlements of human groups in the earliest centuries of the Holocene, at sites such as Hallan Çemi and Göbekli Höyük on the northern fringes of Mesopotamia. We can consider the growth of social complexity in later millennia by studying the material remains of a host of societies that developed within the context of the Mesopotamian past, culminating in the appearance of social and political entities known as states and empires. Empires and their archaeological study will be the subject of the following chapter. For now our main concern is with approaches to the study of complex societies of the later prehistory of Mesopotamia, in particular those of the fifth and fourth millennia BC. The socio-political entities of Mesopotamia in these critical centuries have been characterised in a range of ways, but most observers would agree that we are here concerned with complex chiefdoms and states, at least. In terms of basic approach to these entities we here agree with Earle (1997: 14) that 'the fundamental dynamics of chiefdoms are essentially the same as those of states'.

As archaeologists, how do we approach these highly various and idiosyncratic entities? Does each ancient state or complex society need to be approached and apprehended solely on its own terms, each of its elements studied, described and analysed in an attempt at its particular history, or are there principles and themes underlying the generation, maintenance, death and regeneration of societies that we can approach by means of the archaeological record? Perhaps we need to begin by defining social complexity, a much-used phrase in archaeology. There are no fixed rules or universally agreed criteria to such an end, but some possible areas of general agreement are proffered below. While we may concur with the statement that 'For less well known states, where texts are absent, perhaps the best definition is the most general and simple, so as to encompass marked historical variability' (Marcus and Feinman 1998: 5), even for those states that do have textual sources considerable flexibility in approach is certainly needed.

Recent studies have laid emphasis on power, control and authority as useful analytical concepts in approaches to past complex societies (Earle 1997). In view of an increasing emphasis on the role of 'society', even within Palaeolithic communities (Gamble 1999), the fundamental dynamics of communities of humans can perhaps be approached by means of certain basic concepts rooted in the nature of all human interaction. In all cases we are concerned with approaching the issue of how groups of human beings address the challenges and opportunities generated by living together in close proximity with variable access to resources of material and non-material type. By 'resources' is meant anything from daily bread to holy blessings, and from precious metals to political charisma. The scale and spectacular material residues of the complex states and empires of late prehistory and early history should not lead us into a belief that pre-state human communities lacked structuring principles founded in issues of power, control and differential access to commodities. Nevertheless, there is a world of difference between a hunter-gatherer band of 25–30 individuals who might occasionally promote an individual to act as a leader under specific circumstances, on the one hand, and an urban polity of 20,000 individuals or more whose control extends over thousands of square kilometres and whose social structure is formalised and hierarchical, on the other. But what is the nature of those differences, and how do we locate, identify and study them in the archaeological record?

Let us begin by defining some anthropological characteristics of complex societies, as broadly defined. Amongst the many studies in recent decades of chiefdoms and states, most include at least some of the following elements in their definitions of societal complexity.

Generally agreed anthropological attributes of chiefdoms and/or states

1   Social stratification, whereby at least two, often more, levels of social status exist, at least one of which can be characterised as an elite group;
2   Settlement hierarchy at the regional scale, involving centralisation of some key activities;
3   Specialisation of activity by members of the community;
4   Cultic and ritual elaboration;
5   Historical trajectories of an unstable and fragile nature, invariably culminating in collapse.

What might be the archaeological correlates, or 'clues' in Kent Flannery's phrase (Flannery 1998: 15), that enable us to discern and study these putative characteristics of ancient complex societies? In a pioneering article, Peebles and Kus (1977) proposed the following elements as archaeological correlates of chiefdoms or ranked societies:

Peebles and Kus' (1977) list of archaeological correlates of ranked societies

1   Ascribed ranking of persons;
2   Hierarchy of settlement types and sizes;
3   High degree of local subsistence sufficiency indicating local autonomy;
4   Organised productive activities, such as monument construction or craft specialisation, that transcend the basic household unit;
5   Society-wide organisation in the form of storage and distribution to deal with perturbations in food supply or climate.

While these features correlate reasonably well with the anthropological attributes listed in the first section, it might help to phrase them more explicitly in terms of what is likely to be encountered in the archaeological record. The following list of specifically archaeological characteristics is proposed, numbered in order of agreement with the first list:

Explicitly archaeological correlates of ranked societies

1   Monumental constructions, rich tombs, differential distributions of prestige items, palaces;
2   Regional hierarchy of settlement patterns;
3   Craft specialisation within and between sites, storage, exchange within and between settlements;
4   Temples, priests' residences, cultic paraphernalia;
5   Evidence of growth, flux, collapse.

These loosely defined correlates do not constitute a checklist for identifying complexity in the archaeological record, but are simply some suggestions for the exploration of issues of complexity from what are likely to be patchy and indistinct traces of past societies. Before considering two broad arenas of research for social complexity in ancient Mesopotamia, we shall review some of the approaches employed in the study of complexity in recent decades.

Approaches to the study of social complexity

It is what humans do as social animals, how we interact with each other, with contemporary communities, and with our broad environment, histories and gods, that makes for complexity as understood in this chapter. Approaches to societal complexity in the arena of Mesopotamia have come mainly from the academic context of North American anthropological archaeology, often building on and integrating data and interpretations sought and generated through models of both culture history and anthropology. Approaches to complexity in the context of Southwest Asia have been founded on premises that can variously be described as ecological, evolutionary, systemic, processual, comparative, organisational and chaotic, each of these premises situated in issues of wider humanistic and scientific concerns of their contemporary milieu.

Anthropological traditions, rooted in the positivist New Archaeology of the 1960s and the anthropology of Leslie White and Julian Steward before that, have frequently viewed human societies within a framework of evolutionary development, progressing from simple to complex in a unilinear manner through time (Wenke 1981: 84–7, 111–16). Sometimes this approach has been manifest as a step typology of human society, proceeding from band through tribe and chiefdom to state, so-called 'stage-stops along the road to civilization' (Service 1975: 303; McGuire 1983: 93–5). These often cross-cultural approaches may have an ultimate aim of detecting and delineating general processes, even laws, of development amongst human communities irrespective of time or place. Much of the labour in this area has gone into attempts to define the terminology employed in socio-cultural typologies, often based on broad ethnographic surveys. Criteria employed to define stages of societal evolution have included the size and scale of communities, the nature of social and economic relations between individuals and groups within human communities, and the nature of control and processing of socially significant information. Critiques of evolutionary approaches of the step typology kind have proposed that the complex dynamics of human interaction and development fail to be accounted for or explained by the static, trait-specific strait-jacket of the evolutionist paradigm (Rothman 1994), and that evolutionary studies have so far failed to operationalise their theories into meaningful field and analytical programmes (Yoffee 1979).

But proponents of the step typology approach rejoinder to the effect that its employment is as a heuristic device that does not imply an ineluctable progression of human communities from one simple step to the next more complex step. Moreover, they argue, we should be flexible in assigning human communities to societal categories and we should be ready to adapt those categories as new evidence requires. Above all, we should accept that typologising human communities is no more an end in itself than typologising potsherds or arrow-heads, which can only be worthwhile if the results are employed to tell us something about the ways in which human communities originate, develop and behave (Renfrew and Bahn 2000: 177).

During the 1970s, approaches to the study of states and complex societies were framed within a discourse of systems analysis of the structure and administration of complexity. Leading the way was Kent Flannery, who in 1972 provided a seminal treatment of ecosystemic approaches to complexity in his article on 'The cultural evolution of civilizations' (Flannery 1972; see also Redman 1978: 229–36). Reviewing types of human society, ordered as band, tribe, chiefdom and state, Flannery viewed the human ecosystem as an adaptive mechanism composed of hierarchically arranged elements, or subsystems, the relationships between which fluctuate as socio-environmental stresses and opportunities arise. At the higher end of the complexity scale, the need to process and distribute information within such a system is clearly paramount, and it is from this point that theories which centre on administrative technology and bureaucracy were developed. In particular, the work of Henry Wright and Gregory Johnson focused on issues of the appearance of pristine states in southwest Iran in the fourth millennium BC, where their emphasis fell on tangible aspects of administrative bureaucracy, such as seals and sealed bullae, as evidence for specialisation and levels of decision-making amongst hierarchically arranged settlements (Wright 1977; 1978; 1998; Wright and Johnson 1975). The fortunate fact that much of this evidence survives in the archaeological record, in the form of tokens, bullae, sealed clay pieces and, later, inscribed tablets, grants a unique advantage to Mesopotamia as a field within which to study the unfolding of these processes and their societal implications. Indeed, we might wonder how states could be approached and identified archaeologically without such administrative evidence, given its fundamental significance within Wright and Johnson's interpretive scheme (Wright 1977: 386; Wright and Johnson 1975: 267). The essential argument is that this increasingly complex assemblage of administrative technology was developed and used as a means of control over the production, exchange and redistribution of goods and services by the state or by elite elements within the state. More recently, finds of artefacts such as sealed clay pieces at sites of much earlier date, including late Neolithic Sabi Abyad and Tell Boueid in north Syria, have suggested the early development and application of this administrative technology in a social and political environment devoid of elite exploitation and redistribution of controlled goods, but instead rooted in low-key personal concerns to secure access to private possessions during periods of absence from a base settlement (Akkermans and Duistermaat 1997; Duistermaat 2002). We therefore need to be wary of the assumption that evidence of administrative technology necessarily attests the existence of hierarchical, stratified social entities.

An early critic of the administrative view of complexity was Robert Adams, who pointed out that the administrative routines of a complex political entity could in no way be taken as fully representative of that complexity in kind or degree. Furthermore, Adams argued, such approaches failed to take into consideration the power and role of cult and religious organisations in the development and spread of complexity, even when, as in the Uruk period, there is convincing archaeological evidence for their importance (Adams 1981: 76–8). Pollock has commented that the excessive emphasis upon modes of control and administration tends to reduce the role of the state to that of 'a managerial entity' (Pollock 1992: 319), and Richard Blanton's critique of the systems and administrative approach to state-level societies focuses on its avoidance of significant elements within society, such as commercial enterprise, households and urbanism (Blanton 1998: 138).

Valuable anthropological approaches to complexity in fifth-millennium Mesopotamia have been developed by Gil Stein and Mitchell Rothman (Stein and Rothman 1994), whose work is characterised by a concern with the dynamics of interaction between various spheres of past human activity and experience, and with how those dynamics might be manifest in, and recovered and interpreted from, the archaeological record. Rothman, Stein and colleagues have helped shift the emphasis away from terminological debate and rather fruitless critiques of evolutionary theory and step typologies towards consideration of the substantive dynamics of human society. Defining complexity as 'the degree of functional differentiation among societal units', which may be 'households, economic enterprises, political associations, classes, villages, or urban districts', Rothman and Stein use the concepts of economic, political and ideological integration and centralisation as critical in an approach characterised as 'the organizational dynamics of complexity', which aims to explore the ways in which human communities were structured and how they functioned and developed through time in the context of the Mesopotamian past (Rothman 1994; Stein 1994a).

There is an increasing awareness of the fluidity of Mesopotamian societies and of the flexible dynamic between and amongst elements of those societies that might be sometimes in cooperation, at other times in competition, and that may flit in and out of archaeological visibility, with alternating episodes of centralisation and decentralisation (Blanton 1998: 138–9). Scholars of the Mesopotamian past have frequently failed fully to appreciate the nature and representativeness of the archaeo-historical record, assuming that what they see is the whole picture with nothing missing. Historians, in particular, have constructed overarching theories concerning Mesopotamian temple-states and socio-economic systems on the basis of single archives of material, failing to consider issues of how the evidence was generated, how it may have been manipulated, how it may have been changed and distorted through time, or how it might be seen in a totally different light if less visible forms of evidence could be brought to bear on the problem in question. A realistic and stimulating concern to address these issues has been manifest especially in the work of Marc Van De Mieroop (1999a).

Showing a keen appreciation of the biases inherent in the archaeological record as hitherto explored and recovered, Gil Stein has neatly summarised Mesopotamian complex societies as embodying an ultimately irresolvable tension between the centripetal tendencies of elite power groups and the centrifugal tendencies of other, archaeologically less visible, elements of society, concluding that 'instead of viewing states as all-powerful, homogeneous entities, it is probably more accurate to characterize them as organizations operating within a social environment that, for a variety of reasons, they only partially control' (Stein 1994a: 13). Stein's attempts to redress the balance away from a centrally dominated picture of ancient Mesopotamian societies, with all-powerful temples or palace elites, and to give greater emphasis to archaeologically less tangible elements such as the rural sector or interacting nomadic groups, encourages us to look anew at the structure and development of complexity in the arena of ancient Mesopotamia.

A valuable anthropological approach to the study of complexity in human communities stresses the role of power, control and authority in the processes by which societies become structured and stratified. Based on extensive archaeological, ethnographic and historical researches, the work of Tim Earle, in particular, has situated the rise of complex stratified societies within the context of differential access to, and control of, three sources of social power – economic, military and ideological (Earle 1997; see also Mann 1986). While not necessarily of primary archaeological concern, the driving force or 'prime mover' behind social change is suggested by Earle and others as being biologically rooted in the desire for some individuals to attain prominence as a platform for reproductive success (Earle 1997: 2).

Most recently there has been a hesitant return to a grand-scale comparative approach to the study of early complex societies, or at least those that can be characterised as 'archaic states', in the belief that 'early states as a group do display similarities' (Marcus and Feinman 1998: 7). In the volume *Archaic States* (Feinman and Marcus 1998), authors attempt to take a global view on early states of the Old and New Worlds. The case for comparative study is, however, not obviously apparent. The 'dynamic model' propounded by Joyce Marcus proposes little more than that states go through 'cycles of consolidation, expansion, and dissolution' (Marcus 1998: 60). Furthermore, Marcus' study of ancient Mesopotamia within the context of her model (Marcus 1998: 76–86) fails to take into consideration the potentially critical role of climate and environment in affecting the trajectory of early Mesopotamian states. Thus the 'valleys' of state breakdown evident in her diagram of state development in Mesopotamia, falling at around 3,000, 2,200 and 1,400 BC, all neatly correspond to episodes of climatic adversity and aridification attested in the environmental evidence from Mesopotamia and surrounding regions (Butzer 1995: 136–8).The potential role of climate as a factor in the history of early states is certainly worthy of some consideration in any long-term survey of states in ancient Mesopotamia.

Gil Stein has recently reviewed, with typical insight, the state of current research into complex societies, ranging from chiefdoms to empires, of the Old World (Stein 1998), underlining a renewed emphasis on how complex societies operate rather than on how they originate. Setting out a twofold approach that combines the integration of archaeological and textual evidence, where available, along with regional studies of differential access to and control of resources, Stein promotes the study of the 'dynamic, fluid nature of power relationships and their longer-term transformations' (Stein 1998: 26). At the basis of these approaches lies an analytical framework within which complex societies can be designated as 'segmentary' or 'unitary', at two ends of a spectrum, according to their degrees of scale, complexity and integration (Stein 1994c).

In the remainder of this chapter we shall examine two major areas of the Mesopotamian past where issues of complexity are to the fore: the nature and development of complex societies in the Ubaid period of the fifth millennium, and the Uruk phenomenon of the later fourth

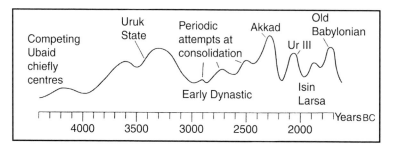

Figure 4.1 Development of states through time in Mesopotamia
Source: after Marcus 1998: fig. 3.8.

millennium. Both these important episodes have received archaeological attention from a wide range of angles, as we shall see.

Complexity in the fifth millennium BC: the Ubaid period

It is fair to say that, despite some important recent studies, Mesopotamia
in the Ubaid period remains a poorly understood research area. What
do we know of this long, vital episode that in Mesopotamia chronologically spans much of the transition from Neolithic village to Early Bronze
Age statehood? Defined originally on the basis of material, including
painted pottery, from Eridu and the site of Tell al-Ubaid in south Iraq,
the Ubaid period in its earliest phases is little known beyond information
provided by the lowest levels of the temple sounding at Eridu and by
excavations deep below the modern alluvium at Tell el-'Oueili near
Larsa (Huot 1989). For the later Ubaid period, spanning much of the
fifth millennium BC, we are better informed by the evidence from a
wide range of sites in south Mesopotamia, such as Eridu, Ubaid, Ur and
Uruk, as well as from those in other parts of Southwest Asia, such as Tell
Abada in the Hamrin region, Tepe Gawra in north Mesopotamia, and
Susa in southwest Iran, amongst many others (Henrickson and Thuesen
1989). Within the overall topic of Ubaid-period Mesopotamia we will
here examine only a sample of the ongoing areas of research, focusing
on cultic structures and pottery.

The significance of the role of cultic structures or temples within
human society is critical throughout the later prehistory and the entire
history of ancient Mesopotamia and, early Neolithic developments in
Upper Mesopotamia at sites like Göbekli and Nevalı Çori aside (see
Chapter 3), it is in the Ubaid period that we first gain some idea of the
physical manifestations that temples could take in Mesopotamia as well
as of their social and economic contexts.

Excavations in the late 1940s at Eridu in south Mesopotamia uncovered a sequence of superimposed temples spanning all the Ubaid
period and beyond, each successive temple increasing in size, grandeur
and architectural elaboration over its predecessor (Lloyd 1963: 57–64;
Safar et al. 1981: fig. 3c–d). By the end of the 1,500-year sequence the
Eridu temples, probably devoted to the worship of Enki, were built on
massive mud-brick platforms and comprised a central open space with
altar or offering table surrounded by suites of rooms. Regular architectural features include niches, buttresses, and orientation of the
building's corners to the cardinal points of the compass.

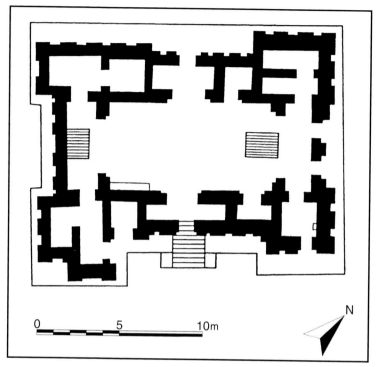

Figure 4.2 Eridu, south Iraq. Cultic building, temple VII
Source: after Safar *et al.* 1981: 88.

The great locational continuity demonstrated by the Eridu temples, their attestation of uninterrupted cultural development in Lower Mesopotamia through the critical centuries prior to the advent of written documents, taken with the Sumerians' own view of Eridu as a source of kingship and one of the first cities to be created after the flood, all argue persuasively for cultural and possibly ethnic (Sumerian?) continuity of occupation of the south Mesopotamian alluvium from a very early date.

Strong similarities in layout, orientation and elaboration of contemporary buildings at Uruk-Warka in Lower Mesopotamia (J. Schmidt 1974) and in Upper Mesopotamia, such as the level XIII Northern Temple at Tepe Gawra (Tobler 1950), moreover, give firm indication of a uniformity of cultural context, presumably manifest in religious creed and practice, across substantial swathes of Mesopotamia, providing a prelude of north/south contact and interaction against which to situate the evidence of the so-called Uruk phenomenon in the fourth millennium, as examined below.

The presence of lapis lazuli and carnelian, probably imported from Iran and Afghanistan, and the first extensive evidence for the use of stamp seals within a system of control of movement of sealed goods, further underline the cosmopolitan and complex nature of Late Ubaid societies across Mesopotamia.

What more can we learn about wider social and economic issues from the study of Ubaid-period temples? Susan Pollock has pointed out that the artefact assemblages recovered from inside the Eridu temples include items such as food and textile processing equipment that would not be out of place in purely domestic contexts. In addition, objects such as elaborate ceramic vessels and stamp seals hint at supra-domestic activities within and focused on temples of the Ubaid period at Eridu and at Tepe Gawra in Upper Mesopotamia (Pollock 1999: 87–8). It may also be the case that traces of food or textile processing within such

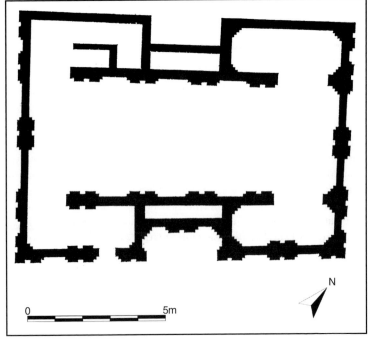

Figure 4.3 Tepe Gawra, north Iraq. Temple of level XIII

Source: after Tobler 1950: 30.

temple contexts relate to activities that might, as archaeological evidence, resemble those of domestic environments but that in fact were transformed through their execution in ritual or ritually mediated contexts. The weaving of a carpet with which to adorn a niche behind a cult statue in a temple, for example, might leave archaeological traces differing little from the traces of weaving a carpet for a domestic sitting room floor, but the social context is completely different. A similar contextualism will apply to evidence for the baking of holy bread or the brewing of sacred beer.

In a stimulating study Gil Stein has proposed that Ubaid-period temples served as agricultural banks or buffers against times of hardship, thus facilitating their own perpetuation as social elements in a long-term atmosphere of stability and ritually mediated control. In these communities the emphasis was not so much on the distribution of wealth, or exotic imports, as a basis for chiefly power, but more on the control and distribution of locally available resources such as agricultural surplus. As Stein puts it:

> the close association between irrigation, socio-economic differentiation, and the appearance of temples suggests that ritual elaboration played an important role in generating and maintaining these economic differences. The particular chiefly strategy of locally-based, ritually generated staple finance resulted in the peaceful spread and long-term stability of small scale chiefly polities throughout greater Mesopotamia in the 6th–5th millennia BC.
>
> (Stein 1994b: 44)

But we need also to consider the occasional presence of beads of lapis lazuli, carnelian and other materials in level XIII at Gawra (Tobler 1950: 192) that do suggest some movement of high-status exotic substances within the community, precursors of the spectacular wealth attested at Gawra in tombs of level X and later (Tobler 1950: 88; Moorey 1994: 88), hinting that Stein's model of low-key, quasi-egalitarian social structure during the Late Ubaid period may not be the full picture. We also need to keep in mind the inevitable partiality of the recovered material record: the discovery of a single wealthy tomb could overturn a theory overnight.

The study of pottery production and distribution in the Ubaid period has led to some important insights into the nature of human societies at this time. Due to its excellent survivability in the archaeological record, its relevance to issues of ancient technology and economics, and its suitability for typological and chronological analysis, pottery features prominently in the study of the Mesopotamian past. As discussed in Chapter 1, approaches grounded in culture history make frequent and detailed use of pottery as a means of descrying and defining cultures across time and space, while the significance and potential variability of the relationships between pots and people are perhaps not often enough explicitly considered:

> Traditionally, however, archaeologists working in Mesopotamia have treated the material evidence, above all pottery, not in technological or industrial terms, but typologically as the primary means for structuring chronological systems or for establishing the identities and relationships of the political and social groups taken to be defined by material culture.
>
> (Moorey 1994: v)

During the Ubaid period there are several notable developments that have encouraged profitable study of the pottery of the period, beyond the definition of cultural horizons in time and space. As Hans Nissen has argued, there is evidence that by the Late Ubaid period some sort of 'pivoted working surface' or tournette was introduced that greatly facilitated the rapid and large-scale production and decoration of pottery. In particular, the ability to produce painted decoration in simple bands, formed by holding the brush against a slowly rotating pot, allowed mass production of repetitively decorated pottery, as occurs widely over the Ubaid world. The widespread success of this technological innovation needs to be interpreted with caution, however:

> the impression could easily arise that this 'Ubaid horizon' was the external indication of the spread of the 'Ubaid' method of painting to the whole of the Near East from one place as a result of a migratory movement.
>
> (Nissen 1988: 46)

The decline in, and imminent abandonment of, decoration of pottery surfaces by the late fifth millennium in Mesopotamia has been connected by Nissen with a shift to forms of stratified society, where the modes of social differentiation could no longer be adequately expressed through painted pottery (Nissen 1988: 63).

At the same time, we may connect the occurrence of mass-produced, or at least repetitively produced and decorated, pottery in the

Late Ubaid period with the development of an artisan class of professional potters, part of a process of increasing craft specialisation and labour division attendant upon the rise of complex societies. Stein's study of the evidence from kilns and pottery manufacture at Ubaid sites in Mesopotamia suggests that, while craft specialisation was of increased significance by the late fifth millennium, there is no evidence yet for the centralised control by elite social elements over such means of production (Stein 1996: 28). Again, the paucity of our evidence on this topic, particularly from Lower Mesopotamia where the most pertinent evidence might be expected, needs to be kept in mind.

Scientific studies of Ubaid pottery have been of major significance as regards issues of production, trade and society. Judith Berman's work on Ubaid pottery in southwest Iran takes as its basis the assumption that 'ceramic style, techniques of production, exchange patterns, and so forth, are sensitive indicators of aspects of sociopolitical organization, contact with other societies, or cultural change' (Berman 1994: 23). Building on Stein's notion of Ubaid society as composed of simple chiefdoms whose power is based on control over staple commodities, Berman proposes that such a model of locally situated, peaceful and egalitarian communities would lead to the production of pottery that is both stylistically homogeneous and locally produced. Employing the technique of neutron activation analysis as a means of characterising the raw materials used in the manufacture of pottery, Berman examined groups of both decorated and undecorated Ubaid pottery from the Susiana plain in southwest Iran. Her results show that Ubaid pottery in Susiana was indeed locally produced, with plain red wares manufactured on a highly localised scale at individual households or small sites within the region. Black-on-buff pottery, by contrast, seems to have been produced by larger-scale village workshops generally exploiting the same or similar clay sources.

Analysis of the clays used in making a series of elaborately decorated beakers and bowls from the Susa Necropole indicates that these vessels were formed from a wide range of differing clays, suggesting that they may have been brought to Susa specifically as burial gifts to accompany regional elite members brought for burial at Susa (Berman 1994: 28). There thus appears to have been a variety of modes of ceramic production in Susiana during the Ubaid period, none of them under centralised control. Given this variety in the modes of pottery production, we are faced with the puzzle of the great stylistic homogeneity of pottery across the Ubaid world. How can this be? Berman's suggestion is that pottery use in the Ubaid period is rooted principally in the context of private food preparation and consumption rather than in the public domain of status display, while the simple and repetitive decoration of Ubaid pottery served to reinforce an ideological identity or group membership shared by all participants in the Ubaid world (Berman 1994: 29).

By contrast, Susan Pollock's study of Terminal Ubaid painted pottery from sites of the Susiana plain explores how stylistic representation in the form of painted elements might be related to social complexity. Working on the premise that, as a means of communication between community groups, style is likely to increase in complexity directly with an increase in social complexity, Pollock studies high-class painted vessels of Susa A date, the later fifth millennium BC. Some problems with representativeness of the evidence notwithstanding, she concludes that these vessels were produced for and used by elite groups within a stratified social context (Pollock 1983).

These various approaches to aspects of the material culture of the Ubaid period and their social, economic and political interpretation are steadily exploring and illuminating this otherwise shadowy period, which lasted for many centuries and culminated in the development of socio-political entities that can be characterised as highly complex, to the consideration of which we can now turn.

Kings, captives and colonies: the Uruk phenomenon

During the fourth millennium BC an extraordinary phenomenon is attested in the archaeological record of Mesopotamia and its neighbouring regions. This phenomenon takes the form of dozens of archaeological sites distributed across Lower and Upper Mesopotamia, southeast Anatolia, and southwest Iran, most known only from survey but a good number also excavated. To varying degrees these sites have commonalities of material culture, including architectural plans and elements, distinctive pottery forms, seals and sealings, and tablets of clay with numerical impressions. Study of these sites, their distributions, and material culture assemblages has been one of the most active fields of research and debate in Mesopotamian archaeology of modern times. For, most researchers would probably agree that in the Uruk period, through more or less the entire fourth millennium BC, the first true states appeared. These states, moreover, were primary states, originating in pristine condition on the plains of Mesopotamia. The fact that this process, or complex of processes, only happened once in the

Mesopotamian past, since every subsequent state could look to an ancestral statehood, lends unique significance to the study of the Uruk phenomenon (Pollock 1992).

The nature of the Uruk phenomenon has been most stimulatingly approached in the context of regional interactions between the polities of Lower Mesopotamia, on the one hand, and those of adjacent regions such as Upper Mesopotamia, Iran and southeast Anatolia, on the other. In particular, debate has centred on the issue of the nature of the relationships, in social, economic, political, and occasionally religious terms, between what is seen as the core zone of Lower Mesopotamia, dominated by the city of Uruk-Warka itself, and the outer regions of the Mesopotamian world through much of the fourth millennium BC. A major stimulus in this debate has been the increased volume of archaeological activity in the outer zones of Mesopotamia over the past twenty years or so (summarised in Rothman 2001a). Large-scale destruction of archaeological landscapes attendant upon construction of dams and irrigation projects along much of the length of the Euphrates and Tigris rivers, in particular, has encouraged the excavation of sites yielding significant new information on the topic of regional interactions in the greater Mesopotamian world. Excavations at sites such as Tell Sheikh Hassan, Habuba Kabira, and Jebel Aruda on the Syrian Euphrates and Hassek Höyük and Hacınebi Tepe on the Turkish Euphrates have provided information and stimulated new ways of thinking about early developments in regional control and interaction at the dawn of urban and literate society. Concurrent with the blossoming of archaeological work in the outer zones of Mesopotamia has been a dramatic decline, for modern political reasons, in the scope and intensity of fieldwork within the Mesopotamian heartland of south Iraq, including at the site of Uruk-Warka itself. Present understanding of the Uruk phenomenon is thus now biased toward those areas of Southwest Asia to which, rather than from which, it spread. Once a full return to fieldwork in Iraq becomes feasible, the many research issues generated by the ongoing debate over the Uruk phenomenon will certainly help to structure the conduct of future fieldwork at sites such as Uruk-Warka and elsewhere.

Any study of complexity in Uruk-period Mesopotamia can reasonably start with the city of Uruk-Warka that, during the centuries of the fourth millennium BC, grew in size and importance to be the paramount political and economic entity of Mesopotamia and beyond (Nissen 1988: 96–103). Hans Nissen has underlined the fact that excavations of the relevant levels at Uruk-Warka were conducted a long time ago, substantially prior to the discovery of Uruk-period sites outside Lower Mesopotamia, and that the excavators, principally historians of architecture, could not have realised at the time the full significance of their findings, especially the pottery sequence (Nissen 2001: 149–50). From modest and poorly understood beginnings in the Ubaid period, the settlement at Uruk-Warka expanded to a size of some 250 hectares with a postulated population of 20–50,000 individuals by the later fourth millennium, and to the phenomenal size of 600 hectares by about 2,900 BC (Nissen 1988: 71–72; 2001: 158, 173). On the basis of calculations of per capita food requirements and availability of suitable agricultural land around Uruk-Warka, Susan Pollock has suggested that the food requirements of the city by the middle fourth millennium significantly exceeded the food producing capabilities of the city's environs and that, therefore, Uruk-Warka must have been exacting tribute from a rural population beyond the city's immediate landscape (Pollock 2001: 195). The political and social ramifications of this postulated relationship will clearly include an element of substantial asymmetry with Uruk-Warka at the top of a steep and highly structured social pyramid.

By the Late Uruk period, Uruk-Warka was four to five times larger than any other settlement in Lower Mesopotamia, and may well have been fortified, if the evidence of seal depictions are accepted as an indication (Algaze 2001a: 32). The region around Uruk-Warka played host to a sudden tenfold increase in settlement density at about 3,200 BC, coupled with the development of a four-tiered hierarchy of settlement, all made possible by increased availability of dry and very fertile land newly freed from constant inundation by an ameliorating climate (Nissen 1988: 66–7). A lengthy programme of survey and excavation at Uruk-Warka has revealed something of the internal complexity of the settlement, dominated by a core of public cultic and administrative architecture in the form of the Anu Ziggurat/White Temple complex.

Hans Nissen has calculated that the construction and maintenance of the Anu Ziggurat/White Temple complex required the input of 1,500 labourers working for ten hours a day over a five-year period (Nissen 1988: 95). These grand construction projects may additionally have served as 'make-work' schemes, keeping potentially idle hands busy and perhaps reinforcing an ideological alignment towards elite ends (Pollock 1999: 180). The construction and use of public monuments are commonly viewed by archaeologists as primarily serving elite ideological ends, but such monuments can also be built and used in ways that convey subversive, non-elite or anti-elite messages. The

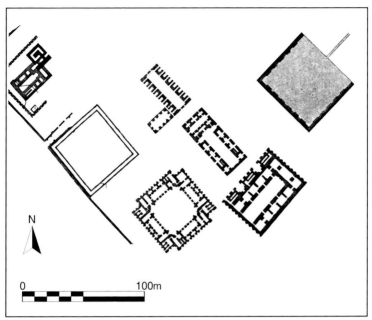

Figure 4.4 Uruk-Warka, south Iraq. Major structures of the fourth-millennium city

Source: after Englund 1998: fig. 6.

conspicuous building of sumptuous mosques throughout modern Turkey, for example, is a social phenomenon arguably situated in non-elite community activity subverting the secular spirit of a ruling political elite. Entire cities, such as Najaf in central Iraq, may be founded and perpetuated on the basis of anti-establishment religious conviction, although such cities are likely to host their own elite/non-elite disparities and divides.

Further evidence of well developed social complexity and hierarchy at Uruk-Warka includes the existence of specialised craft quarters, the earliest convincing iconographic depictions of high-status individuals, perhaps kings, in the media of stone sculpture and cylinder seals (Nissen 2001: 157; Roaf 1990: 61, 71), and glyptic portrayals of human captives bound and maltreated (Boehmer 1999: abb. 16–19). Additionally, thousands of fragments of clay sealings and clay tablets with proto-cuneiform inscriptions attest the overwhelming importance of the city. A survey of Uruk-Warka conducted between 1982 and 1984 recovered surface materials from about 480 hectares of the settlement,

Figure 4.5 Najaf, central Iraq, photographed from 2,000 feet on 30 January 1919

Source: Public Record Office ref. CN 5/2 407.

excluding the fifty or so hectares now severely disturbed by archaeological excavation and spoil disposal (Finkbeiner 1991). Results of the survey show clear areas of, for example, production of carnelian, flint and dolomite objects, supporting the idea of specialised craft areas, although their precise dating is difficult from surface materials. In addition, evidence of specialist metallurgical areas (Nissen 1988: 82), and textual evidence in the form of the so-called Professions List (Nissen 1988: 80; 2001: 156), as well as the practice of writing itself, all underline the trend towards increasing specialisation of labour and social hierarchy by the later fourth millennium BC. As Adams has phrased it, 'In centers like Uruk a highly significant segment of the population must have been given or won its freedom from more than a token or symbolic involvement in the primary processes of food production' (Adams 1981: 80).

Thus, if we look at the material evidence from Uruk-Warka in terms of the early development of literate, urban complexity, it is not difficult to descry an elaboration of power upon the basic tripod of economy, military and ideology, as discussed in the anthropological approach of Earle (1997). The sealings and texts relate partly to economy, concerning themselves principally with the administration and control of agriculture, labour and crafts (Nissen 1995: 800; 2001: 155–6). The seal impressions depict scenes of buildings, prisoners, kings and commodities, readily interpreted within a framework of power in the spheres of economy (herds of domestic animals), military (captives

Figure 4.6 Seal impressions from Uruk-Warka
Source after Englund 1998: fig. 9.

paraded before a king), and ideology (cult building facades and cultic paraphernalia).

The architecture of the great complexes of Anu and Eanna reinforces the picture of ideological domination of an extensive population by a high-status elite, perhaps even testifying to the role of Uruk-Warka as a religious capital for all of Lower Mesopotamia (Algaze 2001a: 32). Social and political developments in the Uruk heartland by the later fourth millennium have been enumerated by Algaze (2001a: 34–7) as the appearance of kingship, an involvement of the state in the production and distribution of certain commodities, industrial-scale craft specialisation, state control over labour, and the development of an ideology and practice of legitimation involving writing and an iconography of heroism. Despite the apparent dominance of the city of Uruk-Warka in the fourth millennium landscape of Lower Mesopotamia, the evidence from Adams' surveys is generally taken to suggest the existence of multiple urbanised communities on the alluvium at this time (Nissen 2001: 158), interaction amongst whom generated a self-reinforcing drive towards urban growth, trade and geographic expansion as means of enhancing and sustaining the prestige of competing elite groups (Algaze 2001a).

As mentioned, some of the most exciting debate has been over the nature of relations between the Uruk heartland and the outer zones of Mesopotamia and beyond. We now turn to a consideration of how this issue has been approached by archaeologists in recent years, in the hope that such a study will elucidate how archaeologists deal with a specific research topic that is at the same time rooted in the minutiae of material culture, including styles of pottery and cylinder seals, and of supra-regional significance. A key figure in the debate is Guillermo Algaze, whose surveys and excavations in southeast Anatolia have contributed greatly to the pool of archaeological material relevant to this issue. In a series of publications (Algaze 1989; 1993; 2001a; 2001b), Algaze tackles the issue from the essential viewpoint of political economy. For Algaze the key element is the natural resource poverty of the Uruk heartland as contrasted with the resource richness of adjacent regions, an asymmetry in resource distribution that underlay the asymmetry in political development of the communities of the heartland and the outer zones. In Algaze's scenario, the high-status elite groups of the sophisticated communities of the south craved the luxury commodities present in the territories of less sophisticated societies of the north and east, and were prepared to go to considerable lengths to obtain them, to the extent that their activities constituted the main engine for change and social development of the Uruk world, a 'momentum toward empire' (Algaze 1993: 114) to be studied as a 'prehistory of imperialism' (Algaze 2001a).

Algaze's argument is that in the Uruk period the Lower Mesopotamian core, including the Susiana plain of southwest Iran, hosted a group of contemporary states, engaging in cut-throat competition for control over the alluvium and over trade routes into the highlands of Anatolia and Iran (Algaze 1993: 115–16; 2001b: 209). Specific outposts or enclaves in the periphery were founded and controlled by individual states of the core, with the location in the core of each state affecting the direction, structure and extent of its outward control. On the basis of this assumed core structure, Algaze prefers to see a modified world system rather than an 'informal empire'. Others have pointed out that 'Our knowledge of a congeries of competing Mesopotamian city-states, however, is practically nil (though theoretically possible) for the late Uruk period' (Yoffee 1995: 287), and posit the alternative view that Uruk-Warka had become in essence the capital of a large territorial state by the later fourth millennium. The evidence for multiple states in the Lower Mesopotamian core comes principally in the form of surveyed settlements found by Adams (1981), with many Uruk-period sites reaching the order of 20–40 hectares (Algaze 2001b: 209). One explanation of the immense size of Uruk-Warka, compared to any other contemporary site, has been suggested by Algaze as the city's function as a religious capital of Sumer through the fourth millennium (Algaze 2001b: 210), partly based on Piotr Steinkeller's idea that the Jemdet Nasr-period city sealings may attest cultic offerings made to Inanna at Uruk-Warka (Steinkeller 2002).

There is no evidence, however, for use of the city seals prior to the Jemdet Nasr period. All the evidence for lists of city names dates to the Jemdet Nasr and later periods, that is immediately after the Uruk period. Furthermore, if Uruk-Warka is seen as the prime cultic city of Sumer at this time, why does its name feature in only fourth place, after Ur, Larsa and Nippur, in the list of city names as attested on evidence from Jemdet Nasr (tablets with seal impressions) and Uruk-Warka itself (a single clay sealing, and at least thirteen Uruk III-type tablets listing city names) (R. Matthews 1993: 39)? Perhaps Ur was the cultic centre of Lower Mesopotamia in the Uruk period, relatively modest though it was in size at that time. The appearance of city lists only *after* the collapse of the Uruk phenomenon around 3,000 BC (although of course earlier instances may one day be found), may suggest that it was the calamity of that great collapse, however it was caused, that encouraged the cities of the alluvium to cooperate and collaborate in order to defend themselves and their interests in the face of a rapidly changing world. As the evidence stands so far, the appearance of lists of Lower Mesopotamian cities coincides with the fragmentation of the Uruk world into the utterly disparate cultural entities of the early third millennium – Jemdet Nasr/Early Dynastic I in the south, Ninevite 5 in the north, proto-Elamite in Iran – that came to replace the considerable cultural uniformity of the Uruk phenomenon. This critical chronological point likewise applies to the argument by Steinkeller (1993: 109–10) to the effect that the evidence from Uruk III tablets, of Jemdet Nasr date, demonstrates that during this period the Lower Mesopotamian core hosted a system of independent city-states with weak theocratic kings who could not have generated the power and expansion attested in the Uruk period. Again, Steinkeller's evidence here is from the subsequent Jemdet Nasr period, by which time there has clearly been a major breakdown in previously obtaining political circumstances across Mesopotamia and beyond. We need to be cautious in using Jemdet Nasr-period evidence to inform us about the preceding Uruk period.

Steinkeller argues against Algaze's Uruk expansion model on the grounds that

> it necessarily requires the existence, in prehistoric Babylonia, of a political system that possessed the organization, ideology, and economic and military resources sufficient to penetrate, colonize, and secure the control of the whole region affected by the Uruk phenomenon.
>
> (Steinkeller 1993: 109)

Strictly, Algaze does not push the argument that far, since colonisation is not detected by him in all areas of the Uruk expansion, being only one of several possible interaction strategies between core and peripheries. In any case, if the physical evidence in all its variety and richness so far recovered from Uruk-Warka in the Uruk period, reviewed above, does not indicate the existence of a extraordinarily well organised, complex, hierarchical, militaristic and outward-looking state, then it is not clear what further evidence is required to that end. A political entity that can organise 1,500 labourers working for ten hours a day over a five-year period, to repeat Nissen's labour figures for construction of the Anu Ziggurat/White Temple complex, as well as organising and controlling so much else at the same time, and overseeing the earliest uses of writing, can only be an entity of immense presence, power and capability.

An explanation of the primacy of complexity in Lower Mesopotamia during the fourth millennium is sought by Algaze, agreeing with Adams (1981), in 'social and "technological" innovations that were selected for and promoted by the unique geographic and environmental framework of the Tigris-Euphrates alluvial lowlands' (Algaze 2001b: 200). Stressing factors such as the variety and wealth of subsistence resources, high agricultural yields and effective water transport, as well as 'ideational technologies' relating to information processing, Algaze underlines 'the Mesopotamian advantage' in the early development of social complexity (Algaze 2001b: 200). This approach, perhaps to be called environmental opportunism rather than environmental determinism, is in general agreement with Nissen's view of the critical significance of the fertility of the Lower Mesopotamian plains and the need for irrigation as factors in the initial rise of complexity (Nissen 1988: 60–1). On the basis of these factors, Uruk communities of the southern plains could produce far greater quantities of foodstuffs per unit of labour and land than contemporary communities in peripheral regions. In this light, Philip Kohl's view that mid-third-millennium interactions between Lower Mesopotamia and its highland peripheries were characterised by a desire of the urban centres of the south to export, or 'dump', surplus staple commodities (Kohl 1975: 48), may have some bearing on the fourth-millennium dynamic between core and periphery. Kohl sees the core position in the mid-third millennium thus: 'Mesopotamian society was organized for the surplus production of certain staple commodities. Its own internal social structure was dependent upon the existence of foreign or external markets' (Kohl 1975: 48). Interactions between the core and highland peripheries of Anatolia and Iran would then stimulate a range of local developments within those communities, altering their social, economic and political structures in varying ways as opportunities for advancement arose on all sides.

Algaze's approach to the issue of Uruk expansion in the fourth millennium employs as its conceptual framework an adapted version of Wallerstein's world systems theory (Algaze 1993: 7), which stresses the asymmetric nature of core/periphery interactions in the development of complex states. Developed originally in an approach to European colonial expansion in the fifteenth and sixteenth centuries AD, Wallerstein's model is adapted by Algaze and applied to the context of interactions between the Uruk core of Lower Mesopotamia and a periphery comprising principally the plains and foothills of Upper Mesopotamia. Algaze defines three categories of Uruk settlement within the peripheral zone, 'enclaves', 'stations' and 'outposts'. Enclaves comprise major settlements such as Habuba Kabira, Jebel Aruda and Tell Sheikh Hassan on the Syrian Euphrates and, arguably, Nineveh on the Tigris and Tell Brak in northeast Syria. At these sites rich assemblages of Lower Mesopotamian material culture are well attested in the form of architecture, pottery, cylinder seals and administrative technology, all according to Algaze's argument evidence of direct colonisation by settlers from the Uruk heartland of Lower Mesopotamia. What were they doing there? Algaze argues that the motivation for founding these gateway communities was a desire to exercise control over land and riverine trade routes along which commodities such as metals, semi-precious stones and slaves were brought into Lower Mesopotamia in asymmetric exchange for perishable goods from the south. Furthermore, the need for Uruk communities of the south to process both imported and exported goods into finished products itself acted as an engine towards increasing social and economic complexity, cooperation and interdependence (Algaze 2001b: 205). One feature of these dramatic processes was a new attitude towards human labour, now seen as an exploitable commodity that could serve the interests of high-status groups as well as any other rare commodity. In Algaze's chilling words: 'Early Near Eastern villagers domesticated plants and animals. Uruk urban institutions, in turn, domesticated humans' (Algaze 2001b: 212).

The dynamics of interaction between Uruk colonial traders and the local communities with whom they dealt have provided a topic for lively discussion within the overall Uruk phenomenon debate. Evidence from a range of sites, including Godin Tepe and Tepe Sialk in Iran, Arslantepe, Hassek Höyük, Tepecik and Kurban Höyük in southeast Anatolia, amongst many others, indicates that there was no single pattern of interaction. Furthermore, given that it is now clear that interactions of Uruk communities endured over very long time periods, up to 700 years, there is great scope for development in the modes of interaction between any of the political entities involved in the Uruk world (Wright 2001). Attempts at outright domination by means of settled colonisation may be manifest in the nature and location of enclaves such as Habuba Kabira, but elsewhere the picture is much more one of mutual co-existence with implanted Uruk communities living side-by-side with well established local communities (Schwartz 2001). One aspect held in common by all sites of the Uruk expansion is their apparently contemporaneous collapse. At some time before the spread of pictographic writing, but after the development of numerical tablets with seal impressions, all the Uruk-related settlements of the periphery were abandoned and an extended period of regionalism set in across the world of Mesopotamia and beyond.

The issue of interaction between Uruk colonial traders and local peripheral communities has been a major focus in the work of Gil Stein, whose fieldwork at the site of Hacınebi Tepe on the Turkish Euphrates has provided the springboard for an alternative view to that propounded by Algaze. Evidence from Hacınebi Tepe has been most conveniently published in a special edition of the journal *Paléorient* (Stein 1999a) with discussion of the broader historical issues in a book (Stein 1999b). Stein has emphasised that the nature of interaction between Uruk Mesopotamians and local communities of Syria, Iran and southeast Anatolia might take several forms, including exchange, emulation and colonisation (Stein 1999a: 15), depending on the specifics of local conditions. At Hacınebi, Stein's excavations have shone unique light on how a small enclave of south Mesopotamians settled within one corner of a local Anatolian town in the middle of the fourth millennium BC, as attested by the presence of Uruk pottery, architectural elements and cylinder seals, all existing alongside, but spatially distinct from, material culture of the local Anatolian community. 'At Hacınebi we appear to have evidence for Mesopotamian colonization and exchange. This exchange appears to have taken place between two encapsulated communities that retained their distinctive social identities, with little or no emulation or transculturation' (Stein 1999a: 19). These distinctions in material culture were maintained, moreover, for up to 400 years of occupation at the site (Stein 2001: 301). Stein's inference is that the local Anatolian community was sufficiently complex and self-confident not to be tempted by acculturation with the small, but long-lived, group of south Mesopotamians whose presence amongst them was dictated by a desire to trade in metals, wood and other commodities of the upland regions (Stein 1999a: 20). According to Stein 'the Uruk enclave at Hacınebi was also economically autonomous in the sense that it produced its own crops, pastoral products and crafts' (Stein 1999a: 20).

It is not altogether easy to share Stein's view of long-lasting, tolerant and economically productive, yet at the same time arms-length and rigidly boundaried, relations between two communities in such close proximity over a time span of at least several generations. Stein's explanation is that 'the foreigners were able to survive and flourish only at the sufferance of the local rulers, most likely by forging strategic alliances with them through marriage or exchange relations' (Stein

1999a: 21), but it is hard to see how such interactions could have flourished without manifesting themselves in the form of some shared traits in material culture between the two communities. Inter-community marriage over a period of at least decades and perhaps centuries might be expected to lead to a blending of material culture distinctions between the two communities. In studying the trajectories and interactions of Lower Mesopotamian and Upper Mesopotamian traditions of glyptic styles through the fourth millennium, Holly Pittman has expressed a comparable sense of bafflement; 'Why then is there virtually no evidence at Hacınebi for the interaction of the two traditions?' (Pittman 2001: 442).

To consider another, later, Mesopotamian example, the existence of enclaves of traders from Aššur living as communities amongst local Anatolian societies in the Middle Bronze Age of the early second millennium BC is best attested by the wealth of textual documentation from Kültepe-Kaneš in central Anatolia, but here the picture is very different from Stein's Hacınebi scenario. While maintaining regular links with families and colleagues in their original homeland, at a distance of six weeks by donkey, the merchant traders from Aššur appear to have adopted almost all aspects of the local material culture, archaeologically distinguishing themselves largely by their habit of keeping written records in Assyrian Akkadian on cuneiform tablets that have survived till the present day (Veenhof 1995). The traders from Aššur clearly took local wives or mistresses, adopted local customs, learnt local languages and blended in as best they could, while at the same time concentrating on their original purpose of engaging in long-distance trade for the sake of their families and community back at Aššur. Many of them died and were buried at Kültepe-Kaneš before they could make the final trip home. Why should this picture be so different from the one conjured up by Stein for Hacınebi?

When Stein talks of a colony as being 'spatially and socially distinguishable from the communities of the host society', with 'artifactual similarities to the homeland' (Stein 1999b: 70–1), these statements have little or no application to the situation at Kültepe-Kaneš. This position is recognised by Stein and explained by him as a result of acculturation by local elites to the material culture of the colonising party (Stein 1999b: 73), but at Kültepe-Kaneš it is the colonisers who have acculturated to local material culture. The broader implication, however, is that such idiosyncrasies of historical process, to which all societies are subject, renders precarious any cross-cultural comparison. On the basis of a Kültepe-Kaneš analogy, for example, we could argue that Uruk

Mesopotamians were present at Hacınebi in the so-called pre-contact phase, but that their material culture identity was not distinguishable from that of the local host. They may have adopted local modes of daily life, local material culture and local means of conducting economic and social relations, and thus have blended in completely with their local hosts. It is for these reasons that Steinkeller's analogy between the Uruk expansion and Old Assyrian trade, suggesting that both were essentially commercial ventures, fails to convince (Steinkeller 1993: 114). The archaeological evidence from these two phenomena is totally different in kind and degree.

One element that needs careful consideration is that of cult or religious devotion. Algaze has hinted that the Uruk phenomenon, although approached largely in economic terms today due to our contemporary biases and interests, might additionally be approached in terms of political and religious ideologies (Algaze 1993: 122; 2001a: 50), and Mitchell Rothman has considered the likelihood 'that religion played roles of sanctification of rule, social integration, and cultural identity in fourth millennium B.C. Mesopotamia' (Rothman 2001b: 360). There might then be scope for an approach rooted in the study of 'the materialization of ideology', to use Earle's phrase (1997: 192), that takes into consideration aspects of surviving material culture, such as architecture, pottery assemblages and cylinder seal scenes, as potential elements within a framework of ideology distinctive to Uruk Mesopotamians (Collins 2000), which were retained and cherished within the physical context of settlement colonialism and other modes of regional interaction. Terence D'Altroy has underlined the possible role of religion, ceremony and corporate architecture within the processes of state formation in Mesopotamia in general, and the Uruk phenomenon in particular. His intriguing suggestion of 'collaborative or competitive sponsorship' by or for religious organisations adds a novel dimension to the possible dynamics of the Uruk phenomenon (D'Altroy 2001a: 467; see also Conrad and Demarest 1984). Clarisse Herrenschmidt has further stressed the significance of social hierarchy and religion as contexts for the early development of writing in Mesopotamia and Elam, particularly in terms of the indebtedness of humans to the gods for maintaining social order (Herrenschmidt 2000: 79–80). In addition, we need to consider the possible roles of newly evolved high-status elite groups in processes of legitimation through ideology, religious and otherwise (Lamberg-Karlovsky 1996: 94).

Stein has at length attempted to repudiate the world systems theory approach to the Uruk phenomenon espoused by Algaze, arguing that the nature of the relationship between the Lower Mesopotamia core and the Upper Mesopotamian periphery, epitomised by Hacınebi, does not fit the requirements of the world systems approach (Stein 1999b). Stein's conviction is that communities of the periphery were engaged in relations with the core that can be characterised as symmetric rather than asymmetric, a conviction based on such evidence as that for sophisticated craft production in peripheral regions, and for a high level of societal complexity in the periphery prior to any contact with the Lower Mesopotamian core. Using models of distance-parity and trade-diasporas, Stein refocuses the debate on the specifics of regional interaction, suggesting that at Hacınebi and other settlements such as Godin Tepe in west Iran, Uruk colonists from the south were too distant from their homeland and too few in number to be in a position of dominance with regard to their host community.

While appreciating Stein's arguments for a degree of social sophistication in peripheral communities of the Uruk world, it is hard to disagree with Algaze that the sheer scale of complexity attested at the site of Uruk-Warka utterly outweighs all the evidence so far put forward for social complexity in the periphery (Algaze 2001a: 66; 2001b: 227). Furthermore, Stein's tight focus on the evidence from Hacınebi has arguably swung interpretation too far in the direction of the dynamics of interaction at the micro scale, as attested in a wealth of data from that site (although often from contexts of dubious or secondary security). Of course, if we look at how a community of colonists interacts with their hosts at a settlement hundreds of kilometres from their homeland, we may be able to detect or postulate social relations at that site founded in mutual respect and symmetry. But if we step back and look at the global picture, we soon appreciate the strong asymmetry of a social relationship whereby one partner, the core, sends out and maintains over periods of time communities of colonists with specific missions of at least an economic nature to settlements of another partner, in the periphery. By its very nature it is a relationship of asymmetry, unless we can argue that there were colonists from Upper Mesopotamia settled in Uruk communities of the south, for which there is no evidence at all. Taken together, the evidence from both Hacınebi and Uruk-Warka, as epitomies of periphery and core respectively, necessitates an interpretation rooted in asymmetry and domination, however transmuted by distance and time.

One aspect of the Uruk expansion is the degree to which we can detect prehistoric precursors to this phenomenon. During the Ubaid period, examined above, there is plentiful evidence for extensive interactions, admittedly often of an obscure nature, between Lower and Upper Mesopotamia, and beyond, manifest at the least in common pottery technology and styles, and both Algaze and Stein make frequent reference to these precursors. Hans Nissen has recently suggested that the Uruk phenomenon was 'nothing but more or less successful attempts to reconstitute older, fifth millennium Ubaid exchange networks that had been disrupted' (Nissen 2001: 167). The adoption of centralised modes of social organisation at the important site of Arslantepe on the Turkish Euphrates, for example, appears to have its roots well back into the early fourth millennium, when there is evidence for massive public structures employing sophisticated administrative technologies that prefigure those of the so-called Uruk expansion of the mid-later fourth millennium (Frangipane 2001). Prior to the Ubaid period, moreover, we can witness broad regional patterns of interaction and development as characterised by the occurrence of Halaf pottery and other items of material culture across a total area of approximately 1,200 by 900km, some two millennia before the Uruk expansion (R. Matthews 2000a: 85). There is a candidate for an early version of the Uruk colonies on the Euphrates, the site of Baghouz on the Syrian Euphrates, which dates to the sixth-millennium Samarra period. Baghouz may have been founded as a trade colony as a means of controlling movement and processing of Anatolian obsidian on behalf of central Mesopotamian Samarra communities, as suggested by finds of obsidian cores and typical Samarra pottery at the site (R. Matthews 2000a: 76–7). Similarly, Algaze's claim for Uruk colonisation of the Susiana plain in the fourth millennium (Algaze 1993: 13–17) is enriched by reference to intensive interactions between Lower Mesopotamia and Susiana in the preceding Ubaid period. Putting the Uruk phenomenon into long time perspective thus helps us to appreciate that the mechanisms for interaction across substantial distances had already been in place for millennia.

It is worth considering for a moment one fundamental plank in the platform of interpretation constructed by both Algaze and Stein in their approaches to the Uruk phenomenon, that of historical analogy. To some extent all archaeological interpretation works by analogy. As Patty Jo Watson says, 'It is simply not possible to dispense with analogies in interpreting the past' (Watson 1980: 57). We cannot directly witness the past and therefore our approach to it will always be by a process of analogy with some familiar thing or process. As archaeologists we are constantly striving to encapsulate the unfamiliar, to 'cage the minute within its nets of gold', in Louis MacNiece's phrase, through the application of analogies, directly or otherwise. But how do we decide when an analogy is good and when bad? The aim of analogy, strongly deployed by Algaze and Stein, is to attempt to understand an aspect of an unknown society by looking for similarities in the effects of a process within a known society. If activity A within society 1 is known to produce result x, then detectable traces of result x in society 2 may also be the result of activity A. The trouble is that such an approach may take inadequate consideration of the importance of context in determining causal and sequential relationships between activities, results, and archaeological traces or correlates of results. As Ian Hodder says:

> we cannot be sure that the societies being grouped together are really comparable. All that is really happening, in this and in all types of ethnographic parallel, is that information is being transferred from society to society on the basis of similarities and differences.
>
> (Hodder 1999: 46)

Moreover, we *can* be sure that the archaeological histories of any two past societies, that is the specific trajectories through which their historical existences have become manifest in the archaeological record today, not to mention the trajectories of their discovery and recovery from that record, are always going to be idiosyncratic and quirky, thus making any explanation flow from present to past and back to present subjective and contestable. It is sometimes claimed that by employing so-called 'direct historical analogies', drawn from ethnoarchaeological observations of peoples living today much as they are assumed to have done in the past, the power of any particular analogy can be strengthened (Watson 1980: 57), but there is still a major element of uncertainty in any such assumption. In an extensive consideration of the subject, Alison Wylie has supported the use of analogy in archaeology, given the ability to control and discriminate the circumstances of its use and the opportunities for testing the validity of an analogy on a case-by-case basis (Wylie 1985).

In Algaze's 1993 book, the historical analogies come from such widely disparate contexts as the Seleucid and Parthian empires, Southeast Asia in the first millennium AD, and European colonialism in Africa in the sixteenth and seventeenth centuries AD, to name only a few (Algaze 1993). Stein's book ranges equally broadly in comparative scope, adopting and applying world-wide analogies from near and far in time and space (Stein 1999b). Agreeing with Algaze that 'it would be foolhardy to extrapolate indiscriminately into the past modes of social relationships and organization that only emerged as a result of specific, nonreplicable historical circumstances' (Algaze 1993: 127), it is fair to comment that both Algaze's and Stein's books lack a full address of the methodological issue of how historical models may be tested or evaluated against given sets of data. Stein's book includes a chapter, entitled 'Testing the models', that approaches this issue within the context of the Uruk phenomenon, containing as it does a discussion of suggested archaeological correlates of both the world systems approach of Algaze and the distance-parity/trade-diaspora approach preferred by Stein (Stein 1999b: 65–81; see also Flannery 1998).

Nicholas Postgate has briefly considered the Uruk phenomenon in the light of textually attested developments in the subsequent centuries of the third and second millennia of Mesopotamia. Making the point that political and cultural regional spheres need not totally overlap, and indeed may drastically diverge, Postgate stresses the unique significance of the Uruk phenomenon, as 'a diffusion of southern Mesopotamian artifacts or production far beyond any comparable diffusion in the later periods' (Postgate 1994a: 10). The implication is that the extent and intensity of the Uruk expansion, as materially attested in the archaeological record, are such that historical analogies, even from places and times historically contiguous to those of the Uruk, totally fail us. Steinkeller makes a similar point:

> Since the Uruk expansion, as we presently understand it, is a purely archaeological phenomenon, the task of correlating the pertinent material record with the testimony of written sources, and of trying to develop a single scenario for them both, is wrought with great uncertainty.
>
> (Steinkeller 1993: 110)

These admissions encourage us to comment that as archaeologists or anthropologists the task must be to approach the archaeological record above all on its own terms, and not to rely excessively on analogies and analytical procedures imported from other disciplines and areas such as history. The Uruk phenomenon as known to us today is an archaeological entity, and our approach to it must be principally as archaeologists. And if we elect to be archaeologists who are happy not to find or develop 'single scenario' solutions to major issues of the past, but rather to explore multiple, sometimes conflicting, interpretations, in the knowledge that such is the way that new perspectives and methods can be assessed and improved, to bring us back to Henry Wright's statement made at the start of this chapter, then the returns are likely to be the greater.

Chapter 5

Archaeologies of empire

Empires in archaeology

Another first often accredited to the arena of ancient Mesopotamia is that of empires, perhaps acceptably defined as 'any large sovereign political entity whose components are not sovereign, irrespective of this entity's internal structure or official designation' (Taagepera 1978a: 113), or 'a supernatural system of political control' (Larsen 1979: 92). Ironically, in historical ancient Mesopotamia there appears to have been no special word for 'empire', only for countries, lands or peoples. Definitions of empire vary greatly, and it is possible to regard some of the complex core/periphery interactions considered in the previous chapter as taking place within a context already containing elements of imperialism, as we have seen. Conventionally the term 'first Mesopotamian empire' (Larsen 1979: 75), or even 'world's first empire', is reserved for that of the Akkadian period of the later third millennium in Mesopotamia, when textual evidence appears to attest an imperial expansion and administration across substantial swathes of Lower and Upper Mesopotamia and beyond. The presence of textual evidence, however, has arguably encouraged an over-hasty definition and detection of imperial modes of power in what is still essentially an ahistoric archaeological environment. In relation to the alleged Tula empire of central Mexico, Smith and Montiel comment that there has been a tendency 'to give too much weight to the native historical record in central Mexico, in spite of its obviously propagandistic nature' (Smith and Montiel 2001: 269), and a similar sentiment might be cast in the direction of some Mesopotamian textual scholars as regards study of the Akkadian period. The notion of ahistoric or prehistoric empires in ancient Southwest Asia has not seriously been entertained, in contrast to studies in the New World on political phenomena such as the aliterate Inka and Wari empires of Peru (D'Altroy 2001b; Schreiber 2001). In truth, the specifically archaeological study of empires in the Mesopotamian context is in its infancy. The apparent wealth of texts surviving from empires of the Mesopotamian past has perhaps encouraged a view that atextual archaeological investigation has little to contribute. In this chapter we hope to show how false that view might be.

How have archaeologists gone about defining and studying empires on the ground? What might be the archaeological correlates of empires, as distinct from those of complex societies engaging in regional interactions? What special approaches or scales of approach might be required, given that we are here considering probably the single largest anthropological entity that an archaeologist might study? Empires are immense phenomena and ought to leave commensurately large traces in the archaeological record. But they are also fickle entities that change shape with unpredictable and sweeping rapidity: 'the spatial scale, geographic and organizational variability, and the rapid rates of change in empires pose considerable challenges to archaeologists, whose focus of research is necessarily a small part of a large phenomenon' (Sinopoli 1994: 173).

Some ideas on approaches to empire are summarised in Table 5.1, compiled on the basis of a broad survey of studies of empires of both the Old and New Worlds, from late prehistory to modern times, including elements presented in those studies as well as original suggestions. What has not been essayed before is the tripartite nature of the approach. Listed in the first column are those characteristics of politics, economy, society and ideology that help to define an empire as an anthropological entity. The presence of isolated characteristics in any particular past society is unlikely to lead to a safe definition, as many of the suggested characteristics may individually be present in non-imperial societies. The more attributes that can be identified, the stronger the case for imperial identification will be, and there is certainly scope for exploration of how some characteristics and correlates might be of greater significance than others. The attributes in Table 5.1 have been gleaned from wide-ranging cross-cultural studies of empires throughout history (Alcock *et al.* 2001; Sinopoli 1994; Smith and Montiel 2001; Taagepera 1978a; 1978b), and others could be added to the list.

The second column represents an attempt to summarise those archaeological correlates that may come to represent, in the recoverable archaeological record, the anthropological reality of empire. Again, the more correlates ticked off the stronger the case that can be made. Rarely will there be a one-to-one correspondence between the first two columns. We are dealing with highly complex political entities, as well

Table 5.1 Empires: characteristics and correlates

Anthropological characteristics	Archaeological correlates	Textual correlates
I IMPERIAL CORE		
Large complex urban centre as capital	Dominant settlement in core region	Archives at capital
	Dominance of capital in local settlement hierarchy	
Occupational specialisation in core	Evidence for craft specialisation	Profession lists Scribes
Social stratification, from elite to slave	Variation in housing	Content – slaves
	Differential distribution of goods	
Ethnic diversity at capital	Clumping of material culture	Multi-lingual? Non-language specific?
Agricultural intensification in core	Irrigation, landscape control, storage	Content – agriculture
Crop management strategies	Changes in archaeobotanical evidence	Content – crops
Animal management strategies	Changes in zooarchaeological evidence	Content – animals
Technological advantage in core	Technologies originating in core	Texts as administrative technology Seals and texts
Imperial ideology at capital Militarism and use of terror	Imagery of battle, conquest, subjugation	
Glorification of state		
Labour investment in public building	Massive public monuments	Content – labour
Glorification of ruler	Imagery of royalty	Content – rulers
Charismatic individual rulers	Imagery of individual	Named rulers – legends
Core appropriation of peripheral ideology	Peripheral cult-status/ images removed to core	

contd

Economic interaction between core and periphery via coercion/exchange	Goods taken/imported from periphery to core	Texts in periphery?
	Goods exported from core to periphery	
Political control of periphery		Language shift?
Military control	Destruction levels in peripheral sites, hoards	Content – war
Imperial infrastructure across entire region	Roads, garrisons, fortresses	Content – geographic
Imposition of tribute/tax on periphery		
Increased agricultural intensity in periphery	Irrigation, landscape control	
intensity/standardisation of craft production in periphery	Evidence for craft specialisation/standardisation	Texts in periphery?
Control of peripheral populations	Nucleation of settlement patterns in periphery Establishment of regional centres	
Imperial co-option of peripheral elites	Core high-status goods in peripheral elite contexts	
Peripheral elite emulation of core elite	Core high-status goods in peripheral elite contexts (e.g. burials)	

3   EMPIRES IN GLOBAL CONTEXT

Economic influence		
Trade/exchange beyond empire	Exotic goods from beyond empire in core zone Goods from empire found beyond borders	Exotic toponyms
Political influence		
Military policing of borders of empire	Fortresses, defences in border zones	Garrison archives
State formation in adjacent zones	Shifts in settlement patterns	
Cultural influence		
Elite emulation of imperial styles	Shifts in material culture in adjacent zones	
Elite emulation of imperial gods/rituals	Copies of temples, cultic paraphernalia beyond empire	

4 CYCLE(S) OF EXPANSION, CONSOLIDATION, COLLAPSE		
Expansion	Spread of material culture/settlement	
Slow-quick-slow sequence		
Consolidation	Continuities in material culture/settlement	
Collapse	Discontinuities in material culture/settlement, hoards	End of texts
Economic downturn	Regional abandonment, no movement of goods	
Environmental downturn	Regional abandonment, environmental evidence	

as an archaeological record subject to various and complex depositional and taphonomic processes. In many cases there will be uncertainty about whether a particular archaeological aspect is diagnostic of empire, of non-empire or, most often, of neither. We need to keep in mind the subtlety of the relationship between cultural and political identity: 'We have no agreed-on criteria for distinguishing archaeologically between conformity imposed by external forces and that arising from the voluntary congruence of an integrated cultural system, independent of political control' (Postgate 1994a: 3). Furthermore, the archaeological impact of empire on any specific region will vary according to the duration and intensity of interaction. Fleeting control might leave no detectable traces, while long-lasting military and administrative intrusion might leave recoverable evidence in a wide range of material culture fields.

The third column of Table 5.1 gives some tentative ideas about how empires might manifest themselves in the written record as recovered from the ground. That is to say, if we look at texts as archaeological artefacts, are there ways in which they are distributed, composed and structured that might betoken an imperial context? This view of texts goes beyond, but will also include, the import of their content. There has been little previous discussion of the potential significance of texts as artefacts in studies of states and empires (but see Postgate *et al.* 1995). As already stressed, texts are archaeological artefacts with meaningful contexts and associations well beyond the nature of their content. As Robert Adams has said, it is up to us as archaeologists to give the body of textual evidence 'the attention that its *anthropological* significance warrants' (Adams 1988: 42; italics in original). It is also up to us to ensure that cuneiform texts found in excavations are published with adequate information concerning their physical contexts and associations within an excavation, so that their full significance can be appreciated (Ellis 1983).

It is vital to distinguish the three elements of a holistic archaeological approach to empires, as represented by the three columns of Table 5.1. In previous studies there has commonly been confusion, particularly as to the first two columns, the assumption being that the definition of an anthropological aspect is sufficient end in itself for the study of empires. The table recently presented by Smith and Montiel (2001: 247, table 1; see also Smith 2001: 131, table 5.2), for example, is entitled 'Archaeological criteria for the identification of empires', but most of the elements listed as examples, such as 'militarism', 'glorification of king or state', 'imposition of tribute or taxes', 'imperial co-option of local elites', are not archaeological criteria at all but anthropological characteristics. Arriving at archaeologically meaningful correlates of these characteristics is the main challenge today facing the researcher of past empires, and Table 5.1 represents a tentative step in that direction. There are doubtless many further characteristics and correlates that could be added to the table.

Empires in Mesopotamia and Mesopotamia in empires

The lands of Mesopotamia have hosted, or participated in, a series of empires through history, as summarised in Table 5.2, largely based on the work of Taagepera (1978a; 1978b). The Uruk phenomenon is included in the table, accepting for now Algaze's characterisation of it as an 'informal empire' at least (Algaze 2001a) and Liverani's assertion that empires existed before Akkad (Liverani 1993: 3). The table has been brought up to the modern era in the hope of underlining the significance of Mesopotamia within long-term trends of imperial history. Imperial areas, of course highly approximate and measured as dry land extent of control, are given as measures of Mm^2, or squared megametres, one megametre being 1,000km.

In his innovative comparative studies of empires of the world through time and space, Rein Taagepera has underlined the fragile nature of Mesopotamian empires, as compared to their Egyptian and Chinese counterparts: 'the special problem with Mesopotamian data is that empires rise and fall so rapidly that it is hard to keep track of all of them' (Taagepera 1978b: 185). He has also pointed to chronological

Table 5.2   Mesopotamia and empires

Empire	Approximate date	Core	Maximum extent (Mm²)
Uruk	3200 BC	Lower Mesopotamia	0.90
Akkad	2250 BC	Northern Lower Mesopotamia	0.80
Ur III	2050 BC	Lower Mesopotamia	0.10
Old Assyrian	1850 BC	Upper Mesopotamia	0.15
Old Babylonian	1800 BC	Northern Lower Mesopotamia	0.25
Mitanni	1400 BC	Upper Mesopotamia	0.30
Middle Assyrian	1300 BC	Upper Mesopotamia	0.40
Neo-Assyrian	700 BC	Upper Mesopotamia	1.40
Neo-Babylonian	600 BC	Northern Lower Mesopotamia	0.50
Achaemenid	400 BC	South Iran	5.50
Seleucid	300 BC	Northern Lower Mesopotamia	4.00
Parthian	100 BC	Northern Lower Mesopotamia	2.50
Sasanian	AD 250	Iran	3.50
Abbasid	AD 800	Northern Lower Mesopotamia	11.00
Mongol	AD 1300	Central Asia	24.00
Ottoman	AD 1550	Anatolia	4.50
British	AD 1920	London	34.00

Source: based largely on Taagepera 1978a; 1978b.

clumping of empires over large regions, as in the later third millennium BC (Akkad, Old Kingdom Egypt) and the later second millennium BC (Hittite, New Kingdom Egypt, Mitanni, Middle Assyrian), alternating with episodes of low imperial activity such as the end of the third millennium BC and the early first millennium BC (Taagepera 1978b: 195), perhaps indicating that, because of their size and complexity, empires rise and fall only as elements in a very broad regional pattern. Environmental factors may also need consideration on this point.

In general, Mesopotamian empires have not received study in the sorts of anthropological ways commonly applied to New World empires, or even to empires of other regions of the Old World, such as the Roman empire. There has perhaps been an assumption that if we have texts from an empire then there is little need to take an anthropological approach and, at the same time, that if there are no texts then there is no need to consider the possibility of empire. North American approaches to New World empires have been more exploratory and innovative in their research aims and methods (Conrad and Demarest 1984), and it may be worthwhile to attempt to import those characteristics into the arena of Mesopotamian imperial studies. Smith and Montiel (2001) try to construct a material culture model for the identification of empires that is then applied to three candidates for empire in central Mexico but, as mentioned, they experience understandable difficulty in distinguishing archaeological correlates from anthropological traits. A recent study by Carla Sinopoli takes a global view of empires as archaeologically approachable phenomena that can meaningfully be compared and contrasted across time and space (Sinopoli 1994). Here, following the structure of Table 5.1, we consider the major elements of Mesopotamian empires and how they might be approached archaeologically.

The imperial core

All empires have a core, a physical focus for political, economic and cultic activity, and regarded as 'the navel of the universe', to use the Inka term for their sacred capital of Cuzco (D'Altroy 2001b: 201). Since the nineteenth century, Mesopotamian archaeology has focused strongly on major urban settlements that have frequently turned out to be the centres of empires. Excavations at cities such as Nimrud, Nineveh, Khorsabad, Aššur, Susa, Babylon and Ur have all explored core cities of long-dead empires. Here could be found the massive palaces and temples of the imperial elite, formally planned and constructed as the physical manifestation of their administrative, military and ideological supremacy, 'a symbol-laden statement of awesome power' as Sennacherib's Nineveh has been described (Lumsden 2000: 820). Here also might be the residences of elite representatives of subjugated populations, and here might we find a material culture diversity and richness to correlate with the ethnic and cultural dominion of the empire. But despite the input of labour and time that has gone into the investigation of these centres, we still have much to learn about the functioning of core centres within their imperial contexts. Our knowledge of them is dictated by the research aims and field programmes, insofar as they existed, of the excavators of the time and their funding institutions. We know a great deal about the architecture and art of imperial Assyrian palaces, for example, but much less about the quality of daily life of the common individuals who dwelt in humbler abodes in the imperial core. We know much about the import and use of exotic raw materials and finished goods to the centre, but less about the political and economic means by which those commodities were obtained, or the maintenance of routes of communication along which they were traded.

The investigation of an imperial core city is not a simple task. By definition such a settlement will be extensive and likely to have been occupied through more than one period, often millennia, as an imperial or at least regional point of focus, as is the case with Nineveh, Aššur, Susa, Babylon and Ur, for example. Such long-term occupation makes archaeological exposure of contemporary structures time-consuming and difficult. It may be impossible to expose earlier levels without destruction of overlying buildings. The implementation of massive building programmes in antiquity, such as frequently occurred at core centres as successive rulers built new palaces and temple complexes, is also likely severely to have disrupted archaeological levels belonging to earlier phases, so that there may be no prospect of attaining a detailed diachronic picture of settlement and activity at an imperial core. Furthermore, the immense and carelessly executed excavation programmes of the early modern era have themselves inflicted significant damage and destruction to the archaeological integrity of many of these sites. Ancient imperial cores may lie buried and largely inaccessible under major modern cities, as is the case with the 'Abbasid Round City of Mansur under modern Baghdad. Another factor is that few of the major imperial capitals have been directly threatened by modern civil engineering projects, such as dam construction, and therefore have not attracted multi-national rescue programmes such as have been routinely conducted along much of the river valleys of Mesopotamia in recent decades. We know less about settlement history in the immediate environs of Nineveh or Babylon, for example, than we do about many peripheral regions of the Assyrian empire and beyond (Parker 1997). Threatened flooding, within the near future, of the Assyrian state capital at Aššur by construction of a dam across the Tigris may lead to an international response and, at the expense of the city itself, an increased understanding of it and its regional context.

The foundation of an imperial capital may in itself serve as an affirmation of power and charismatic identity by a specific ruler, 'the apex in the action of the creator king' comparable 'only to the works of basic creation, owed to the gods' (Liverani 1979: 309). Movement to a new capital may be a means used by rulers of disempowering subsidiary elite groups entrenched in the old capital (Sinopoli 1994: 170). Perhaps the best hope for holistic exploration of an imperial core city lies with single-period settlements founded by individual rulers and abandoned at the death or demise of that ruler. At these charismatic capitals we can gain an impression of the scale and variety of activity envisioned for a capital of empire. An example that has been identified and extensively excavated, and where in March 1843 Botta first discovered an Assyrian palace, is the city of Khorsabad, ancient Dur-Šarrukin, 'built, occupied and abandoned in the space of a single generation', as Seton Lloyd puts it (Lloyd 1978: 201–2).

Let us then look for a moment at Khorsabad as an example of an imperial core centre from ancient Mesopotamia.

Sargon II founded Dur-Šarrukin, 'Fortress of Sargon', in the later eighth century BC as a deliberate statement of his own power and magnificence. Of paramount importance in the layout of the city was the king's palace, located on a high platform dominating the city on the northwest side. The relief-clad palace and the rest of the citadel, with its temples, ziggurat and elite residences, and its immense gates with guardian human-headed bulls, give imposing physical form to the ideology of great kingship of the Assyrian ruler.

At the core of the core, so to speak, lay the throne room of Sargon's palace, its entrances from the courtyard protected by winged bulls. The walls of the throne room rose over 12m in height and were decorated with coloured murals offsetting the relief scenes around the throne emplacement itself. The reliefs in the throne room depicted scenes of the king presiding over the torture and execution of important rebels, an unambiguous message for any visiting dignitary (Reade 1979: 338). Monumental city walls, 24m thick on stone foundations, seven-gated, and enclosing an area of around 280 hectares, define the imperial core in a stark and undeniable manner. Were we to look at other Assyrian capitals, Aššur, Nimrud and Nineveh, the story of imperial greatness manifest in stone and mud-brick would not substantively differ from what we see at Dur-Šarrukin, and it is thanks to the nineteenth-century excavators, and some of their twentieth-century successors, that we know so much about this particular aspect of imperial cores.

What we know far less about can readily be appreciated by a glance at Figure 5.1, which reveals that almost the entirety of the lower town within the city walls, let alone any area outside the walls, has remained

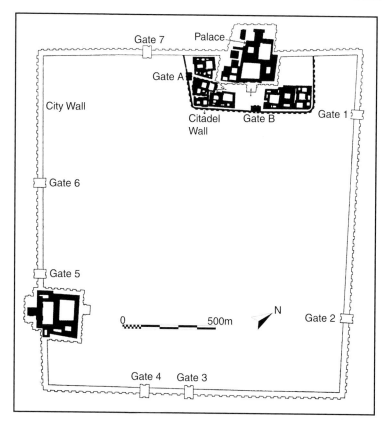

Figure 5.1 Khorsabad, north Iraq. Plan of the city
Source: after Lloyd 1978: fig. 143.

largely unmolested by archaeological exploration. In fact Victor Place did put some small soundings into the lower town of Khorsabad but the techniques of the day did not enable him, nor Botta and Layard at Nimrud and Nineveh, to discern and excavate structures built entirely of mud brick (Liverani 1997: 88–9). We therefore know next to nothing about urban structure, household density, distribution, and differentiation by district within residential areas of ancient Mesopotamian capital cities. We have little or no understanding of such issues as the role of centres within their contemporary and diachronic local settlement hierarchies, where we might expect intensification of land use and enhancement of storage facilities as means of ensuring food supplies

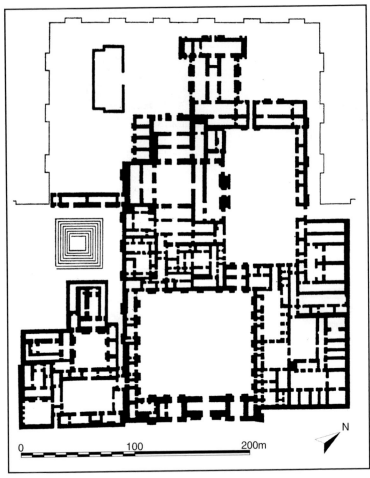

Figure 5.2 Khorsabad, north Iraq. Plan of Sargon's palace
Source: after Lloyd 1978: fig. 143.

against times of conflict (Sinopoli 1994: 170). We also know little about the nature and variability of urban/rural interactions, the scope of labour and craft specialisation within and around the core city, the evidence for social stratification and perhaps ethnic grouping within residential areas of the city, as well as the possibilities of technological innovation and dispersal in and from the imperial core. A unique anthropological study of animal management as attested in the texts of the Ur III empire indicates the possible effects of imperialism on central management strategies, and at the same time provides pointers for how a truly interdisciplinary research programme might tackle such issues, employing the evidence of both texts and material culture remains (Zeder 1994), while study of highly organised grain processing institutions suggests how increased productivity was achieved in order to meet burgeoning imperial demands (Grégoire 1999).

We know from texts that the city wall of Dur-Šarrukin was built in segments assigned to workers from different provinces of the empire (Postgate 1979: 203). Where did these workers live, and what are the prospects of excavating their residential quarters within or around the city and identifying ethnic or cultural groups in the archaeological record? In order to address this and many other issues, we need to investigate the daily practices of diet, economy, codes of living and of ritual and burial that may aid in more sharply defining and exploring the variety and richness of human life to be found in a great imperial capital. Similar approaches might also be employed in investigations of craft quarters or neighbourhoods such as we know existed within imperial cities such as Aššur and Nineveh (Lumsden 2001: 42). This journey has barely begun. The major consolation, as we can see from the unexcavated swathes of the city in Figure 5.1, is that the evidence relating to such questions has so far remained largely untouched by the insensitive hands of early explorers. There is no doubt that future programmes of research will eventually turn their attention in these directions.

As another example of an imperial core, let us glance at the city of Samarra, another city founded, partially settled and abandoned in very short order. Samarra was the capital of the 'Abbasid caliphate from AD 836 to 892 and has been claimed as 'maybe the largest archaeological settlement in the world' (Northedge 1997: 473), extending over 57km² along the bank of the Tigris north of Baghdad. Some 5,700 buildings, many unfinished when the city was abandoned, have been identified at the site, and they include a wealth of high-status court facilities such as immense palaces, mosque complexes, military cantonments, racecourses and hunting parks (Northedge 1997). Here again we see the core of empire materialised as a monument to the glory of the ruler and his associates, including the army.

Imperial core cities, then, have hitherto been approached by archaeologists largely in terms of the elements in them that serve to glorify the state and the ruler, that is in terms of their monumental structures. One aspect is the use of art in the service of royal and imperial ideology, a field of increasing interest in recent years (Winter 1997). In the imperial context there is no 'art for art's sake'. Every picture tells a story of imperial grandeur in the form of military achievements of the ruler

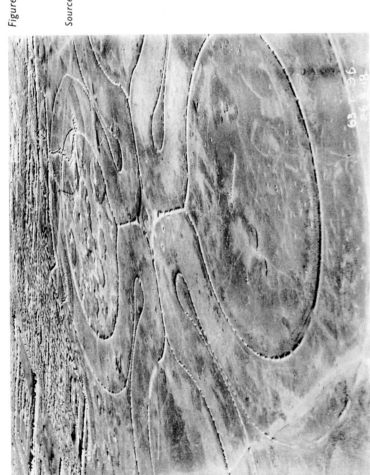

Figure 5.3 Samarra, central Iraq, imperial racecourse in cloverleaf plan, photographed from 1,500 feet on 26 August 1918

Source: Public Record Office ref. CN 5/2 385.

and his role as priest-king in the meticulous conduct of state ritual, essential to the prosperity of the empire. Julian Reade has discussed how every detail of the layout and decoration of an Assyrian palace was planned and executed to the individual design of each ruler. The impulse of successive kings to carry out this massive operation led either to a movement to a new, or previously used, capital or to the construction of an immense new palatial complex at an existing capital every time a ruler ascended the throne: 'we therefore have a magnificent succession of palaces, each the memorial of one man' (Reade 1979: 330). More than that, each capital city, and indeed the entire empire through that city, is dedicated to the charisma of a single individual, and the diversity of empire is unified through the ideology associated with that individual, or such might at least have been the wish of that person.

In a hard-hitting essay Mario Liverani has summarised the function of imperial ideology as 'the systematization of unbalance, and in this respect it is the apex of all forms of exploitation ... the dominion of the few over the many, the surrender of wealth by classes or groups of producers in favour of non-producing consumers' (Liverani 1979: 297). Like others (Yoffee 1995: 300), Liverani sees the condition of imperialism as being 'not natural' and therefore in need of intensive ideological reinforcement in order to become palatable to the many oppressed and reluctant participants in empire. Political views apart, it is hard to see what is unnatural about a form of political entity that arose time after time in Mesopotamia and many other parts of the world, however fleeting any individual manifestation may have been. In any case, asymmetric relations between individuals and groups of individuals appear to have characterised the entirety of human history, and empires are just one extremity of that human historical spectrum.

Royal inscriptions and titulary can also inform on the developing significance of individual rulers, epitomised by 'Naram-Sin, the mighty, king of the four corners of the world' (A. Westenholz 1979: 111) or the divine ideology of the Ur III kings (Michalowski 1991), but how might imperial ideology impact upon the non-elite elements of an empire? By laying unremitting stress upon an assumed unnaturalness and political repulsiveness of ancient imperial ideology, without at the same time attempting to approach and apprehend the ways in which the messages of ideology were received, transformed and resisted by those for whom they were designed, we run the risk of an excessively 'presentist' view that imposes our own post-colonial stances on the distant past. Before we pronounce too firmly on the iniquities of an ancient ideology, we need to learn more about how that message was constructed, mediated and acted upon by those who came into contact with it, contested it and reformulated it, and that process has barely begun. Further exploration of these concerns will require the recovery and nuanced study of the full range of artefacts from the past, including written documents, in a new holistic and integrated manner that encourages rich interpretations of the past that give voice equally to the oppressed as to the oppressor, such as may come from truly contextual investigations of both palace and hovel approached in the same spirit of integrated enquiry.

One aspect of imperial core cities is the likely presence of archives of written documents, potentially of great importance in understanding the workings of empire. Almost all Mesopotamian imperial core cities have yielded textual archives, and may have been defined as imperial cores principally on that basis. The use of multiple languages in archives of core cities may be a good indication of the scope of interactions engaged in by the core, as well as of its ethnic constitution. In the case of archives from the Hittite capital, Hattusa, for example, seven different languages are attested in imperial documents. While vastly informative on matters of imperial administration and bureaucracy, such evidence needs to be viewed in context. Excavations have hitherto focused on imperial cores and on royal palaces and cultic centres within those cores, with very few published discoveries of private archives from imperial cores, let alone from peripheral contexts (Postgate 1979: 195), so that the textual picture is highly biased towards 'history from above' (Van De Mieroop 1999a). Again, systematic long-term investigation of private residences at core cities might go some way to righting this imbalance.

Domination of peripheral polities

Relations between core and periphery are likely to be of an asymmetric nature in an imperial context, but that does not severely limit the variety of such relations that can exist. For the rather exceptional Ur III empire, it has even been suggested that core and periphery interacted economically in a symmetrical fashion (Steinkeller 1991: 33). In fact a single empire can entertain a host of different sorts of relations with contemporary neighbours, and each of those relations can change through time. Important factors affecting core/periphery relations will include the nature of pre-contact political and social conditions in the periphery, as we have seen in the case of differing responses to the Uruk expansion (Chapter 4), as well as the natural distribution of resources

(Sinopoli 1994: 160–1). Feinman and others have distinguished between territorial and hegemonic empires, the former employing more direct and intrusive means of control and tribute exaction than the latter (Feinman 1998: 109).

Further factors influential in shaping and changing core/periphery relations include the physical distance between core and a particular periphery, where the importance of communications as related to exaction of tribute or suppression of disquiet through military movement, for example, can be critical. Taagepera has pointed out that the radius from core to periphery of the largest pre-Achaemenid empires of Southwest Asia, taking some account of topography, comes out at about 650km, or about one week in terms of fastest available communications (Taagepera 1978a: 121), or two weeks for a round trip. The importance of fast and reliable communications cannot be overstated in this context (Barfield 2001: 30), and surviving evidence may include dramatically improved modes of communication across large areas, exemplified by the Roman and Persian roads of Asia Minor as well as by the textual evidence for imperial Assyrian communications (Kessler 1997). The study of what Adams has called 'the calculus of pre-industrial transport costs' (Adams 1979: 401) has hardly begun. As ever, common-sense assumptions are not necessarily the best guide on this issue. Research on movement and portage by foot in the hills of eastern Nepal demonstrates that human porters regularly carry on their backs loads of 70–80kg, occasionally more than 100kg, over distances of 8 to 11km per day across difficult terrain, principally in order to exchange agricultural surpluses for salt and other products, covering one-way total distances of at least 150km. Applying these ethnographic observations to the pre-Hispanic American Southwest, Nancy Malville deduces much greater potential ranges of contact and interaction than had previously been envisaged (Malville 2001). Nevertheless, the types of commodities transported, whether by foot, animal, river or other means, are likely to vary with distance, luxury items predominating over bulk goods as the distance increases (Stein 1999b: 59).

Once an empire has expanded there may follow a phase of consolidation, during which the management by the core of the periphery is implemented by means of administrative and military control, asymmetric economic interaction and ideological imposition (Sinopoli 1994: 163–8). In this phase, peripheral ideologies may be appropriated by the core, perhaps involving the transport of cult images, and core ideologies may be manifest in the culture of the periphery. Peripheral elites may adopt elements of core ideologies in the way of dress, architecture and rites of religion and burial. Such interactions may be manifest in the form of high-status goods present in peripheral elite contexts, such as residences and burials (Smith and Montiel 2001: 249). But the degree to which a core controls its peripheries is highly variable, an extreme version being the implementation of a provincial system of bureaucratic control administered by officials originating from, and directly controlled by the core city, as occurred in the later phase of the Assyrian empire (Larsen 1979: 92). As an empire stabilises, if it does, there may be a shift in emphasis from military to civil administration in some provinces, as in the case of the Assyrian empire (Postgate 1979: 194). In the case of the Ur III empire, strict bureaucratic control of provincial administration was maintained by the provincial governor, a royal appointee who could oversee production and transport on behalf of the imperial core (Steinkeller 1991).

Imperial domination of peripheries might be manifest in changes in settlement and subsistence patterns (Sinopoli 1994: 171; Parker 1997), including the foundation of regional nodes of power to act as foci for tax and tribute gathering and as delegates of military and ideological control. There may also be intensification of peripheral settlement as a response to the imposition of an imperial peace and/or as a means of achieving tax and tribute targets. In areas of less direct rule, the means of production may remain largely in local hands with an obligation to produce certain quantities of tribute. Storage facilities and physical evidence of land management, such as large estates, terraces, field systems and irrigation technologies, may show themselves in the archaeological record of dominated peripheries (Smith and Montiel 2001: 249; Weiss and Courty 1993: 141), a process of 'ruralization' complementing that of urbanisation (Yoffee 1995: 284). Peripheral estates may be allotted to elite families chancing their hand in the provinces, as with Assyrian families around Harran (Larsen 1979: 97). Populations may be moved around the empire for political and military purposes, with an emphasis on nucleation in controllable towns as nodes of imperial domination (Weiss and Courty 1993: 139). Such a pattern may be contrasted with that of settlement dispersal and contraction associated with the collapse of sophisticated political entities (Peltenburg 2000).

The intensification and standardisation of craft production in peripheral centres is also a possible outcome of imperial control, which may manifest itself as increased scales of production and homogenisation of elements of material culture (Weiss and Courty 1993: 140). There may be a distinction between items of elite material culture whose production and raw material procurement may be under strict centralised control, as against production of non-elite items conducted outside central control (Lamberg-Karlovsky 1996: 77–9). Such a distinction between attached and independent specialists is made by Stein and Blackman in their innovative study of production at later-third-millennium Tell Leilan in Upper Mesopotamia, where they suggest that ceramics, as low-status objects, were produced by multiple independent workshops, while high-status commodities such as textiles and metals were produced by attached specialists under central control (Stein and Blackman 1993). In the Ur III empire there is textual evidence for massive specialisation in commodity production directly under central control (Steinkeller 1991: 17).

In terms of exchange of commodities, imperial domination of peripheries should entail the movement of peripheral goods, often as raw materials, to the core, countered by the movement of core goods, often as finished products, to the periphery. Kohl has suggested that in the case of mid-third-millennium Mesopotamia the exchange of commodities may have been stimulated principally by a desire of the core urban centres to 'dump' their staple surpluses onto peripheral markets (Kohl 1975: 48). But these exchanges are notoriously difficult to detect in the surviving record, especially when so many of the finished products – textiles, clothing, spices – are likely to have been perishable or, in the case of high-status artefacts of metal and semi-precious stone, intrinsically of high value and therefore likely to be reused through time. In the case of the Akkadian empire the prominence of geographical terms such as the 'silver mountains' and the 'cedar forest' might be taken to indicate the importance of these peripheral regions as sources of raw materials for core consumption (Larsen 1979: 79). Careful consideration of both textual and archaeological evidence for Akkadian imperial presence in Anatolia tends to support such a view (J. G. Westenholz 1998).

As regards the Assyrian empire, the principal commodities extracted from peripheries for benefit of the core included metals, dyes, processed foodstuffs (wine, honey), fibres, resins and lapis lazuli, as well as slaves for imperial building projects and horses for the army (Postgate 1979: 207). The processing of raw materials into elite luxury goods at the imperial core is expressed by Liverani as part of the ideological process whereby chaos (the periphery) is transmuted into cosmos (the core) through the channel of the king (Liverani 1979: 314). The assumption that ancient empires engaged in maximum milking of peripheries for minimum input has been rightly queried by Adams, who underlines the paucity of our existing data on the scale of tribute exaction from conquered territories (Adams 1979: 395).

Peripheries may be directly dominated through the imposition of military might, manifest in such form as improved communications for the rapid deployment of troops, and the construction of garrisons and fortresses at strategic locations. There are suggestions, for example of a strong Akkadian military presence, alongside merchant colonists, at Susa in the later third millennium (Foster 1993: 35). Destruction levels at specific peripheral sites may be associated with core/periphery conflict (Smith and Montiel 2001: 249), although there is perhaps too strong a temptation to connect such destructions with historically attested incidents.

At the edge of empires

Empires have effects well beyond their own borders. In material terms, such effects may include the movement of high-status commodities and artefacts between imperial entities, and the conduct of trade or diplomacy with regions beyond imperial control, such as Akkadian and Ur III trade with the Arabian Gulf and beyond. In textual terms the occurrence of exotic place-names, such as Dilmun in the earliest Uruk texts, and Dilmun, Magan and Meluhha in Akkadian texts (Michalowski 1993: 73) may be a suitable material correlate here. High-status artefacts may travel across very large distances, perhaps through exchange between elites of contemporary empires, as in Assyria and Phrygia (Muscarella 1998). Such may be an explanation for the occurrence of Indus Valley artefacts in third-millennium Mesopotamia (Potts 1997). The variety of possible relations between an empire and its external neighbours may receive ideological treatment in the art of the core, as in differing depictions at Assyrian palaces of representatives of foreign states such as Babylon, Urartu, Elam and Egypt (Reade 1979: 332).

The border between an empire and its exterior may be marked by a militarised zone (Barfield 2001: 32), with all the associated trappings of border control, such as the defensive walls constructed along the north and northwest boundaries of the Ur III empire (Larsen 1979: 80). Borders and frontiers can also be highly charged areas where dynamic social, economic, and military interactions take place (Lightfoot and Martinez 1995). Outside the Mesopotamian context, a clear example of a long-term attempt at military domination of a contested border zone at the limits of empire occurs in the northern border of the Hittite empire in the Late Bronze Age, now north-central Turkey. Here the Hittites attempted to bring a dangerous and difficult landscape under control by implanting strategically located fortified settlements at

regular intervals across the landscape, which could serve both as permanent garrison settlements and as temporary bases and store-house cities
for the royal army as it marched through on campaign beyond the
borders of the empire against the hostile peoples of the hills (R.
Matthews 1999/2000). The recovery of an archive of cuneiform documents from the site of Maşat Höyük (probably ancient Tappiga) in the
same border zone throws into unusually sharp relief the nature of relations between the core city of Hattusa and the frontier garrison town,
with references to movements of troops, animals and chariots, the
storage of crops and metal objects including weaponry and captured
arms and armour, and the disposition of platoons of troops at vital
points across the landscape, such as bridges (Alp 1991a; 1991b; Özgüç
1978).

A further effect of the existence of empires may be the stimulus
towards political complexity of adjacent communities, the emergence of
'shadow empires' as secondary political phenomena (Barfield 2001). A
good example is that of the east Anatolian empire of Urartu whose rise,
florescence and demise are inextricably connected with the history of
the Assyrian empire to its south. Without the Assyrian empire there
would not have been an empire of Urartu, located as it is in a region
where no other centralised state has ever existed (Zimansky 1985: 1).
Without detailed excavation of multiple contexts in settlements in both
empires, however, it will be extremely difficult to distinguish a
secondary but independent political entity outside imperial control from
a periphery totally subject to imperial control (Smith and Montiel 2001:
250). As always, the more correlates that can be established the sounder
the argument will be.

Empires in time and space: expansion, consolidation, collapse

Adams has commented on the fact that ancient empires are 'character-
ized by wide variability and constant flux' (Adams 1979: 393). Work some
time ago by Rein Taagepera on comparative study of the world's empires
provides some intriguing pointers to trajectories of imperial development
(Taagepera 1978a; 1978b). His study of over one hundred historically
attested empires stressed the fragility of empires as political entities,
invariably collapsing after relatively brief periods at near-maximum
extent. He also pointed to a growth rhythm of slow-quick-slow as empires
approached maximum size, and intimated that the slower the rate of
growth the longer the duration at maximum extent. Certain key points

can be made, based on Taagepera's figures. First, there is a clear trend towards increasing size of empires through time, albeit with severe fluctuations. Second, it is possible to discern three major phases of imperial development on a worldwide basis (Taagepera 1978a: 119). Phase 1 spanned the late fourth millennium (if we accept for now the Uruk phenomenon as imperial) to around 600BC, during which time empires ranged in size from 0.15 to 1.4Mm^2. Phase 2, from 500 BC to AD 1600, saw the largest empires range in extent from 2.3 to 24Mm^2, while in phase 3, the modern era, empires continued to grow in area. Taagepera's deduction is that there was 'a limited number of crucial organizational inventions or breakthroughs during human history, instead of a gradual development' (Taagepera 1978a: 121).

The trigger for phase 1 may have been the pristine formation of complex urban societies on the Lower Mesopotamian plains with their associated technologies of administration and new ideologies of political control. The leap to phase 2, marked by the enormous spread of the Achaemenid empire (Kuhrt 2001), may have been accountable to a shift in the ideology and practice of bureaucratic control: 'the successful introduction of satrapies may have been the secret weapon which suddenly enabled the Medes and the Persians to build an empire of 5Mm^2 in a world that up to that time had seen no empire surpass 1.3Mm^2' (Taagepera 1978a: 121) or, as Adams puts it, a 'more voluntaristic, harmoniously integrated synthesis of plural cultural and political systems' may have enabled the Achaemenid empire to grow as large as it did (Adams 1979: 403). The inception of phase 3 brings us into the age of widening horizons and globalisation in the fields of industry, commerce and communications in the modern era.

Taagepera comments on the relationship between technological innovation and imperial expansion, making the key point that technological advances may give a core area significant advantages over its peripheries, and that as expansion proceeds the increasing technological disparities between conqueror and conquered can make conquest easier (Taagepera 1978a: 122). Subsequent diffusion of technology, however, can later erode these disparities and undermine established political relationships between core and periphery. We could use this model to view the Uruk phenomenon, seeing advances in administrative technology, such as seals and writing, as epitomising a level of organisational sophistication that enabled large-scale expansion into neighbouring areas to the east, north and northwest. In regions such as the Susiana plain where the new technologies quickly spread, as manifest by Proto-Elamite writing and seals, previous political realities were soon overturned and new relationships established. There are numerous other instances where empires might be defined as a fleeting political entity existing only in the time lag between diffusions of ideology and technology.

As to the stimulus for expansion, there is much debate on this point, with issues such as military security, economic aims and ideological fervour all to the fore. For the Assyrian kings, expansion appears to have been regarded as a religious duty owed to the national god Aššur (Larsen 1979: 90), much as Akkadian kings viewed their conquests as sanctioned by the Mesopotamian gods (Foster 1993: 26). Weiss and Courty (1993: 150) have suggested that, where technological innovation is lacking, agricultural development may require expansionary activity. Early Hittite expansion may have been little more than military adventurism (Gurney 1979: 154). One clear and consistent element is something of a paradox. As already mentioned, empires constitute perhaps the single largest anthropological entity studied by archaeologists, and yet even here there appears to be a special place for the role of the individual. Almost all empires can be traced to the actions of a single charismatic individual, right from the start of imperial history. The role of the leader in acting as a focal point for highly various groups within the empire, as well as a diplomatic and military node for interactions beyond the empire, may well have been vital (Sinopoli 1994: 163). Did every empire start with a personal vision? Was the Uruk phenomenon stimulated by the vision and action of a single individual, perhaps the person represented as 'priest-king' on cylinder seals and other art media, or the legendary rulers of Uruk-Warka, Lugalbanda and Gilgameš, venerated by the kings of the Ur III dynasty a thousand years later? Or is it that imperial ideology works most effectively by means of the glorification of the individual as a unifying motif for disparate elements of the empire, and that the successful propagation of such an ideology has continued to make sense even to us today, who thus continue to be taken in by the notion of ancient empires as concrete manifestations of individual vision and will, suckers still for an eternal ideology of empire?

From the Mesopotamian point of view there can be no doubting the significance of a major resource imbalance between the heartlands of Lower Mesopotamia and the world without. Not only basic resources such as timber, stone and metals, but also all raw materials with which to manufacture luxury materials, had to be imported into Lower Mesopotamia from surrounding regions. Larsen has pointed to the open nature of Mesopotamia, accessible on almost all fronts and therefore amenable both to internally inspired attempts at control of routes of trade and communication and to potentially catastrophic incursions from the wide world outside (Larsen 1979: 99). These basic elements of the Mesopotamian condition suggest that, whatever the prevailing ideology of holy war in pursuit of expansion, hard economic logic underlay attempts at empire through time. In this light Larsen has suggested that the Akkadian empire may at root have been an attempt to secure trade routes to the north and west in the face of the emergent power of Ebla in that very region (Larsen 1979: 99). In the same way, the Uruk expansion of a thousand years earlier may have been stimulated by the rise of sophisticated polities along the northern fringes of Mesopotamia by the middle of the fourth millennium, now well attested at Tell Brak and Arslantepe, period VII (Frangipane 2001), which could have threatened Lower Mesopotamian access to invaluable raw materials. Explanations for imperial expansion need to consider multiple possible causes: one scholar has described Spanish imperial expansion into the sixteenth-century Americas as 'simultaneously an invasion, a colonization effort, a social experiment, a religious crusade, and a highly structured economic enterprise' (Deagan 2001: 179).

Empires ineluctably collapse. How often we read of empires in western Asia in terms such as these, used of the Ur III empire of the late third millennium: 'the phenomenal rise of this empire was matched only by the suddenness and completeness of its demise: in less than a century after its creation, no trace of it remained' (Steinkeller 1991: 15), or 'people in ancient Mesopotamia seem to have been well accustomed to cohabiting with collapse' (Liverani 2001: 377). It seems that without infinite and continuous expansion empires become economically and administratively unviable, the costs of maintaining control soon reaching prohibitive levels, 'declining productivity for investment in complexity' (Tainter 1988: 110; see also Liverani 2001: 387–9). But perhaps there is also something in the ideology of empires that underscores the dialogue between expansion and ideology and that precludes the possibility of an essentially static empire. In all cases a range of factors can be delineated in the collapse of empire, ranging from foreign incursions, environmental change and collapse of trade networks, to communication breakdowns, and ethnic, religious and factional conflict (Sinopoli 1994: 169; Yoffee 1988; Weiss and Bradley 2001). A swift change in settlement pattern from nucleation and dispersal may also follow on from, or occur in concert with, the collapse of empire (Peltenburg 2000). Rarely, bodies of those killed in the final hours of an empire may be excavated, as in the case of Nineveh (Stronach 1997).

Collapse of empires at the peripheries may be archaeologically attested by hoards of precious objects and commodities. Hoarding is likely to have been a regular activity in antiquity, as a means of temporarily secreting wealth, but it may be highly significant if for some reason hoards were not recovered by their owners and therefore find their way into the archaeological record. We can almost certainly impart some significance to the discovery by archaeologists of hoards of later-third-millennium date across much of the periphery of the Akkadian empire, including at Tell Brak, Tell Taya and Tell Asmar (R. Matthews 1994). Complexities in dating associated seal impressions and pottery render it impossible to connect these hoards with textually attested incidents such as the revolt against Naram-Sin, but the fact of their deposition and the failure of the owner or relatives to recover them is in itself indicative of substantial disruption. In the case of the HS3 hoard from Tell Brak, the building under whose floor it was buried was subsequently abandoned and there was an accumulation of wind-blown deposits indicative of a major episode of settlement interruption (R. Matthews 1994: 301).

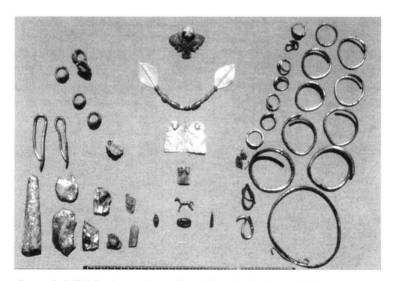

Figure 5.4 Tell Brak, northeast Syria. Hoard of silver, gold, lapis lazuli, carnelian and other items of later-third-millennium BC date

Source: photo by R. Matthews.

Hoarding along the northern frontiers of the Hittite empire, as attested by the spectacular find of silver vessels from Kınık-Kastamonu (Emre and Çınaroğlu 1993), almost certainly indicates raiding and frequent military activity in a highly unsettled border region (R. Matthews 2000b).

An important material corollary of the fact that empires rise and fall with rapidity is the complexity of associating surviving material remains with textually attested political sequences. An extreme case is that of the Achaemenid empire, well known from textual evidence but over much of its large territory poorly or not at all known from archaeological evidence (Moorey 1980: 128). The problems of fitting material culture assemblages, especially pottery, into historical sequences are epitomised in the ongoing debate over what, if anything, characterises Akkadian material culture in Lower Mesopotamia (Gibson and McMahon 1995; Nissen 1993; J. G. Westenholz 1998). Uncertainty in identifying exclusively Akkadian pottery has made it impossible to reconstruct Akkadian settlement patterns with any confidence (Nissen 1993: 100). The bleakest view has been put thus: 'If we didn't know from the texts that the Akkad empire really existed, we would not be able to postulate it from the changes in settlement patterns, nor ... from the evolution of material culture' (Liverani 1993: 7–8). The inference is either that we are failing to isolate and identify the specifics of Akkadian material culture, or that a political entity apparently so large and sophisticated as the Akkadian empire can rise and pass without making a notable impact on settlement patterns or any aspect of material culture. On the basis of this dilemma, Liverani has argued for the possibility that archaeological 'methods of proto-historical reconstruction (based on the spatial analysis of settlements and artefacts) prove to be fallacious as soon as we have an outer and comparable set of data' (Liverani 1993: 8).

Liverani's view of the nature and potential of both archaeology and the written record in this context appears to be a further instance of the assaying of archaeology against the 'trueness' of the written record. One could turn his argument on its head and suggest that the existence of a written record, however scant, for the period 2,350–2,150 BC has seduced scholars into believing that they are looking at a principally historical phenomenon when in fact the Akkadian empire is much more an inhabitant of prehistory, or better ahistory, than it is of history. The Akkadian empire falls right on the chronological fault line between archaeology and history identified by Brinkman as existing around 2,350 BC (Brinkman 1984: 170). We have barely begun to look at the

Akkadian empire as an archaeological entity, of which the written records might form only one element of the surviving evidence, but where initial steps have been made through careful analysis of a range of data and hypotheses from all the disciplines at archaeology's disposal, the preliminary conclusion has been that:

> the archaeological and paleoclimatic data suggest, however, the unrepresentative and essentially ahistorical quality of the epigraphic record, particularly for early historic Mesopotamia. Here the cuneiform record misses the early historic climate change, the structure and goals of Akkadian imperialism, the native historical screen enveloping adaptive responses, and the spatio-temporal dynamics of nomadism.
>
> (Weiss 2000: 92)

In short, if we want to approach a reality of the Akkadian empire, or of any past empire, it will be most productive to employ interdisciplinary archaeological approaches that will naturally include hypotheses rooted in written documents as part of their battery of methods, but will not serve solely or principally as a support-act to the headlines of textual history.

It behoves us to recall how little specifically archaeological investigation has been conducted into the phenomenon of the Akkadian empire. The capital of the Akkadian empire has not been located, yet alone excavated; extremely few Akkadian sites have been excavated and adequately published (Nissen 1988: 166), certainly to modern standards. From those that have been excavated, distinctive assemblages of Akkadian material culture have been recovered, even if there are many problems with regard to the details of absolute and relative chronology (Nissen 1993). Material correlates of the Akkadian empire are lying still in the soil of Iraq, the subtleties of their characteristics awaiting investigation through appropriately nuanced archaeological methods. Finally, Adams has forcefully expressed the potential for specifically archaeological contributions to the study of ancient Mesopotamian empires:

> although not the kind of archaeology that is conceived as a process of archival discovery subordinated to strictly Assyriological strategies ... the seriously skewed, palace-temple-urban orientation that continues almost wholly to encompass historical Near Eastern archaeological efforts, [but rather an] archaeology that examines

the mechanics and specifics of empire in terms of demography and the economics of interaction between cores and peripheries.

(Adams 1979: 396–7)

As yet, we have hardly begun to conceive, formulate and execute such strategies with regard to the great empires of the Mesopotamian past.

Chapter 6

People's pasts

'Humble people who expect nothing'

In this chapter we examine the role archaeology plays, and might further play, in approaching the everyday lives of common people in the Mesopotamian past. Everything we have considered so far has been about people, however indirectly, but here we focus the archaeological lens somewhat more sharply on the lives of common peoples themselves. The social value of studying everyday life has been celebrated by Giddens as revealing 'how humans can act creatively to shape reality', as well as comprising a means of shedding light on the structures and institutions of societies (Giddens 2001: 80–2). We have perhaps already gained a sense that this broad subject, in all its manifold complexity and diversity, has hitherto not been adequately treated by archaeologists working in the Mesopotamian arena, as has also been the case in other parts of the world, particularly once we consider periods for which textual evidence exists. In the past century and a half much effort has gone into the exploration of capital cities, palaces, temples, royal cemeteries and other aspects of socially dominant elements, often in the hope of recovery of spectacular material culture such as palace reliefs or rich grave goods, the so-called 'old-fashioned archeology of digging royal tombs for fine-arts museums' derided by Robert Braidwood many years ago (Braidwood and Howe 1960: 7). Less effort has been expended on the investigation of the more mundane and quotidian aspects of living in the Mesopotamian past, although in recent decades there has been some redress of the balance, principally under the influence of the innovative and interdisciplinary approaches of economic and anthropological archaeology pioneered by Braidwood himself. Extensive areas of private domestic quarters have been excavated at several sites, from various periods, thus allowing us to explore issues of everyday life for the common people of ancient Mesopotamia.

By 'common people' we mean those elements of society who did not belong to dominant and elite groups, who did not live in palaces or high-status residences, whose daily activities were centred on the practice of child-rearing, agriculture, animal husbandry, and domestic food procurement and processing, with varying additional concerns such as cult, trade and perhaps military service. Common people enabled and shaped the existence of complex societies and empires simply by being there, by having and rearing children, by forming the bulk of the core population, by producing and processing food for all, by serving in armies and garrisons, by labouring on domestic and elite projects of construction, and by receiving, transmuting and opposing elite ideologies imposed from above. We should not give the impression, however, of common people in the Mesopotamian past as being a voiceless, shapeless entity that drifted through the millennia like a cloud blown hither and thither by the force of ideologies thrust upon them by elite groups. Despite the fact that the surviving, or at least so far recovered, written documents stem often from elite contexts, there is nevertheless infinite scope for the study of common people in terms of the particularities of their existence from place to place and time to time, and of their ways of resisting and shaping ideologies imposed from above, even if archaeological approaches along such lines have scarcely begun in Mesopotamia.

What evidence have the common people of ancient Mesopotamia left for us to recover? We have their houses and homes, some of which have been excavated, and within those buildings we have, with newly developed and refined techniques of investigation, manifold items of material culture and increasingly accessible traces of the activities conducted inside and around those homes. In many cases we have the skeletons of the common people themselves. In the way of written records we have a range of resources, but in this volume we are concerned with what the non-textual archaeological record has to tell us, and how we can best access it, and so we deal here with the physical and social contexts of everyday life and how they might be approached via the archaeological record. Text-based approaches to 'history from below' have been treated in Marc Van De Mieroop's thoughtful study (1999a: 86–105), in Marten Stol's survey of 'private life in ancient Mesopotamia' (1995) and, with more archaeological input, in Karen Nemet-Nejat's informative study *Daily Life in Ancient Mesopotamia* (1998). In the following discussions we hope to show, nevertheless, that the archaeological position is significantly healthier than as represented by Van De Mieroop in his study of 'the silent subjects of history':

Excavations could reveal equally well the hovel of a day laborer as the palace of a king and show us what living conditions were. But, sadly, virtually no houses have been excavated, and none allow us to reconstruct how many people shared the same roof, how many pots and pans, and tools they had, where they slept, what they ate, and so on.

(Van De Mieroop 1999a: 86)

It is arguable, furthermore, that the notion that people who do not feature in as yet recovered documentary evidence constitute a 'people without history' is an unwarranted admission of failure on the part of the historian or archaeologist, and a misapprehension of the nature of the archaeological record and of archaeology itself:

The silencing of the oppressed is not simply a product of their 'absence' from texts. Rather they were silenced through the operation of various technologies of oppression which drew upon the resources provided by the material world *and* by the written word. To hear their voices, however faintly, we must abandon our fixation with texts and artefacts simply as *evidence* in the present (although they certainly are that) and consider more carefully how words and things were used, manipulated, and imposed *in the past*.

(Moreland 2001: 77–8; italics in original)

It is up to us as archaeologists and historians to give history to those whom we choose to study.

Cities

Subsequent to the pristine developments towards complexity, literacy and urbanism in the Uruk period (see Chapter 4), for most of its duration Mesopotamian history can be characterised as essentially urban, and hitherto the vast majority of our sources, archaeological and especially textual, come from urban contexts. Most people lived in cities, and city-states have rightly been called 'the basic building block of Mesopotamian society' (Stone and Zimansky 1992: 212). We should at the same time be aware that each ancient city existed on its own terms along a trajectory through time unique to that city. As Mario Liverani has expounded, the cities of Mesopotamia in the Old Babylonian period – Aššur, Mari, Sippar, Ur, Ešnunna, Babylon, Nippur – can all be characterised in distinctive ways, each different from all the others

(Liverani 1997: 105–6). And yet we need also to focus on the points of similarity between Mesopotamian cities in order to generate useful approaches with which to apprehend their archaeological and historical significance. The work of Robert Adams (1981) on the rise and development of cities in the Mesopotamian heartland has focused especially on the broad similarities and trends of urban life within a framework of adaptation and cultural ecology.

For the archaeologist urban sites are easier to locate and they promise more in the way of spectacular and significant finds, and so since the birth of the discipline excavators have favoured cities or towns over rural landscapes. Almost no excavation projects have focused principally on rural settlement, although in the past few decades many have included the countryside as an integral element in their scope of study, as we shall see below. In approaching the Mesopotamian city from a specifically archaeological angle we are in some ways complementing a body of knowledge about urban life that is contained in the contemporary written record, however patchy that record might be (Van De Mieroop 1997b). We have already seen in Chapter 2 how integrated archaeological and textual approaches can sharply illuminate segments of life in ancient urban contexts, when we are fortunate enough to have written documents from secure archaeological contexts and someone eager to approach them in that way.

But such occasions have so far been uncommon and, for several reasons, as archaeologists we cannot rely on the discovery and interpretation of written texts in our basic approach to Mesopotamian cities. First, the significance and preponderance of literacy varied considerably across time and space in the Mesopotamian past, to the extent that many aspects of urban life, especially quotidian in nature, never found their way into a written record. Only the archaeologist, if anyone, can speak to these topics. Second, even where we know or suspect that written records existed in the context of a past urban society in Mesopotamia, there is no guarantee of recovering such texts in archaeological investigations. For the period 3,000–1,500 BC archives of texts have been excavated from secure contexts within houses at only a handful of Mesopotamian cities, principally Ur, Nippur and Sippar-Amnānum (Van De Mieroop 1999b: 255), as well as at Kültepe-Kaneš in Anatolia. A wry example is the important site of Tell Brak in Upper Mesopotamia, known through texts from Mari, Ebla and Tell Beydar to have been the major regional power of Nagar through the later third millennium, but where many seasons of excavation have so far failed to yield textual evidence in significant amounts. The texts may not have survived as archaeological artefacts, they may have been recycled in the past or, most likely, they may yet lie in the vast bulk of the mound waiting their moment of discovery next year or in a century's time.

We need to employ, therefore, specifically and explicitly archaeological approaches to the study of cities if we are profitably to investigate them in all their depth and richness. During the last fifteen years or so before the caesura in fieldwork in 1990, several archaeological projects were underway in Iraq that were explicitly tackling the manifold issues of Mesopotamian cities through interdisciplinary and innovative archaeological approaches, and here we shall focus on a couple of them – the work of Nicholas Postgate at the small Sumerian city today known as Abu Salabikh, and that of Elizabeth Stone at the early second-millennium city anciently known as Maškan-šapir.

A major loss in recent times to the development of the discipline of Mesopotamian archaeology was the abrupt halt brought to a budding programme of innovative investigations at the second-millennium city of Maškan-šapir, located 25km north of Nippur in the heart of the Mesopotamian alluvium. From the start the project was unusual: the director had a research programme in mind and was looking for a site to fit the bill of her archaeological agenda. Often the process happens in reverse, with archaeologists falling prey to temptation to tackle specific sites that swim into view, creating their research design *ex post facto*.

Stone's aim was to reconstruct 'a picture of a single, living city' from the Mesopotamian past (Stone 1994: 15), in order that issues of political, economic and social organisation could be explored. In particular, Stone felt that integrated investigation of a city could test her ideas on the consensual, as opposed to coercive, nature of urban society in Mesopotamia, perhaps rooted in the control of labour rather than control of land, whereby social mobility appeared to be fluid and specific segments of urban society operated with respectable autonomy (Stone 1997; 1999). How might these ideas be approached through the archaeological record? To such an end her requirements were for a site with the following characteristics: small enough to tackle in its entirety yet large enough to have been of some significance; more or less single-period occupation to enable large-scale investigation and exposure of contemporary parts of the city; dating to the early second millennium BC that could thus be slotted into known or suspected historical and archaeological frameworks already partially constructed for the region; with immediately accessible surface remains facilitating extensive investigation without the need for excavation at all points. Drawing on the alluvial survey work of Adams, Stone selected Tell Abu Duwari as a candidate for inspection. A preliminary trip to the site, difficult to locate in the seamless spread of sand, dust, and sky, confirmed its great potential. Three seasons of fieldwork followed, and the account here is based on the reports and discussions published so far (Stone 1994; 1997; Stone and Zimansky 1992; 1994). Finds of inscribed clay cylinders gave the ancient name as Maškan-šapir, thus establishing the site's place within a known historical context as a city built, or at least aggrandised, by Sin-iddinam of Larsa on behalf of the god Nergal in the mid-nineteenth century BC and abandoned little more than a century later following its destruction by Hammurabi of Babylon.

In approaching Tell Abu Duwari and attempting to reincarnate, or pre-incarnate, it as Maškan-šapir, Stone employed a wide range of archaeological techniques. Satellite imagery was used in order to detect gross features of the urban morphology and traces of waterways, including a possible old bed of the Tigris. Geomorphological coring supplemented these investigations. A camera attached to a kite took hundreds of photographs in a 50m grid across the entire 72 hectares of the city, enabling accurate plans to be drawn up, with buildings showing especially clearly after rain. The surface of the site, as with all Mesopotamian mounds from the later Neolithic onwards, is covered in potsherds, anything up to 30 million of them and no systematic collection of these sherds has yet taken place. Future investigations might explore issues of chronological or functional differentiation of pottery across the surface spread of the city. Apart from pottery, large numbers of artefacts were collected and plotted on the site plan, and any surface features were mapped. Clearance of surface earth exposed traces of buildings. Excavation was conducted at highly selective points in order to test ideas about urban organisation and to recover elements of the archaeological record, such as plant and animal remains, that would not have survived on the surface of the site.

On the basis of these approaches, Stone has constructed a picture of the nineteenth-century city at Maškan-šapir. The city is divided into areas by five major canals, with two substantial harbours or quays located within the city wall, which itself encloses the entire city and is pierced by at least three gates. Streets within the city run parallel and at right angles to the canals. In the southwest area a series of substantial brick platforms, along with egregious numbers of fragments from terracotta guardian lions and naked women, suggests the existence here of a religious quarter, immediately to the north of which there appears to be a walled cemetery, attested by sherds from large burial

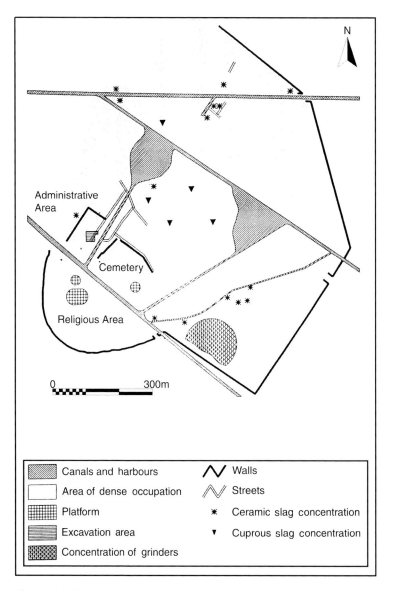

N

Administrative
Area

Cemetery

Religious Area

0   300m

	Canals and harbours		Walls
	Area of dense occupation		Streets
	Platform	*	Ceramic slag concentration
	Excavation area	▼	Cuprous slag concentration
	Concentration of grinders		

Figure 6.1 Maškan-šapir, south Iraq. City plan
Source: after Stone and Zimansky 1994: fig. 2.

pithoi and grave goods of weapons and jewellery. To the west, spreads of apparently non-domestic architecture, unusually constructed with baked bricks, and finds of clay sealings with seal impressions, as well as cuneiform tablet fragments, hint at the presence of an administrative quarter. The remainder of the city appears to have been devoted to residential neighbourhoods for the bulk of the population, the common people of this chapter, with no evidence from either surface architecture or the distribution of surface artefacts for separate elite quarters. Possible high-status objects, such as copper items, stone bowls and cylinder seals, are not isolated in clumps but occur at all points of the site, suggesting to Stone that 'the rich and powerful were represented in all parts of the city' (1994: 24).

The distribution of surface artefacts reveals aspects of craft organisation, with clearly demarcated areas for production of pottery around the edges of the city, and for high firing of clay perhaps to make substitute grindstones. Other traces of manufacture, including basic metallurgy and stone working, suggest that craft activity took place within residential neighbourhoods. From residential areas multiple finds of fish-hooks and net-weights, as well as bones from fish, fowl, pig, and sheep, amongst others, along with carbonised remains of cereals and fruits tell us of diet and economy. The picture, and most elements of it are still highly provisional, is one of a decentralised yet highly organised society, with urban regions demarcated for the purpose of specific activities such as worship, burial and trade, but also with a wide range of craft and social activities taking place within significant numbers of contemporary residential neighbourhoods. Such an urban layout fits well, Stone feels, with her notion of the Mesopotamian city as shaped by consensus, with a strong mix of rich and not-so-rich citizens living together in the same neighbourhoods: 'both tablets and archaeological data indicate that an important official could live beside a humble fisherman and that large, well-appointed houses were nestled alongside small, poor structures' (Stone 1997: 20).

At Tell Abu Duwari/Maškan-šapir we have an exemplary instance of archaeology in action, with the fieldwork structured and executed in pursuit of a specific and academically stimulating research agenda, the whole aimed towards a major issue of the Mesopotamian past: the nature of urban social structure in the second millennium BC. Despite the enforced brevity of the field element of the project, the structured and targeted nature of the research meant that plausibly coherent answers or scenarios were constructed towards the original research design. Future fieldwork would of course modify, perhaps in fundamental ways, many aspects of these provisional results and interpretations.

Our second urban archaeological case study concerns a project that, although like Maškan-šapir in enforced abeyance in field terms since 1990, enjoyed a longer period of development as a coherent research programme: the Abu Salabikh project. The low mounds at Abu Salabikh, only 25km to the southwest of Maškan-šapir, constitute the surviving remains of a small Sumerian city of the third millennium BC, ancient name uncertain but perhaps Eresh. Excavations in the 1960s by a team from the American Schools of Oriental Research had established the general dating of the site to the Early Dynastic period, as well as recovering a collection of over 500 Sumerian cuneiform tablets, comparable in date and style to those already known from the city of Fara, ancient šuruppak (Biggs 1974). From 1975 to 1989 Nicholas Postgate directed a large-scale British programme of investigations at the site, much of which has been published in preliminary and final forms (Green 1993; Postgate 1990b; R. Matthews and Postgate 1987). A wide range of objectives and issues was integrated under the overall aim 'to describe life in a small Sumerian city-state through the eyes of a visiting social anthropologist' (Postgate 1992–3: 410) and 'to encompass the whole city, from temple and palace down to the poorest and most emphatically illiterate family dwelling' (Postgate 1982: 61). At Abu Salabikh the explicit intention has been to match 'the record in the ground and the record on the cuneiform tablet' as 'different aspects of a single set of human activities' (W. Matthews and Postgate 1994: 171). The net result of fifteen years' investigations is that we know more about the daily lives of ordinary folk at Abu Salabikh than at any other contemporary site. In this chapter we can do no more than sample the many aspects of archaeological exploration at Abu Salabikh, as an indication of how interdisciplinary approaches can recover highly detailed and contextualised information on ancient lifeways.

Like Maškan-šapir, Abu Salabikh lends itself to extensive aerial investigation by virtue of the broad contemporaneity of its surface remains, although there are some complicating factors caused by eroded traces of occupation later than the main Early Dynastic levels. The site was settled from Uruk times through the entire Early Dynastic period and up to the end of the third millennium, with the city reaching its peak during the Early Dynastic III period around the middle of the third millennium. A probable bed of the Euphrates has been traced by coring to the west of the Main Mound, and it is likely that the westward movement of this bed by the early second millennium was instrumental in leading to the abandonment of the city by that time. The core of the city lay on the 12 hectares of the Main Mound, enclosed by a city wall against which piles of rubbish had accumulated.

A technique used to considerable effect at Abu Salabikh has been that of surface scraping, a careful cleaning and planning of the mound's surface after removal of pottery and other artefacts. By this means a total of 4 hectares, or 40 per cent of the intra-mural surface of the Main

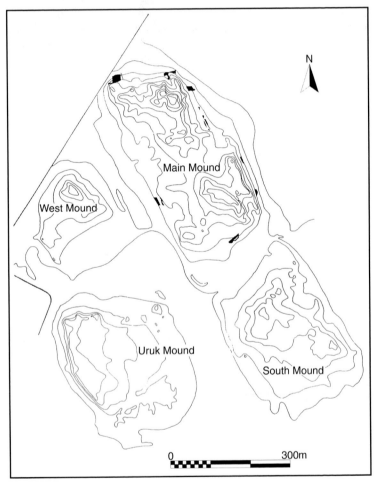

Figure 6.2 Abu Salabikh, south Iraq. Plan of the mounds, detected city wall around Main Mound shown in black

Source: after Postgate 1994b: fig. 5.

Mound, has been exposed and recorded, giving a broad view of the internal layout of the city. The city plan comprises a lattice of streets running along and across the city, defining blocks of urban housing. Major streets lead to gates in the city wall. Mud-brick houses occupy most of the city space, with occasional areas given to the disposal of

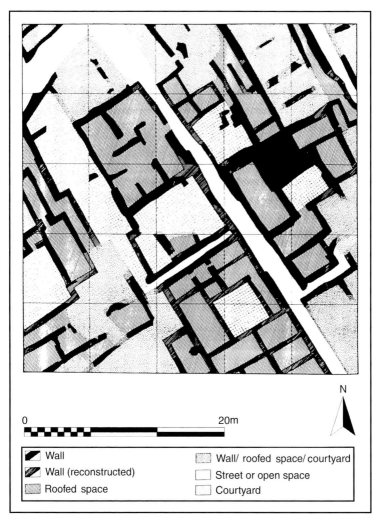

0   20m

N

Wall	Wall/ roofed space/ courtyard
Wall (reconstructed)	Street or open space
Roofed space	Courtyard

Figure 6.3 Abu Salabikh, south Iraq. Plan of Early Dynastic buildings in Area A of the Main Mound, depicting use of space

Source: after Postgate 1994b: fig. 7.

rubbish. There are few convincing candidates for buildings of a non-domestic nature, although the collection of cuneiform texts recovered in the 1960s and the distinctive assemblage of cultural material excavated from the 'ash tip' both appear to have originated from temple contexts at the south end of the Main Mound, and there may have been an administrative building at the northern end of the city. An area of pottery kilns was detected and excavated at the northern limits of the city, just within the city wall, and other kilns were located well outside the wall out of harm's way. The finding of clay sealings in a potter's workshop may suggest that pottery production here was at least partly under the control of an institution above the household. Surface traces of a typical Early Dynastic III palace or administrative building with double outer walls detectable on the largely unexplored South Mound, suggest that the ruler or administrative elite may at that late stage in the city's history, at least, have resided in a separate complex outside the main city walls.

On the basis of results from application of a range of techniques at Abu Salabikh, some of which feature below in the section on houses and households, and taking into account also ethnographic analogy, Postgate has tackled the vexing issue of Sumerian urban population in a novel way (Postgate 1994b). In considering proportions of urban space devoted to public use (streets, open spaces) as against residential use (houses) at different sectors of Abu Salabikh as well as at Old Babylonian Ur, Postgate derives a figure of approximately 90 per cent residential and 10 per cent public. Given that an average Abu Salabikh house occupies $343m^2$, he arrives at a figure of about twenty-six houses per hectare of urban space, with 10 per cent of each hectare reserved for public use, making a total of some 250 houses for the 9.5 hectares of urban space contained within the city wall around the Main Mound. But how many people were living in each of these quite spacious residences? Here is where the results of micro-analyses, discussed in the following section, come in, because they allow us to assign, at least provisionally, functions to many of the rooms, such as sleeping, eating, cooking, storage, washing, reception, and so on, and thus to distinguish actual dwelling space, pertinent to the number of inhabitants of the house, from what one might call redundant social space, pertinent to the social status of the householder. An analysis of correlations between courtyard area and house area, on the one hand, and reception room area and house area, on the other, showed clearly that courtyards correlate strongly with house area while reception rooms stay more or less the same in area regardless of total house area, perhaps indicating the significance of reception rooms as formal dwelling areas used by all householders whatever their status (Matthews and Postgate 1987). In his speculative essay, Postgate concludes that the population of the Early Dynastic Main Mound at Abu Salabikh could have been anything between 2,120 and 10,303, depending on a range of variables still subject to much uncertainty but at least more sharply focused as research issues through the exercise of being defined and explored in the field.

Other approaches to urban layout and household in the Mesopotamian past have focused on sites where the recovery of information was not so meticulous and fine-grained as in the case of Abu Salabikh, but where coarser-grained approaches enabled the uncovering of large areas of domestic housing. A pioneering study was that of Elizabeth Henrickson on households of the Early Dynastic period excavated during the 1930s (Henrickson 1981; 1982). Through analysis of house plans and artefact distribution within houses, Henrickson discerns chronological and spatial patterns of family structure and wealth distribution at the sites of Khafajah and Tell Asmar in the Diyala region northeast of Baghdad. The principal methods employed by Henrickson are analysis of house plans in terms of areas and arrangement of rooms, and the occurrence and distribution of artefacts within rooms and houses. As Henrickson herself points out, a significant drawback of this approach is the fact that many so-called utilitarian objects and traces of daily life were not included in the room-by-room catalogue of excavated objects upon which her work is based, or were not recovered at all during excavation. Nevertheless, Henrickson evaluates evidence for activities such as food preparation, serving and eating of food, ablutions and drainage, storage, sleeping and reception of guests, and craft work, concluding that back and central rooms of houses were used for serving and eating of food, storage, relaxation and sleeping, front rooms for cooking, while in central rooms guests were entertained and business transacted. Burials occurred principally under floors of back rooms, perhaps affirming a connection between sleep and death.

In terms of urban layout, Henrickson concluded that large, multi-suite residences, presumed to house extended families, were more commonly situated close to non-domestic structures such as temples or palaces, and that such extended families were likely to be high status and wealthy, with the corollary that urban nuclear families were not wealthy and lived in cramped conditions. There is a danger of circularity of argument here, however, as it is on the basis of the small size of any particular house that Henrickson has identified them as housing nuclear families in the first place. Additional elements perforce missing from her study include data on animal and plant exploitation that would doubtless have significantly enhanced ability to discern patterns of wealth, consumption and family type. Nevertheless, her study represents a stimulating and successful attempt to make some sense of large quantities of data excavated by the standards of the 1930s (see also Pollock 1999: 123–37).

It is noteworthy that when we turn our attention to the few smaller settlements of historic Mesopotamia that have been excavated extensively we find a pattern of households and structures that is in no way different, apart from aerial extent, from that pertaining in large cities. Small settlements of only one hectare, such as Tell Harmal and Haradum (Kepinski-Lecomte 1996), have their surrounding walls, their temples and literate, administrative foci, and their archives of texts in private households in the same way as urban settlements ten or a hundred times larger: 'they are structured as cities in miniature rather than as villages that are functionally differentiated from the larger cities' (Stone 1999: 218). This structural identity in the archaeological record of settlements with only a few hundred individuals with those of many thousand inhabitants materially underlines the fact that in written texts of ancient Mesopotamia the same word is used to refer to what we would call, based solely on population count, large towns and small villages.

Looking at the question of urban layout and its potential social significance, a study by Marlies Heinz of fourteen settlements on the Euphrates in Syria, spanning fourth to second millennia BC in date, discerned three categories of settlement, graded according to the degree and type of planning attested in their ground plans (Heinz 1997). On the basis of social and geographic approaches to urban layout, stressing the significance of factors such as the division of a settlement into distinct areas, the distances between buildings, the extent of planning, and routes of access and communication through settlements, Heinz underlines how archaeological evidence from extensively excavated sites can indicate social and economic status from house to house and area to area. Interestingly, many of the houses at the Uruk 'colony' of Habuba Kabira (Kohlmeyer 1996) are structurally very similar to the temples in the religious quarter at the site, perhaps suggesting that the house-dwellers played a role of some importance within the system of religious power, an interpretation that accords well with intimations of religious or cultic aspects to the Uruk phenomenon (Chapter 4). Additionally, the temple/house resemblance may signify an intention to build temples as dwellings or houses of the gods.

Houses and households

In her 1837 book *Society in America*, the sociologist Harriet Martineau wrote 'The nursery, the boudoir, and the kitchen are all excellent schools in which to learn the morals and manners of a people' (cited in Giddens 2001: 15). More recently, a social theorist has written

> As an extension of human being, the material form of housing reflects the cultural boundaries between different dwelling activities – working, resting, eating, sleeping, bathing, defecating. In this sense the building *contains* the customs and conventions of the particular culture as well as the people who dwell together and their belongings.
>
> (Dant 1999: 65; italics in original)

It has taken archaeology a while to apprehend the notion that study of the household might make a major contribution to study of societies. But there can be no doubting the significance of the household as a fundamental element in ancient Mesopotamian society, however low it has been on the archaeologist's agenda for much of the duration of the discipline. Few today would gainsay the words of Lamberg-Karlovsky:

> It is important to recognize that throughout the vast majority of Near Eastern antiquity the private household remained the primary focus of economic activity. A concentration upon the temple and the palace distorts the social order of the greater Mesopotamian world. The individual household contributed its own labor and/or service in return for commodities obtained by barter from other households, or alternatively, produced a substantial amount of its own food and goods from its own lands and craft production.
>
> (Lamberg-Karlovsky 1999: 183)

Beyond this, Joy McCorriston has pointed to the household as the critical level of cultural and social activity, where grand processes of social change operate in evolutionary perspective, thus emphasising the importance of detailed, high-resolution investigations of Mesopotamian households, not only as a means of exploring ideas of social evolution but also as a way of balancing previously top-heavy emphasis on elite elements of ancient societies (McCorriston 2001: 221). Patricia Wattenmaker has further emphasised the significance of the household for studies of the structure and development of complex societies: 'the household, the lifeblood of the state, may prove to be one of the best sources of information on the rise and organizational dynamics of complex societies' (Wattenmaker 1998: 205), and a recent analytical model proposed by Daniel Snell situates the household at the hub of social and economic development in ancient Southwest Asia (Snell 1997: 154–8). In terms of urban layout, the domestic house played a key role in organically shaping the ways in which cities developed through time, there being little convincing evidence for systematic town planning in ancient Mesopotamia (Lampl 1968).

Michael Roaf's detailed work on an Ubaid-period house at Tell Madhhur in the Hamrin region of central eastern Iraq has provided insights into house use in the fifth millennium BC (Roaf 1989). The level 2 house at Madhhur had been destroyed by fire and subsequently dug over in order to recover valued commodities before being deliberately knocked down and abandoned. Large quantities of intact pottery vessels were excavated from many rooms of the house, in some cases so many in a room that 'there would have been little floor space unoccupied by pots' (Roaf 1989: 122). Other artefacts such as bone, stone and baked-clay tools, and vast quantities of clay sling bullets, were recovered from within the burnt house and are used as far as possible to ascertain the nature of activities within or beyond the house as listed by Roaf on the basis of ethnographic analogy (1989: 135):

- food preparation and cooking
- eating
- reception of guests
- religious activity
- food and water storage
- storage of other goods, tools, etc.
- washing of bodies and clothes
- sleeping
- cultivation of crops
- looking after domestic animals
- hunting and gathering
- manufacture of artefacts

Roaf's conclusion to the effect that, even with such rich and detailed information as is provided us by the Madhhur house, we still can do little more than speculate about Ubaid social structure seems overly bleak, not least in view of the hypotheses on house use and family

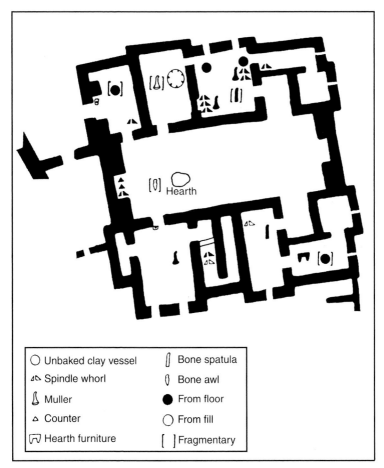

Figure 6.4 Tell Madhhur, east central Iraq. Distribution of small finds within the excavated house

Source: after Roaf 1989: fig. 15.

structure he himself generates in the course of his article, many of which are capable of further assay and exploration through future excavation at contemporary and other period sites, and which are attractively portrayed in his reconstructed depiction of the house in use (Roaf 1990: 54–5).

We have already seen how combined archaeological and textual approaches can most profitably be employed in the study of households (Stone 1981). In the absence of textual records, however, and also in conjunction with them, interpretation of household space, as with all interpretation of the archaeological record, may be enhanced by and rely upon ethnographic and ethnoarchaeological study (Aurenche 1996). The more explicit and structured the connections between these approaches, the more readily we can evaluate and appreciate their conclusions. In her work on early-second-millennium BC houses at Nippur, Elizabeth Stone attempts to link the ancient past with patterns of urban residence in Islamic cities of the Middle East, such as Damascus, Aleppo, Cairo and Baghdad, arguing on the basis of architecture, artefacts and texts for the existence in Areas TA and TB of Nippur of 'neighbourhoods' of adjacent households where the tensions between kinship and institution, settled and nomadic, urban and rural, were played out over the decades (Stone 1987). A problem with the Nippur study is the small areas of housing featured in the analyses. Again, we can only regret that Stone has not had the chance to explore her ideas more fully in the context of work at Maškan-šapir. Detailed studies on carefully excavated houses in Upper Mesopotamia, supported in part by reference to ethnographic studies, have also provided insights into activities and social practice within households of the third millennium BC (Pfälzner 1996; Lebeau 1996).

A principal contribution of the Abu Salabikh project has been towards our understanding of house and household in a Sumerian city. Arguably, we know more about life in a typical Abu Salabikh house than in perhaps any other domestic context of ancient Southwest Asia, although there is still a great deal to learn. The focus of research at the site has been on identifying use of space within domestic structures of the city, and to that end innovative interdisciplinary approaches have been employed. The research agenda has been not only to attempt to reconstruct the intricate patterns of Sumerian daily life in a small city, of major significance in itself, but further to use such reconstructions as a basis for consideration of more far-reaching issues in the fields of demography, urban structure and urban/rural dynamics.

In the first place, certain buildings, selected from those revealed by surface scraping, have been excavated and sampled in meticulous detail, enabling rigorous reconstructions of the sequences of construction, use, alteration and abandonment of buildings and their component parts through time. Deposits and artefacts recovered from within and around buildings, as well as burials of humans with grave goods under floors of internal rooms, contribute further to the picture of domestic life. Let us look for a moment at the most extensively investigated building of the city, House H.

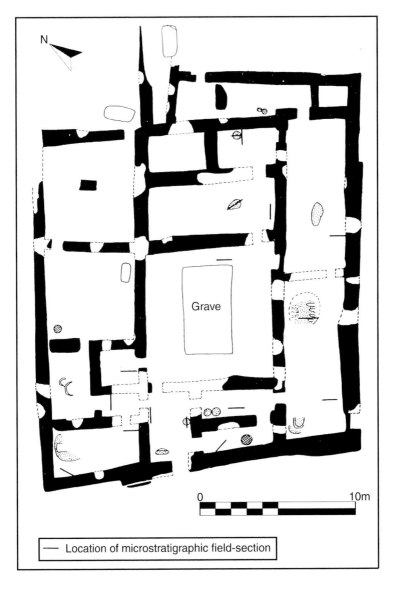

N

Grave

0   10m

— Location of microstratigraphic field-section

Figure 6.5 Abu Salabikh, south Iraq. Plan of House H, Main Mound
Source: after W. Matthews and Postgate 1994: fig. 15.6.

Here we have a classic Abu Salabikh mud-brick house, quite large in area, with sets of rooms arranged around a square courtyard. At the gross level several features of the building can be readily identified, including a door and entrance porch on the west side, a reception room, and a series of cooking facilities in at least one room, as well as massive disruption of floors and sub-floor deposits by the digging and re-digging of intra-mural graves.

But beyond these often impressionistic interpretations, what more might we say about the use of space in this building and others like it at the site? Artefacts which might tell of room functions are rarely found by archaeologists in their original context of use – 'cocktail shakers in the lounge and chamber pots in the bedroom' as Postgate puts it (W. Matthews and Postgate 1994: 172) – and so it will be the minute waste products and microscopic traces of activities that might remain to give away the game of household room use. Using integrated approaches of qualitative and quantitative analysis of artefacts and animal and plant remains from tightly defined domestic contexts, along with microstratigraphic characterisations of the accumulation and modification of deposits within the building, increasingly detailed answers to such questions are being formulated and proffered (W. Matthews and Postgate 1994). In addressing such issues through systematic application of techniques previously applied almost exclusively within the context of prehistoric archaeology, if at all, the research programme at Abu Salabikh has been of major methodological significance in Mesopotamian archaeology.

The field and laboratory procedures underlying these analyses (summarised in W. Matthews and Postgate 1994; for procedures and results see also *http://ads.ahds.ac.uk/catalogue/exc_arch/TellBrak/index.html*) involved the extraction of whole earth samples of sixty litres from each excavated context, ten litres of which was wet-sieved through a mesh of 1mm before the entire sixty litres were passed through a 3.5mm mesh. Items recovered thereby comprised, in common order of frequency, pottery, bone, shell, flint, charred plant remains, and assorted bits and pieces, all of which were quantified per context in terms of their type, abundance and degree of fragmentation. Using a preliminary classification of space categories based on macroscopic observation, the objective was to see if characteristic bundles of attributes could be assigned from the archaeological record to each of those space categories. Some notable results, which themselves can only be sampled here from the wealth of generated deductions, include: the high correlation of frequencies of pottery and bone fragments in rubbish deposits;

the low frequency of artefacts found within interior rooms; the relatively high frequency and fragmentation of artefacts in streets and corridors, suggesting rubbish disposal; the recovery of pig milk teeth, suggesting these animals ran free in the city streets; the discrete disposal of noisome fish-heads in burnt rubbish dumps; and the mixing of plant species and component parts in almost all deposits, suggesting that most of the recovered plant remains originated as particles in dung cakes used for fuel by the city dwellers.

A complementary technique applied at Abu Salabikh, arguably for the first time in a systematic way to a settlement site anywhere in the world, is that of micromorphology. The work of Wendy Matthews has focused on analysis of sequences of sediments and deposits within the urban settlement. Investigated sections through deposits – floors, occupation debris, rubbish strata, street make-up – were meticulously cleaned using an artist's palette knife, a matchless tool for the job, and then photographed and drawn at scale 1:5, itself an act of considerable interpretation. Then intact blocks of deposits were removed, wrapped securely in tough paper and tape, and exported to the laboratory where they were impregnated with a crystic polyester resin that, upon hardening over a period of weeks, allowed the cutting and mounting of massive thin sections, 13.5 by 6.5cm, that can then be studied under varying light conditions through the microscope: 'thin section observations uniquely enable simultaneous analysis of the nature and relationships of artefacts, biological remains and sediments in occupational sequences' (W. Matthews and Postgate 1994: 187). Ideally, such analyses can be coordinated with other scientific approaches, including chemical investigations, in order to provide as full as possible a picture of the history of deposits within and around buildings.

Using this and related techniques, Wendy Matthews has considered in detail issues relating to the preparation and laying of plaster floors and surfaces, the origins and use of constructional materials, the occurrence of trampling on floors, the use of rugs and mats, and variations in type and depth of over-floor occupation deposits according to room type. An important realisation from this work at Abu Salabikh and elsewhere is the extent to which archaeological mounds in Southwest Asia are composed of ancient plant stuffs in the forms of pseudomorphic voids of decayed plants, silicified phytoliths of plant elements, calcitic ash crystals from burnt plants, and charred remains. In terms of identifications of the use of urban space, micromorphology at Abu Salabikh has enabled characterisation of room and space types, roofed and unroofed, through often subtle definitions of bundles of attributes, such as thickness of under-floor packing, frequency of floor application, cleanliness of floor surfaces, thickness and type of occupation deposits overlying floors, and evidence for transformation of floor surfaces through actions such as burning, trampling, washing, and disposal of micro-debris from activities such as food preparation, cooking or craft work. This approach has for the first time allowed us to make quantitative, concretely contestable and essentially non-impressionistic interpretations about the questions posed by Van De Mieroop and already quoted: 'how many people shared the same roof, how many pots and pans, and tools they had, where they slept, what they ate, and so on' (Van De Mieroop 1999a: 86).

Excavations at Abu Salabikh have informed not only on the life of everyday people but also on their death, or at least their burial, the site yielding hundreds of burials so far. During the Early Dynastic period the dead were buried under household floors, in many cases while occupation of those houses was still current. In House H, bodies were buried at several points under the floors, the richest burial being in the form of a large shaft in the central courtyard that, despite having been robbed in antiquity, still contained items of jewellery and the remains of an equid deposited with the dead person. Another burial from the same building comprised three children buried in a single pit with offerings of simple beads and pendants. Elsewhere, in the northern sector of the city, some 12–14 individuals, mostly adults, were buried together in a grave that may originally have lain in a large courtyard, the circumstances of their death now unknown.

One of the most stimulating approaches to ancient households, integrating analyses of archaeological, ethnographic and textual investigations, is a recently published study by Paolo Brusasco of Old Babylonian houses at Ur (Brusasco 1999–2000). Here Brusasco studies houses from four excavated parts of the city, totalling seventy-nine buildings, using textual and archaeological/ethnographic approaches as complementary and mutually heuristic devices. Firmly rooted in modern studies of social space and social theory (Hillier and Hanson 1984; Hanson 1998), Brusasco's analysis looks at issues such as accessibility of rooms within houses and social solidarity of family groups, as represented in degrees of similarity in spatial relations in terms of house plans. Then applying ethnographic insights from studies of societies with both patrilocal and matrilocal residence traits, in concert with detailed exploration of the distribution of fittings and artefacts within the Ur houses (as far as is possible given often patchy recording), Brusasco looks at patterns of domestic activity on a room-by-room

Figure 6.6 Abu Salabikh, south Iraq. Adult and child burial within Early Dynastic house

Source: photo by R. Matthews.

basis, detecting a relatively low degree of segmentation of activity, that is a strong representation of multi-function rooms, which he attributes to a survival of tribally based social organisation:

> both the archaeological evidence and the ethnographic sources suggest that one is dealing with a system of social solidarity with a relative lack of tension in the relations among brothers, in the relations between men and women, and finally in the interaction with outsiders.
>
> (Brusasco 1999–2000: 106)

Finally turning to the evidence of archives of texts found within many of the Ur houses, although often unsuitably recorded in terms of exact provenance, Brusasco constructs parallel histories of families and their architectural contexts. On the basis of all these approaches, applied individually and collectively, Brusasco detects the presence at Old Babylonian Ur of several different family types, ranging from poor nuclear families to rich extended families.

A major study of households in a complex urban context is the work of Patricia Wattenmaker on household economics in the Upper Mesopotamian town of Kurban Höyük on the Euphrates, dating to the later third millennium BC (Wattenmaker 1994; 1998). By approaching urban complexity solely through the eyes of political elites and their actions in antiquity, she argues, we have ignored the power of non-elite production and consumption as agents of change and creation in the social process. Wattenmaker studies evidence for change in domestic production and consumption over a 500-year period at Kurban Höyük, explicitly assuming that in increasingly complex societies, 'because there is more variability in identity, status, and wealth, there is a greater need for symbols of social identity, and use of goods becomes more important as a means of conveying social information' (Wattenmaker 1998: 13). Specialisation and standardisation are viewed as socially motivated strategies, employed in order to define and reinforce the clarity of whatever social message might be conveyed by the production and consumption of goods in their social contexts, such messages potentially including rank, gender, age, marital status and ethnic or geographic identity amongst others. On the basis of these ideas Wattenmaker deduces that the archaeological record of societies undergoing a process of increasing complexity should include evidence for increasing consumption of specialist-produced goods by non-elites, continuing self-sufficiency by non-elite households in the production of goods not viewed outside the household, and increased non-elite consumption of goods likely to be viewed by interacting social groups, including items such as serving vessels, textiles and ornaments.

Through detailed study of household production of ceramics, stone tools and textiles, as well as patterns of food production and consumption attested above all by animal bones, Wattenmaker carefully delineates patterns of interaction between household and state concomitant with increasing social complexity. Suggested developments include the increased involvement of households in specialised production, increasing reliance of households on pottery and textile producing specialists, and household production of surplus goods perhaps in order to provide tribute to the state. An unusual feature of Wattenmaker's research into household economy is that excavations were conducted specifically in order to address her concerns with domestic modes of production and consumption, so that she was able to shape, test and modify her ideas in the field as well as at the desk. This two-way inter-action of theory and practice makes her study especially significant, and a model for future explorations of non-elite social elements, the common people of this chapter.

A relatively recent trend in the archaeology of Southwest Asia, as elsewhere, has been towards the application to past urban contexts of models and approaches from contemporary geographical studies, often with a major ethnographic element (Blanton 1993). Such approaches have been applied at the level of the house and neighbourhood as well as at the broader level of urban layout, providing insights into possible clustering of households into what may be social or lineage-related units (Banning 1997). Bleda During's close study of housing, access and use of space at Neolithic Çatalhöyük detects a shift through time in social practice from neighbourhoods with associated shrines to indi-vidual buildings with public spaces, a trend seen as 'a detachment of history via locality and buildings' involving the contraction of social interaction from clusters of up to thirty buildings to, in the later phases, the inhabitants of single buildings (During 2001: 16).

Post-processual and interpretive archaeological approaches to houses and households have been pioneered in the context of the Neolithic of southeast Europe, as well as at Çatalhöyük in Turkey (see Chapter 2). Viewing architecture as 'both a container and arena of social action', Ruth Tringham has outlined a tripartite strategy involving the consider-ation of material culture as an active element in society, of architecture as social arena, and of individual social actors (people!) as essential participants in the narratives of the past constructed by the archaeolo-gist, narratives that by the nature of the archaeological record and our relationships with it are bound to be multiple and polysemic (Tringham 1995: 81). Applying these ideas to her study of the use, alteration, aban-donment, destruction and replacement of Neolithic houses, often well preserved due to their deliberate destruction by fire, Tringham exam-ines the individual histories of houses, and areas within houses, that have been meticulously excavated in order that their full complexity, or something approaching it, be apparent and apprehensible, culminating in reconstructed narratives concerning individual actors within the household and social drama. Such approaches necessitate multi-scalar interpretations that consider similarities and differences between houses, and between areas within and through houses, at a range of scales of analysis and meaning, ranging from the microstratigraphy of floors and occupation deposits to the architectural plans of houses and groups of houses:

> in such an exploration, the lives and actions of individual families and members of those families are given equal priority to the longer, and wider-scale view in which these individual acts and perceptions are normalized and homogenized.
>
> (Tringham 1995: 95)

In this approach there is an explicit conviction that the daily domestic actions of men and women within and around their homes are not simply passive elements dominated and shaped by omnipotent elite ideologies, but themselves have the power to generate and shape modes and rules of social interaction.

In the context of the early Neolithic of the Levant, Brian Byrd has produced a thoughtful and stimulating study of households at a time of critical change (Byrd 2000). Defining a household as 'a task-oriented residence unit that shared a combination of production, coresidence, reproductive tasks, and consumptive tasks' (2000: 66), Byrd tackles the thorny issue of how the spatial characteristics of buildings might relate to social organisation and ideology. A strong feature of Byrd's analysis is his critical awareness of the processes through which the archaeological record is created and shaped through time. Thus artefacts found within buildings do not necessarily relate directly to use of space within those buildings, and there needs to be a subtle appreciation of how artefacts get into the archaeological record before meaningful spatial analyses can proceed. Byrd identifies four categories of floor artefact assemblages, including items left at sudden abandonment, items left at gradual abandonment, caches of discarded items, and trash dumping after abandonment. Highly detailed excavation and recording practices are essential for the identification and investigation of these categories and processes, leading in turn to consideration of the complex question of how artefacts found on floors relate to behavioural processes going on within and around the house.

The study of houses and households is likely to be high on the agenda once a full return to archaeological fieldwork in Iraq becomes possible. Through meticulous and innovative excavation and analysis there is every prospect of significant advances in our apprehension of the lives of common people, not only as elements in the rise and fall of complex social and political entities, but more significantly as players in their own right whose daily habits have a poignancy and relevance to our modern world. The alternative has been well put by Susan Pollock:

> By ignoring the vast majority of people, their labours, and the routines and dramas of their daily lives, we participate in ideologies that, both then and now, work to make these people and the inequalities of the societies in which they lived invisible.
>
> (Pollock 1999: 223)

One area in which significant developments might be expected is in the contextual study of ancient material culture. We have seen here how multi-scalar approaches to excavation of households have attempted to tease maximum information and interpretation from buildings. Sadly for us the householders of the past often kept their houses very tidy, repeatedly building new dwellings on top of old ones, sweeping their floors immaculately clean, and so in the macro sense within houses we find very little in the way of artefacts, such as pots, stone tools, or animal bones, as potential evidence for activities and social interaction. Only when houses are unexpectedly destroyed, preferably by fire, do we encounter significant quantities of objects in potentially meaningful positions within houses. In the case of Mesopotamia such destructions are relatively commonplace, either as single dwellings within settlements or as entire settlements put to flame by accident or intent. Artefact-rich structures such as the Ubaid dwelling excavated by Michael Roaf at Madhdhur, discussed above, are not isolated examples.

Such buildings and the artefacts within them offer immense potential for the study of how objects are constructed and consumed in their social contexts. How are they distributed within houses? Are there notions of age, gender, status at play in terms of their location, type and frequency? What correlations can we make between specific artefacts and the microscopic traces of activity within houses? How do artefact distributions and attributes vary from house to house within the same settlement? At the larger scale, if we have two or more excavated sites of the same archaeological period, how do artefacts differ from site to site, region to region, in any of their aspects? How does the same artefact, such as an identical pot form, perhaps take on differing significance from one site or region to another? Are they really identical? We conventionally assign the same value and meaning to artefacts that resemble each other and by instinct we look for unitary explanations.

Thus attempts to explain that humblest of pot type, the bevelled-rim bowl of the Uruk period, have generally been all-encompassing, unitary theories that seek a single role or function for the pots, whether as bread-moulds, salt containers or ration bowls. But the same object can have a host of different meanings depending on its context. What was a ration bowl at Uruk-Warka may have been a cherished curiosity at Hacınebi Tepe. The more information we have regarding context the richer our interpretations can be.

Town, country and nomad

The undoubted significance of the city as an element of Mesopotamian society notwithstanding, there is no question that urban life existed only as a part of an integrated urban/rural interaction. The city could not have existed without the countryside, and any adequate study of Mesopotamian urbanism needs to look beyond the city walls as well as inside them in order fully to apprehend the nature of the life of common people. Ibn Khaldun's fourteenth-century study of urbanism stressed the importance of this urban/rural discourse as a fundamental driving force for historical change. He discerned an evolving relationship between city-dwellers and the inhabitants of the desert and countryside, whereby a stage of mutually beneficial interaction was inevitably succeeded by the conquest, by battle or subtle infiltration, of the city by nomadic tribes, who themselves in time assumed the civilised characteristics of their urban hosts, facing up in turn to an unwinnable struggle with new inhabitants of the desert (Mahdi 1964: 212).

Almost all the foodstuffs of a city came from its surrounding countryside in the form of water, plant stuffs and animal products. Additionally, building and furnishing materials such as wood, straw, mud and reeds were obtained from the environs of Mesopotamian cities. Work at Abu Salabikh (Postgate 1992–3: 416) has shown that locally available timbers such as tamarisk, willow/poplar and date palm were used for roof timbers, while interior features included mats of reed or palm leaflet and, not surviving in the archaeological record but highly likely to have existed, chairs and beds of palm frond ribs, as commonly used today. Locally produced textiles may also have decorated interior surfaces of houses. All these products would have been obtained by urban dwellers either through management of their own resources, or through exchange of commodities with other parties to the urban/rural compact, or through more elaborate social mechanisms generated in the context of urban life such as employment within a supra-household institution. Based on his urban population estimates referred to above, Postgate has calculated that the rural hinterland of Abu Salabikh, needed to produce crops to support a maximum of 10,000 people, would have extended up to 10km in any one direction from the city itself (Postgate 1992–3: 435). Future progress in more concretely exploring and understanding the nature of urban/rural interactions in and around the small city of Abu Salabikh will partly depend on increasing success in 'matching the patterns of plant and animal exploitation attested in the texts with the excavated remains' (Postgate 1992: 159).

The precise ways in which city dwellers might have managed their rural resources is still an open issue. Textual information, often from poorly documented sources, indicates that urban individuals as well as institutions such as the temple could own and manage their own rural resources, but from an archaeological point of view the lack of investigation hitherto of small rural sites in an integrated programme of urban/rural research means that our information is seriously deficient. One significant attempt to approach this concern archaeologically, at the same time considering relevant textual data, was made by Henry Wright in his study of the rural site of Sakheri Sughir near the city of Ur (Wright 1969). Wright's project stands out as almost unique in Mesopotamian archaeology in being explicitly conceived, executed and published in order to address questions of urban/rural intercourse, production and administration. Centred on a study of interactions between the city of Ur and a nearby small rural site at Sakheri Sughir in the Early Dynastic period, Wright sets out an agenda for anthropological archaeology that encompasses in one succinct publication most of the significant approaches and trends in the modern discipline, including political theory, ethnoarchaeology, epigraphy, regional survey, site excavation, and a range of statistical analyses on many aspects of material culture. The excavated village comprised a settlement of perhaps fifteen families living in houses associated with hearths, ovens and items of material culture indicative of involvement in rural production, particularly the practices of crop cultivation, animal herding, fishing and field maintenance, while at the same time receiving goods and objects produced elsewhere within the urban/rural network.

Holistic analysis of relevant texts can give ideas of the sorts of urban/rural/nomadic interactions that should, given close enough attention to the full range of evidence, be recoverable from the archaeological record to some degree, despite the fact that many of the commodities involved are highly perishable and only likely to survive in

charred condition. Postgate's chart (1979: 198) of city/village intercourse for the cultivated plains of Upper Mesopotamia in the
Neo-Assyrian period encourages us to consider the sorts of interactions
that are likely to have existed, at least in periods when strong centralised
states existed, which is for much of Mesopotamian history (Figure 6.7).

Similarly, an integrated approach to the study of social and
economic archaeological evidence that relates to urban/rural interactions is still in its infancy, but it is through such means that we are
likeliest to understand the full significance and subtlety of the
city/countryside relationship. 'Urbanocentric' approaches to the past of

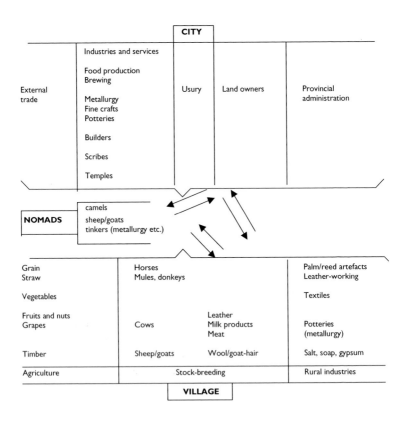

Figure 6.7 Resources and production in terms of city/village/nomad
    interactions

Source: after Postgate 1979: chart 2.

Mesopotamia, undertaken in the implicit belief that we can learn everything about an ancient complex society by studying its core with minimal or no reference to its hinterland, have had their day and recent years have seen a new appreciation of the significance of rural approaches to complex societies and states (Schwartz 1994; Schwartz and Falconer 1994; van Driel 2001). In these approaches there is a concern to stress that, in times of increasing social complexity, village communities are liable to undergo processes of specialisation and differentiation, commonly associated solely with urban centres, and that they have the power to engage in an often fractious dialectic with their urban partners that belies the conventional view of the countryside as a passive and immutable resource to be exploited at will by elite urban groups.

Studies that benefit from appreciation of both textual and archaeological evidence in approaching urban/rural concerns feature in issues of the *Bulletin on Sumerian Agriculture* (e.g. Postgate and Powell 1988; see also Potts 1997: 56–90). In the field, however, there have been few systematic programmes of recovery, study and publication of faunal and plant assemblages from Mesopotamian sites of the historic era, but those that have been undertaken have hinted at the richness of information and insight available from these previously neglected resources (Wattenmaker 1998). Patterns of culling of animals, based on age at death figures, suggest how the inhabitants of Abu Salabikh herded goats for meat, wool and milk, for example, while the absence of bones from very young animals argues for the possibility of herds being maintained long-term in rural areas at some distance from the city itself, perhaps according to seasonal patterns, a tantalising hint at one element of interactions between city dwellers and a more rural populace. These mixed strategies of sheep and goat herding have also been detected in an unusual study by an Assyriologist and an archaeozoologist of Old Babylonian texts concerning shepherds and flocks (Postgate and Payne 1975). Another respect in which faunal and plant remains might be induced to inform us on social and economic practices and relations will be by the analysis of quantities and types of animals and plants consumed or otherwise used according to rooms within houses, houses within quarters, quarters within cities, and so on, particularly if coordinated with equally rigorous study of contemporary rural communities. Diachronic studies along similar lines are also certain to produce results of note, as adumbrated in Susan Pollock's review of Early Dynastic and later evidence from the limited number of sites that have yielded relevant material (Pollock 1999: 140–7).

A fine example of zooarchaeological work can be found in the innovative approaches of Melinda Zeder, where the evidence of animal bones from excavations is as far as possible considered in the light not only of any relevant textual evidence, as in the case of the Ur III empire referred to in the previous chapter, but also in terms of its bearing on wider issues of urban-rural intercourse and early state development, as best shown in Zeder's work on animal economy at the site of Tal-e Malyan, ancient Anšan, in southwest Iran (Zeder 1991). Such approaches are rooted in a rounded understanding of animal ecology and the built and natural environment, the development and application of systematic recovery, recording and analytical procedures, and a willingness to situate often tightly focused studies within a broad context of social, economic and political development.

The significance of pastoral animal-herding nomads and of interactions between them and the more sedentary peoples of Mesopotamia is attested in the textual record, with pastoral nomads providing animal products to sedentary populations in exchange for agricultural and craft products (Schwartz 1995). The roots of this intimate and complex symbiosis have been seen in the rise of canal irrigation for crop production, leading to increased yields at the same time as a requirement to remove domesticated animals at seasonal intervals well away from irrigated and farmed land (Lees and Bates 1974). The work of Michael Rowton has focused on the relationships between nomadic and sedentary elements of ancient Mesopotamia, the tribe and the state (Rowton 1973). Rowton stresses the significance of pastoral nomadism within a political and social entity that stemmed from two roots, one the city-state, the other the nomadic tribe. Almost all our knowledge of ancient Mesopotamia relates to the city-state root rather than the nomadic root, largely because that is where our physical evidence originates, and it therefore takes an effort to conceive of the great significance of nomadic elements in the past. Rowton has characterised ancient Mesopotamia as having 'dimorphic structure' whereby interactions between nomad and sedentary, tribe and state, took place at a highly integrated level, with ever-shifting emphases upon urban, rural and nomadic elements contingent upon historical circumstance, a version of Ibn Khaldun's original city/desert idea referred to above. Pastoral nomadism could serve as an economic alternative during tough or unsettled times when harvests were inadequate to support high levels of sedentary people, and thus there might be a quite fluid relationship between settled and nomad. Frank Hole has additionally argued that a specialist pastoral nomadic lifestyle, with minimal or no interaction with agriculturalists, would also be possible in certain resource-rich regions (Hole 1974: 237). But how can we approach these issues archaeologically in view of the considerable difficulties involved in detecting, understanding and dating traces of nomads in the archaeological record? The answer is with great difficulty, and although some pointers as to how to detect and apprehend archaeological traces of pastoral nomadic activity have been generally agreed upon (Cribb 1991a; 1991b), the fact is that in the Mesopotamian context there has been little fieldwork conducted so far that might make a serious impact on this topic. Nomads have received even less archaeological attention than villages, and it will be only be through the execution of high-resolution, intensive survey of parts of the plain or adjacent uplands not totally wasted by erosion and/or alluviation that any progress may be made.

The closest and hitherto most profitable approach to pastoral nomadism as an archaeologically represented phenomenon is the work conducted by Frank Hole in his travels and excavations in the company of Luri pastoralists in southwest Iran, where traces of Neolithic camp-sites showed remarkable similarities to those of modern pastoral nomads (Hole 1995: 2722–3). Hole's conviction that 'sedentary villages, old or young, have relatively little to tell us about pastoralism which, by its nature, occurs away from such settlements' (Hole 1979: 195), encouraged him to look for traces of pastoralism in areas sited at some remove from arable land, developing survey techniques tailored for the job. These techniques included use of aerial photographs, in which modern tracks and springs could be detected, topographic maps, highly intensive field walking, and an intimate familiarity with modern practices of pastoral nomadism gained through targeted ethnoarchaeological fieldwork. On this platform of approaches, Hole's excavation of a nomad camp at Tula'i in Khuzistan revealed alignments of stones, areas of ash, and scatters of pottery and other artefacts all indicative of a campsite regularly used by Neolithic pastoral nomads with their dogs and herds of goat (Hole 1974; 1979; see Cribb 1991a: 214–5 for some doubts about the identity of the site as a pastoral nomad camp). Hole's manifesto for an archaeology of pastoral nomadism, whereby 'we need to fan out over the Zagros mountains (or elsewhere) with aerial photos, maps, and questionnaires and to gather and record information about nomad structures, facilities, and patterns of movement, *in extenso*' (Hole 1979: 214) stands a quarter of a century on as a challenge yet to be adequately met.

One possible angle is to study modern nomads in the hope of gaining insight into how they interact with settled communities, and how those interactions might manifest themselves in archaeological terms. Nomads in Mesopotamia existed in a form of symbiosis with their settled neighbours, characterised as 'enclosed nomadism' by Michael Rowton in order to distinguish it from the freer nomadism of the steppe. In this complex relationship, political as well as economic factors could be to the fore, and Rowton has stressed that nomads of Western Asia in the twentieth century AD lack the 'armed autonomy' of their ancient ancestors and cannot be viewed in the same, or similar, light (Rowton 1981). For this and other reasons, we therefore need to approach ethnographic studies of nomads with great care when attempting to use such analogous insights to throw light on the ancient Mesopotamian nomad. Here, as with all aspects of the lives of common people in ancient Mesopotamia, there remains an immense amount of research to design, execute and publish.

Chapter 7

Futures of the Mesopotamian past

AD 2084: a vision

> The countryside is badly ruined: all the remains of ancient settle-
> ments – still clearly visible one century before – have totally
> disappeared. The human alteration of the surface of Mesopotamia
> during the last 150 years has exceeded by a factor of 1000:1 the
> effects of all previous human activity during the past 10,000 years.
>
> (Liverani 1996: 283)

In Liverani's apocalyptic vision of the year 2084, the exploitation of
Mesopotamia for resources such as oil, water and agricultural produce
has by that time, a century on from George Orwell's *1984*, reduced the
countryside to a barren, wasted bleakness. Revealing his faith in the
dedication and ingenuity of archaeologists, however, Liverani goes on
to describe how a team of archaeologists might in that same year
attempt to put a sounding through 20m of silt, deposited by the lapping
waters of one of the dammed lakes of the Tigris or Euphrates, in order
to locate a known Early Bronze Age tell on a twentieth-century land
surface, buried for a hundred years. In the topsy-turvy world of 2084,
the sites flooded and buried by the massive civil engineering projects of
the later twentieth century have turned out to be the only sites to have
survived the ravages of the twenty-first century. Those sites not rescued
by salvage archaeology of the twentieth century have become the only
sites preserved for future investigation.

In this final chapter we consider some possible directions in which
Mesopotamian archaeology might profitably move in the years ahead,
assuming that Liverani's 2084 vision may not imminently come to pass,
as well as selected issues relating to the wider context of Mesopotamian
and Near Eastern archaeology. Some of these hoped-for developments

will depend on the lands of Iraq opening up before too long for further investigation by archaeological teams from all over the world. But other trends are certain to take shape even in the absence of further field-work, as has already been the case over the past decade and more.

Telling tales and painting pictures

The future of archaeological interpretation lies increasingly in narrative and images, 'a more explicit use of creative imagination', in Ruth Tringham's words (1995: 97). The factual accounts of architectural levels, pottery assemblages, chronological niceties and cultural processes that have hitherto been the end-product of our labours serve their own end, which has been to generate and maintain an academic discourse on agreed topics in agreed formulae for an agreed audience. This discourse, which differs in many respects from public discourses on archaeology, can be viewed as part of the professionalisation of archaeology during the twentieth century, whereby increasing degrees of specialisation and professional definition have dominated the discipline, in Southwest Asia as elsewhere. The academic discourse has been dictated largely by institu-tional, male, white and Western interests and concerns. Despite being an institutional, male, white Westerner, I nevertheless have the right to make some comments about other possible directions. For a truly engaging and multi-vocal discourse to develop, one that traverses, or better dissolves, the divides between academic and public, male and female, Western and non-Western, white and non-white, there is a need for radical change in the ways that archaeology is planned, executed and publicised/published. Here is not the place to expound an exhaustive manifesto of how archae-ology might change in these directions, but some pointers can be made.

There is an increasing realisation of the significance of narrative in archaeological interpretation. In fact, archaeological reporting is usually in the form of narrative, even if dressed in a sombre suit. A few bolder archaeologists have made attempts at explicit, empathetic narrative as a means of interpreting and re-presenting the past in the present (Tringham 1995). In the context of Southwest Asia such essays have been rare, perhaps heeding Marc Van De Mieroop's sceptical stance:

> The lack of narrative sources in Mesopotamian historiography makes it impossible to do more than imagine how one of the innumer-able men and women known to us by name spent the day at work, at home, with friends, or wherever. Except for a few kings, whose personality is to some extent revealed to us, the Mesopotamian

person we study is a faceless one, a name with a profession, some records and earthly goods. We can develop vivid images of a citizen of Uruk or the like, but most of that would be in the realm of fantasy.

(Van De Mieroop 1997b: 262)

But should not the very anonymity of the peoples of the Mesopotamian past encourage us, oblige us, to resurrect them and to consider their daily practices, fears, beliefs, however tentatively? Are not the personalities of the long dead somehow revealed to us through the artefacts made and used by them, the houses that they lived in, the skeletons that survived their dreams? Are there not ways to connect our archaeological interpretations in coherent, cohesive, sometimes contradictory, narratives that tell us and our audiences and public how it *might* have been? Is there not an onus on the archaeologist to deliver visions of the past that transcend traditional boundaries and territories? And if we as archaeologists fail to generate and deliver such visions, on what grounds may we criticise those non-archaeologists who are bold enough to try?

Attempts by academics at narration concerning, or inspired by, ancient Mesopotamia and the Near East have not been common. The most considered and stimulating essay along these lines so far is Jack Sasson's 'Thoughts of Zimri-Lim' (Sasson 1984), an engaging reconstruction of life as seen through the mind of a king of Mari in the eighteenth century BC, based principally on textual evidence with some archaeological input. While showing how texts might be used to reconstruct an empathetic 'history from above', Sasson's tale has the commendable aim of imparting vision and narrative imagination to the study of the past. Archaeologists and historians need to follow this path with greater enthusiasm and rigour than has hitherto been displayed. Lack of evidence should not prevent, perhaps should encourage, speculation. It is a duty for archaeologists, once more descending from their ivory towers, to explicate and formulate their studies in engaging narrative terms that can reach out to their colleagues, to the public of their own countries and, in appropriate languages and media, to the peoples of the countries in which they work. Here again might be particularly fruitful ground for archaeologists, historians and others to cooperate across disciplines and nations.

At this point we can mention a further approach to writing about Mesopotamian and Near Eastern archaeology that has led a rather unacknowledged and unofficial life within the context of academe. In a conventional way it has little to do with narration but much to do with the way we approach the past as people and as archaeologists. In the decades of the mid-twentieth century there appeared a number of books dealing with the subject of conducting fieldwork in Mesopotamia and the Near East, written largely by women. The most famous instance is Agatha Christie's book on digging in Syria, *Come, Tell Me How You Live* (Christie 1946). Such books were written by the wives of senior archaeologists, as Christie herself was, or by women working in various roles on field projects, and they are generally highly readable and engaging accounts of the vagaries of life on an excavation. In addition they provide sensitive and lucid insights into the academic contexts of the field projects themselves. First-class examples include Mary Chubb's *City in the Sand* (1957, reissued 1999), Margaret Wheeler's *Walls of Jericho* (1956), Sylvia Matheson's *Time off to Dig* (1961) and, perhaps best of all, the study by Linda Braidwood, wife of Robert, *Digging Beyond the Tigris* (1953), subtitled *An American Woman Archeologist's Story of Life on a 'Dig' in the Kurdish Hills of Iraq*. In his foreword to *Time off to Dig*, Mortimer Wheeler characterised these works as 'inverted archaeology', concerned with aspects of the archaeological process normally ignored by the professional practitioner, but he conceded that their public appeal was likely greatly to exceed that of 'the cultural setting of the broken mud buildings of Mundigak' (Matheson 1961: 9). Within their historical context these books may be seen as the product of a male-dominated academic system that excluded female voices from formal academic discourse in the mid-twentieth century. Today they enable us as readers to share in the practice and rigours of archaeology, and give an extra life-enhancing dimension to the process that is missing from conventional reports. The practice in some modern field projects of publishing online diaries, rarely as readable as the above-named accounts, is another outlet for unconventional elements of discourse.

In addition to textual narration, there is infinite scope for the use of modern GIS (Geographic Information Systems) and computing technology to be put to use in the reconstruction and visualisation of the Mesopotamian past. Steps have already been taken in this direction on several fronts (Forte and Siliotti 1997), but the potentially rich visual significance of ancient Mesopotamia has barely begun to be explored. One step has involved innovative explorations of the Northwest Palace at Nimrud, where initial online reconstructions of the building and its decorative elements are underway (*http://www.learningsites.com/NWPalace/NWPalhome.html*). For ancient Egypt, where the visual impact of the monuments is today still plain to see, there have been many successful attempts at reconstructing in depictions the monumental architecture of the past, most attractively in the series of volumes *L'Egypte restituée* (Aufrère *et al.* 1991), where numerous buildings, large and small, are depicted in full colour within their landscape settings. A major project of reconstruction of Mesopotamian buildings, including their contents, their human inhabitants and their landscapes, could explore issues of architecture, social space, urban layout and landscape structure in concrete and exciting ways. Such a project might comprise a high-quality printed series of volumes and/or multiple images on CD-ROM with a dedicated website. The ability to take virtual tours round such buildings, city-scapes and landscapes would be not only an enlightening experience but also a phenomenal teaching and learning aid.

Mesopotamia in England AD 2002

In a comparative study of empires, in which he shows that the largest empire in the world at any one time has been in what is today the Muslim world for 2,700 out of the past 5,000 years, Rein Taagepera has made the following telling statement about the way the past is studied in the modern West:

> We arbitrarily ignore some of our roots. The treatment of the Middle East is especially striking. Its most ancient history is well represented in our history texts: Egypt, Babylon, and Assyria figure prominently, and even the Hyksos are mentioned. But after the rise of the Greek civilization our textbooks implicitly suggest that the culture that started in Egypt, Anatolia, and Mesopotamia completely shifted to Greece, leaving behind a cultural vacuum. Achaimenid Persia marginally enters our 'world history' but only as far as it attacks Greece or is briefly taken over by an adventurer originating from the European marches of the empire. … It is as if the scientific-technological-cultural phoenix flew from the Middle East to Greece, then to Rome, and then died, only to arise from the same Italian ashes a thousand years later. But the phoenix did not die – it returned to Byzantium, spread out all over the Arab world, picked up a few feathers from India and China, and then returned to Italy.
>
> (Taagepera 1978a: 123–4)

The standing today of ancient Mesopotamia, and of the Near East in general, within the educational system of England, at least, is little short of disastrous. Let us follow the educational trail from infancy to adulthood that a pupil in a state school in England might take while studying history under the remit of the National Curriculum (introduced by the Education Act of 1988; the following quotes are from their website: *http://www.nc.uk.net*), followed by their studies in history and/or archaeology in upper secondary education. Up to the age of fourteen, education is divided into three 'key stages'. At key stage 1, ages 5–7, there is no specific mention of the ancient Near East nor, in fact, of any geographical region outside Britain.

For key stage 2, ages 7–11, pupils are obliged to study 'the everyday lives of men, women and children, of a past society *selected from*: Ancient Egypt, Ancient Sumer, the Assyrian Empire, the Indus Valley, the Maya, Benin, *or* the Aztecs' (italics in original), with a commendable coverage of a range of aspects such as houses and cities, technology, food, health and medicine, rulers and ruled, and wealth and economy. This particular element is situated within a key stage 2 requirement to study in total one topic of local history, three topics of British history, one topic of European history, and one topic of world history. Our initial surprise and encouragement at seeing both Sumer and Assyria explicitly mentioned amongst a list of only seven options for the world history element of key stage 2 is promptly deflated when we learn that in practice only a tiny proportion of pupils end up studying either of these two Mesopotamian choices. There are no centralised statistics available for what gets taught in UK schools, but informed estimates indicate that something like 95 per cent of all key stage 2 pupils study the ancient Egypt option for their world history element, and that of the remaining 5 per cent virtually none study the Sumer or Assyria options. Why is this so?

The choice, of course, is made not by the pupils themselves but by their teachers, and one cannot blame teachers for focusing their efforts on topics that can be taught through use of well produced, attractive and easily obtainable teaching aids. In this respect, ancient Egypt wins hands down. A quick browse through the British Museum bookshop, through which hundreds of teachers and pupils pass every day, reveals multiple shelves of educational books and activity materials devoted to ancient Egypt, with lesser amounts of material addressing the Roman empire, the Vikings, and one or two other topics. For ancient Mesopotamia, and the Near East beyond, there is almost nothing available to attract a potentially interested teacher, let alone pupil, into the fold, with the exception of a couple of titles, neither on sale in the British Museum bookshop (Oakes 1994; 2001). The British Museum has produced a range of leaflets aimed at key stage 2 teachers, including ones on the Sumerians and the

Assyrians, and the recently opened website *http://www.mesopotamia.co.uk* is designed as one of a series of linked sites (funded exclusively by Japanese corporations!) all addressing key stage 2 world history options of the National Curriculum, as well as some key stage 3 topics.

These developments are welcome, but it is still a matter of some concern that production of teaching aids for key stage 2 topics is an *ad hoc* affair, as it seems. Should there not be an impetus from the board of the National Curriculum actively seeking ways to generate, even commission, good teaching aids that might enable a genuine diversity of choice for teachers and pupils at key stage 2? All seven of the featured options ought to have at least a basic range of approved teaching materials that prospective teachers, even pupils, can browse on and chew over before making a selection. Materials could include activity packs, well constructed, thoughtfully illustrated and challengingly written, such as have been produced by the Commonwealth Institute for the Indus Valley and the Kingdom of Benin, for example (Aronovsky and Aafjes-Sinnadurai 1995), as well as a greater wealth of appropriate websites. On this note, one teacher, herself a scholar of ancient Mesopotamia, relates how she attempted to interest the Department of Education and Skills, whose suggested history syllabus 'schemes of work' are offered on an optional basis to English schools (*http://www.standards.dfee.gov.uk/schemes/*), in the production of study materials for ancient Mesopotamia, either Sumer or Assyria, but was told that they would not be required.

But the problems with key stage 2 fade into insignificance once we move on, aged eleven, to face the challenges of key stage 3 and beyond. During a pupil's key stage 3 years, ages 11–14, arguably the most formative of any in terms of shaping academic character and skills, obligatory elements of the history curriculum comprise three British topics, one European topic, and two world studies, these last split either side of AD 1900. Paragraph 12 of key stage 3 specifies that pupils will pursue 'a study of the cultures, beliefs and achievements of an African, American, Asian *or* Australasian society in the past (other than those included in the programme of study for key stage 2)'. This bracketed stipulation means that, even if they were not selected for study in key stage 2, both Sumer and Assyria (and ancient Egypt, come to that) may not be studied in key stage 3. Suggested topics include Islamic civilisations, Chinese dynasties, and a range of African, American and Asian options. The only pre-Islamic Near Eastern element specifically mentioned is the Phoenicians.

We are now aged fourteen and, stimulated by a range of consistently good TV programmes such as *Time Team* and *Meet the Ancestors*, we are eager to continue our studies of the past into key stage 4, up to age 16. In some schools we may be fortunate enough to be able to take a GCSE (General Certificate of Secondary Education, formerly 'O' level) in archaeology, but for most interested pupils history will be the only option and, in any case, ancient Mesopotamia and the entire ancient Near East will not feature in any of our studies, whether it be of archaeology or history. Indeed, the GCSE in archaeology is concerned exclusively with the archaeology of Britain and Ireland. Let us progress rapidly to our final two years of full-time secondary education, formerly as devoted to 'A' levels, now divided into a first year of Advanced Subsidiary (AS) studies and a second year of Advanced Level (A2) studies. At this level, history courses will not concern themselves at all with the ancient Near East, the closest optional topic being 'Crusading Europe and the Latin East, 1095–1192'. The syllabus for archaeology in both these years of study in England is now overseen principally by the Assessment and Qualifications Alliance or AQA (*http://www.aqa.org.uk*). Under the current AQA syllabus there is obligatory study of a thematic topic, 'religion and ritual', to be taught in the context of one of the following: prehistoric Britain and Ireland, ancient Egypt, the Roman world, or the Maya. Until 2000 there were two archaeology syllabi, one under the Northern Examinations and Assessment Board (which has since become part of AQA), the other under the Cambridge Board. But the Cambridge Board has since folded and now there is only the AQA, who have taken all ancient Near Eastern elements out of the archaeology syllabus for AS/A2 studies, whereas previously the ancient Near East played a reasonably significant role within the Cambridge Board syllabus.

The result has been catastrophic for the study in English schools of ancient Mesopotamia and the Near East. One example may serve to demonstrate how drastic this collapse has been. In 1999 the British Museum Education Department held a study day on the ancient Near East, open to all 'A' level students, and a total of 140 students from all over England attended. In 2000, the last year of the Cambridge Board, sixty students made the effort. In 2001 the same ancient Near East study day was offered. Not a single AS/A2 student or teacher expressed interest and the day passed with an attendance of zero. We could hardly imagine a sharper comment on the death of a discipline at a level where it cannot afford to die. Our French neighbours have in like spirit excluded the study of ancient Mesopotamia entirely from their secondary school programmes (Bottéro 1992: 26).

These figures contrast strongly with the high attendances at adult education events concerning the ancient Near East held at the British

Museum and at colleges throughout England, some of which draw larger crowds than any other field of study. Thus, Ancient Near East Week at the British Museum in November 2001 attracted over 1,000 people, with up to fifty at each gallery talk. Whether such attendance levels will be maintained as the current school generation evolves into the future adult generation remains to be seen. Current adults went to school when Sumer and Assyria were taught, however fleetingly, as integral elements of an education that featured the Bible and a unitary sense of 'the rise of civilisation'. A return to such an education programme is not here being advocated, but it is absurd to excise Sumer and Assyria as part of a de-privileging of the Bible in education.

The parlous state of education in the ancient Near East in the UK has many knock-on effects. One consequence is the small numbers of first-year university students in archaeology or history with a basic knowledge of the geography, history and archaeology of the ancient Near East, hardly surprising given that their most recent exposure to ancient Mesopotamia and the Near East may have been when they were eleven, and then only if they happened to be in the tiny proportion of pupils who did not study ancient Egypt at key stage 2. And yet, happily, once university students are exposed to the excitement and challenge of studying ancient Mesopotamia and its neighbours, especially if they can travel to those parts of the modern Near East that remain accessible, many of them find the attractions strong enough to keep them in the discipline for at least a few years, and some for much longer.

A related long-term concern is the low level of public awareness and knowledge, even in well educated circles, of what and where Mesopotamia is, and how it relates to the modern state of Iraq, and how Britain and Iraq have interacted through the nineteenth and twentieth centuries. We have successfully detached Mesopotamia from Iraq, the past from the present, in the eyes of our compatriots. It is now our duty to reverse this process, to reconstruct the bridges broken by the smart bombs of our modern intellects. Writing as a Briton, I am ashamed at the degree of national ignorance of our own history and of the relations between Britain and Iraq in the twentieth century that pervades our country. In 1922 it was estimated that Iraq had cost the British taxpayer the immense sum of £100 million in the previous four years, and Bonar Law stated in the House of Commons, 'I wish we had never gone there!' (Barker 1967: 457). No doubt the feeling was mutual, but the point here is to stress how little we seem to have learnt from our undeniably special relationship with Iraq. We have sent thousands of our armed forces to Mesopotamia, in both World Wars and in 1991, as well as troops from lands under our imperial control, generally with a diffidence that has led to, or closely approached, disaster. In the First World War, a 'forgotten army' fought 'the neglected war' against the Ottoman occupiers of Iraq with ammunition labelled 'Made in the USA. For practice only' (Barker 1967), while in 1941, with decrepit aeroplanes of a bygone era, the Royal Air Force achieved a 'hidden victory' over local and German forces (Dudgeon 2000). By the 1990s British intelligence on Iraq was so poor that nobody knew it got cold at night in the desert, and SAS crack troops died of exposure in inadequate clothing (McNab 1993). Press coverage of Iraq during the Gulf War made little or no mention of previous British involvement in Iraq and, on both sides of the Atlantic, discussed the archaeological heritage of Iraq principally in terms of its significance within the western, biblical, orientalist paradigm, 'civilized art in primitive places' (Pollock and Lutz 1994: 280).

An uncertain future: transcending history?

What of the practice today of archaeology in the modern lands of Mesopotamia? Since the Iraqi invasion of Kuwait in August 1990 there has been a more or less complete moratorium on western fieldwork in Iraq, with a few exceptions. Field activity has swung away from the heartlands of Sumer, Akkad, Babylonia and Assyria, all within modern Iraq, to regions such as the Syrian Jazirah. There has been a healthy increase in our appreciation and understanding of cultural developments in areas of Mesopotamia that had not previously been so well understood. A good example is the issue of urbanisation and state development in the later third millennium BC in Upper Mesopotamia. Excavations and surveys in northeast Syria, at sites such as Beydar, Brak, Mozan and Leilan, much of which had been underway before 1990, increasingly underline the importance of local elements in the development of literate urbanised society in this part of Southwest Asia. But many other major concerns of Mesopotamian archaeology have stayed on ice for over a decade, issues such as the transition from mobile hunting and gathering to permanent sedentism in Upper Mesopotamia as attested at sites such as Qermez Dere, M'lefaat and Nemrik, the earliest settlement of the Lower Mesopotamian alluvium, as tantalisingly hinted at by French excavations at Tell 'Oueili in the 1980s, or the long-term investigation of Sumerian urban structure at the small third-millennium city of Abu Salabikh.

All archaeologists working in this region do so within the context of the history of the discipline. Everyone is free to write or imagine their own history of the discipline, but there are certain elements that need to be considered. One of these is the origins of the archaeology of Southwest Asia within a context of Western imperialism and colonialism from at least the nineteenth century onwards. All of us who originate in the West need to be acutely sensitive to what that means for the exercise of our discipline today. At the same time, we may also choose to accept the great advances made through this tradition. Conducting research in a post-colonial world means being sensitive to the past, but also being creative in imagining and implementing ways to transcend inherited history. No-one has to be a prisoner of the past, and indeed there is everything to learn from it – why else be an archaeologist or historian?

Future Western work in Southwest Asia will go forward only as a fully collaborative exercise, where academics and interested parties of the host country are involved at every level. This involvement needs to go well beyond, as well as including, the training and recruitment of local specialists to fulfil specific project roles. It is vital that sensitivities and intellectual alignments of the host country that may or may not be rooted in the Western positivist, scientific tradition are considered, discussed and integrated into research designs at the conception of long-term collaborative projects. Iraqi Mesopotamian archaeologists may not wish to operate within an intellectual, conceptual and methodological paradigm imported wholesale from the West, for example, but may desire to explore their pasts in entirely different ways that have not been formulated or adopted in the West. Have we even asked? As Charles Redman stated twenty years ago, 'It is unrealistic for us as foreigners to expect to continue research under what is largely a colonialist paradigm' (Redman 1982: 382). Some encouraging developments have taken place (Masry 1981: 237), but every Western field project in Southwest Asia needs to make constant effort to stimulate and engage local communities, academic and otherwise, in all stages of the planning, execution, publicisation and publication of projects.

Archaeology needs to be removed from its ivory towers of the West and integrated on local terms in local languages amongst local peoples. British, and other foreign institutes based permanently abroad are uniquely placed to generate and implement such programmes of cooperative research and interaction, despite what some see as their post-colonialist context. Western archaeologists will bring the cause forward by involving themselves intimately in the life of the communities and countries in which they conduct research. Academics who turn up in Turkey or Syria or Iraq, spend a couple of months digging, then return to their Western universities to study and publish their discoveries without involving host academics are operating at a morally unacceptable level. In order to give some idea of the problem as seen from the side of a host country, here is a passage from the editorial of a recent issue of the journal *Adumatu*, produced in Riyadh:

> Perhaps one ought to wonder: why should foreign expeditions impose their cultural and epistemological orientations on our archaeological sites? Is it because they know more about them than we? Or is it because they have the oldest, more advanced and developed experience in the field of excavation? Or is it because expeditions arrive armed with funding and professionals in all dimensions of technologies? The answers to these could very well be 'yes'; yet one may ask: has the Arab world been unable to afford its own able professionals in areas of excavation, periodization, analysis and insightful interpretation? Although we know there have been enough of them, still we ask: where have they been and what roles have they played?
>
> (Al-Ansary 2000: 5)

A similar sentiment has recently been expressed by a Western scholar: 'we must perhaps wonder whether the West's endless conquest of its own past and of that of other civilizations should not be accompanied by similar research undertaken by those civilizations into their own origins' (Zabbal 2000: x). Al-Ansary pleads with Arab archaeologists to break out of the historical trajectory that the seniority and authority of the West have imposed on them. By publishing exclusively in foreign languages 'we deprive our nation of the ability to read its own heritage and history in its own language' (Al-Ansary 2000: 6). In a complementary vein, Western archaeologists are under an obligation to meet Al-Ansary's challenge from the other side, to learn the languages and sensitivities of the countries in which they work. This statement may sound otiose, but it is alarming how many Western archaeologists claim 'not to have the time' to learn Turkish or Arabic, and who therefore deal exclusively in their own tongue with their hosts. It would be unthinkable for a British archaeologist to direct or co-direct an excavation in France without knowing French, or for a German archaeologist to work in Britain without knowing English. Why then do we impose the unthinkable on countries outside the West? When I studied archaeology and ancient history as an undergraduate in England, the compulsory language was Latin. Today all departments of archaeology with courses in the archaeology of Southwest Asia should be able to provide access to courses in the modern languages of the region, and should consider making them compulsory at certain levels.

Fieldwork is an activity that unites past and present realities through its execution, in particular through 'close working relationships with the very much living people in whose villages, towns, and homes we reside for a short time and into whose lives we inject our unsolicited and often very alien presence and life-styles', engaging in 'interpersonal and inter-cultural understandings that far surpass the capabilities of any purely academic discourse to describe or explain' (Pollock 1992: 303–4). Anyone who has excavated in Iraq, Syria, Turkey, or any country of the modern Middle East, will know what Susan Pollock is talking about and, moreover, will appreciate the benefits to be had all round by sincere efforts made at learning and respecting the languages and customs of host communities.

Another means by which Western archaeologists might build the piers on their side of the bridge is through greater involvement in, appreciation of, and sensitivity to the archaeology of the Islamic era, including that of the Ottoman empire (Baram and Carroll 2000), often treated as somehow disconnected from the past of earlier periods. The generation of this sense of discontinuity is doubtless rooted in Western attempts, conscious or not, to expropriate the past of Mesopotamia and environs for the biblico-classical tradition, as discussed in Chapter 1 (Van De Mieroop 1997a: 289). As Kohl puts it, 'An evolutionary archae-ology of the ancient Near East has so far been conceptualized only within an Orientalist mode that distances present realities from past concerns' (Kohl 1989: 245). Part of this process has involved the exclu-sion, intentional or not, of the modern peoples of the region from any meaningful involvement in the investigation of their own countries' pasts. One of the great evidential strengths of the past of Southwest Asia is the diachronic richness of material to be interpreted by the modern student of the past, a richness immensely enhanced by inclu-sion of the often highly detailed evidence from more recent episodes of that past, as Kohl cogently argues. Here again there is great scope for collaborations with host country scholars.

It may seem trite to say that Western archaeologists are bound to respect local customs and manners. We need to be aware of the impact on local communities, not solely in financial terms, that may be brought about by the sporadic invasion of Western archaeologists with their alien ways. Of course much of this impact can be positive and all to the good for both parties, if carefully handled, but many of the behaviour traits of Western archaeologists currently active in Southwest Asia are more invidious and truly colonialist than those of the dedicated colonial professionals of a century ago. We cannot be too sensitive on this and many other issues: 'Archaeology, as cultural practice, is always a politics, always a morality' (Shanks and Tilley 1987: 212).

There is another area in which modern archaeology might one day quietly contribute to a process of healing and bridge-building in the context of Mesopotamia. One of the most poignant duties in which some archaeologists are currently involved is that of the excavation of mass graves of humans slaughtered in ethnic conflicts of the modern age. Sadly for the Iraqi people, who, as one author recently put it, 'have not had a decent break for eight hundred years' (Hamza 2000: 7), there is considerable scope for the application of archaeology within Mesopotamia to this end. Here is an opportunity for archaeology to act as part of a cleansing and healing process that could be of value to all, if delicately handled. On or around Iraqi soil in modern times there have taken place several major conflicts, including the Mesopotamia campaign of the First World War, the Rashid Ali conflict of the Second World War, the Iran-Iraq War, and the Gulf War. All these episodes were immensely painful and tragic for the Iraqi people, as well as for soldiers and civilians of other nations. Rather than assign blame, even decades on, for the cause and conduct of these terrible events, is there some role archaeology can play in bringing sides together, building bridges, and moving on?

Is it conceivable one day for a team of Iraqi and Iranian archaeologists, united under a UN umbrella and comprising human remains specialists, to work to retrieve, identify and return to their families in Iraq and Iran the bodies of some of the thousands of soldiers killed in the 1980s? If such practices are deemed valuable, even essential, in a European context, then why not in a Middle Eastern context? What about the possibility one day of archaeologists from Iraq, Britain and Turkey together excavating some of the First World War trenches of the Ottoman and British imperial forces, for example at Kut al-Amara, in order to create a peace park with palm groves and quiet memorials, as the Turks have so impressively done at Gallipoli? Here might be a way of confronting and transcending the colonial past, Ottoman and British, in a concrete and cathartic fashion.

As this book draws to its end, there is talk of the flooding within the next few years of the great Assyrian city of Aššur on the Tigris river in north Iraq (Bailey 2002). A dam is being constructed downstream of

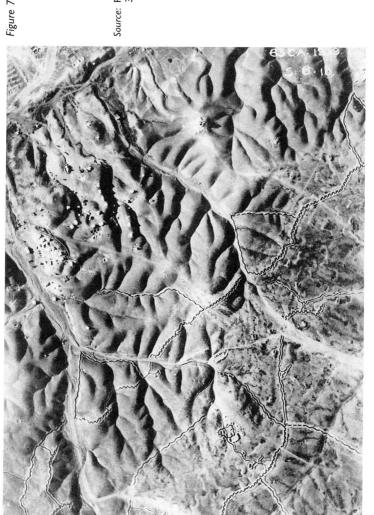

Figure 7.1 Daur, central Iraq, photographed from 6,000 feet on 18 June 1918. Traces of military trenches, supply lines and encampments of Ottoman forces can clearly be seen cutting across the natural erosion features

Source: Public Record Office ref. CN 5/2 369.

the city and Aššur, along with at least seventy other archaeological sites, will disappear under the waters of a new lake, perhaps to be safely smothered under metres of soft silt, as in Liverani's AD 2084 vision. But, on the assumption that the city will disappear forever, we of the West may hope to join with our friends and colleagues of Iraq in planning and executing a programme of research and rescue survey and excavations across the entire flood zone. Together we might devise an integrated programme of fieldwork where sites of all periods are excavated according to comparable procedures of excavation and recovery, allowing long-term diachronic explorations of issues such as landscape use, settlement layout, architecture, diet, economy, technology, and a host of other concerns within a specific geographical environment, covering periods from early prehistory up to modern times, with the close involvement of local communities. Indeed, such a programme of integrated, diachronic study in the rescue context was conceived and at least partially executed thirty years ago in southeast Turkey (French 1973). In this and so many other respects, the potentials for future archaeological explorations in Mesopotamia, for creating, reshaping and casting our theories and approaches, are as unbounded, stimulating and politically situated as they have ever been.

Bibliography

Adams, R. McC. (1965) *Land Behind Baghdad. A History of Settlement on the Diyala Plains*, Chicago: University of Chicago Press.

——(1979) 'Common concerns but different standpoints: A commentary', in M. T. Larsen (ed.) *Power and Propaganda. A Symposium on Ancient Empires* (Mesopotamia Copenhagen Studies in Assyriology 7) Copenhagen: Akademisk Forlag, 393–404.

——(1981) *Heartland of Cities. Surveys of Ancient Settlement and Land Use on the Central Floodplain of the Euphrates*, Chicago: University of Chicago Press.

——(1988) 'Contexts of civilizational collapse. A Mesopotamian view', in N. Yoffee and G. L. Cowgill (eds) *The Collapse of Ancient States and Civilizations*, Tuscon: University of Arizona Press, 20–43.

Adams, R. McC. and Nissen, H. J. (1972) *The Uruk Countryside. The Natural Setting of Urban Societies*, Chicago: University of Chicago Press.

Akkermans, P. M. M. G. and Duistermaat, K. (1997) 'Of storage and nomads: The clay sealings from Late Neolithic Sabi Abyad, Syria', *Paléorient* 22(2): 17–44.

Al-Ansary, A.-R. T. (2000) 'Editorial', *Adumatu* 2: 4–6.

Alcock, S. E., D'Altroy, T. N., Morrison, K. D. and Sinopoli, C. M. (eds) (2001) *Empires. Perspectives from Archaeology and History*, Cambridge: Cambridge University Press.

Algaze G. (1989) 'The Uruk expansion: Cross-cultural exchange in early Mesopotamian civilization', *Current Anthropology* 30: 571–608.

——(1993) *The Uruk World System. The Dynamics of Expansion of Early Mesopotamian Civilization*, Chicago: University of Chicago Press.

——(2001a) 'The prehistory of imperialism. The case of Uruk period Mesopotamia', in M. S. Rothman (ed.) *Uruk Mesopotamia and its Neighbors. Cross-Cultural Interactions in the Era of State Formation*, Santa Fe: School of American Research Press, 27–83.

——(2001b) 'Initial social complexity in Southwestern Asia. The Mesopotamian advantage', *Current Anthropology* 42: 199–233.

Alp, S. (1991a) *Hethitische Keilschrifttafeln aus Maşat-Höyük*, Ankara: Türk Tarih Kurumu.

——(1991b) *Hethitische Briefe aus Maşat-Höyük*, Ankara: Türk Tarih Kurumu.

Ammerman, A. J. (1981) 'Surveys and archaeological research', *Annual Review of Anthropology* 10: 63–88.

Anderson, P. C. (1999) 'Experimental cultivation, harvest, and threshing of wild cereals', in P. C. Anderson (ed.) *Prehistory of Agriculture. New Experimental and Ethnographic Approaches* (Institute of Archaeology Monograph 40) Los Angeles: University of California Press, 118–44.

Andrae, E. W. and Boehmer, R. M. (1992) *Bilder eines Ausgräbers. Die Orientbilder von Walter Andrae 1898–1919*, Berlin: Gebr. Mann.

Andrén, A. (1998) *Between Artifacts and Texts. Historical Archaeology in Global Perspective*, New York: Plenum.

Aronovsky, I. and Aafjes-Sinnadurai, U. (1995) *The Indus Valley. National Curriculum History Key Stage 2*, London: Commonwealth Institute.

Ataman, K. (1999) 'Threshing sledges and archaeology', in P. C. Anderson (ed.) *Prehistory of Agriculture. New Experimental and Ethnographic Approaches* (Institute of Archaeology Monograph 40) Los Angeles: University of California Press, 211–22.

Auden, W. H. (1976) *Collected Poems*, ed. E. Mendelson, London: Faber and Faber.

Aufrère, S., Golvin, J.-C. and Goyon, J.-C. (1991) *L'Egypte restituée: sites et temples de haute Egypte (1650 av. JC–300 ap. JC)*, Paris: Editions Errance.

Aurenche, O. (1996) 'Famille, fortune, pouvoir et architecture domestique dans les villages du Proche Orient', in K. R. Veenhof (ed.) *Houses and Households in Ancient Mesopotamia* (papers read at the 40e Rencontre Assyriologique Internationale Leiden, 5–8 July 1993) Leiden: Nederlands Historisch-Archaeologisch Instituut te Istanbul: 1–16.

Bahrani, Z. (1998) 'Conjuring Mesopotamia: Imaginative geography and a world past', in L. Meskell (ed.) *Archaeology Under Fire. Nationalism, Politics and Heritage in the Eastern Mediterranean and Middle East*, London: Routledge, 159–74.

——(2001) *Women of Babylon. Gender and Representation in Mesopotamia*, London: Routledge.

Bailey, M. (2002) 'Tigris dam damns Assur', *The Art Newspaper* 125: 24.

Baird, D. (1996) 'The Konya Plain survey: Aims and methods', in I. Hodder (ed.) *On the Surface: Çatalhöyük 1993–95*, Cambridge: McDonald Institute for Archaeological Research and British Institute of Archaeology at Ankara: 41–6.

Banning, E. B. (1997) 'Spatial perspectives on early urban development in Mesopotamia', in W. E. Aufrecht, N. A. Mirau and S. W. Gauley (eds) *Aspects of Urbanism in Antiquity from Mesopotamia to Crete*, Sheffield: Sheffield Academic Press: 17–34.

Baram, U. and Carroll, L. (eds) (2000) *A Historical Archaeology of the Ottoman Empire. Breaking New Ground*, New York: Kluwer Academic/Plenum.

Barfield, T. J. (2001) 'The shadow empires: Imperial state formation along the Chinese/Nomad frontier', in S. E. Alcock, T. N. D'Altroy, K. D. Morrison and C. M. Sinopoli (eds) *Empires. Perspectives from Archaeology and History*, Cambridge: Cambridge University Press, 10–41.

Barker, A. J. (1967) *The Neglected War. Mesopotamia 1914–1918*, London: Faber and Faber.

Bar-Yosef, O. (2001) 'PPNB interaction sphere', *Cambridge Archaeological Journal* 11: 114–17.

Bar-Yosef, O. and Meadow, R. H. (1995) 'The origins of agriculture in the Near East', in T. D. Price and A. B. Gebauer (eds) *Last Hunters – First Farmers. New Perspectives on the Prehistoric Transition to Agriculture*, Santa Fe: School of American Research Press, 39–94.

Belfer-Cohen, A. and Bar-Yosef, O. (2000) 'Early sedentism in the Near East. A bumpy ride to village life', in I. Kuijt (ed.) *Life in Neolithic Farming Communities. Social Organization, Identity, and Differentiation*, New York: Kluwer Academic, 19–37.

Bell, G. (1953) *Selected Letters of Gertrude Bell*, Harmondsworth: Penguin.

Bender, B. (1978) 'Gatherer-hunter to farmer: A social perspective', *World Archaeology* 10: 204–22.

Berman, J. (1994) 'The ceramic evidence for sociopolitical organization in 'Ubaid southwestern Iran', in G. Stein and M. S. Rothman (eds) *Chiefdoms and Early States in the Near East. The Organizational Dynamics of Complexity* (Monographs in World Archaeology 18) Madison: Prehistory Press, 23–33.

Biggs, R. D. (1974) *Inscriptions from Tell Abū Salābīkh* (Oriental Institute Publications 99) Chicago: University of Chicago Press.

Binford, L. R. (1968) 'Post-Pleistocene adaptations', in S. R. Binford and L. R. Binford (eds) *New Perspectives in Archeology*, Chicago: Aldine, 313–41.

Blanton, R. E. (1993) *Houses and Households. A Comparative Study*, New York: Plenum Press.

——(1998) 'Beyond centralization. Steps towards a theory of egalitarian behavior in archaic states', in G. M. Feinman and J. Marcus (eds) *Archaic States*, Santa Fe: School of American Research Press, 135–72.

Blumler, M. A. (1996) 'Ecology, evolutionary theory and agricultural origins', in D. R. Harris (ed.) *The Origins and Spread of Agriculture and Pastoralism in Eurasia*, London: UCL Press, 25–50.

Boehmer, R. M. (1999) *Uruk früheste Siegelabrollungen* (Ausgrabungen in Uruk-Warka Endberichte 24) Mainz am Rhein: Philipp von Zabern.

Bogucki, P. (1999) 'Early agricultural societies', in G. Barker (ed.) *Companion Encyclopedia of Archaeology*, London: Routledge, 839–69.

Bökönyi, S. (1986) 'The equids of Umm Dabaghiyah, Iraq', in R. H. Meadow and H.-P. Uerpmann (eds) *Equids in the Ancient World* (Beihefte zum Tübinger Atlas des Vorderen Orients Reihe A 19/1) Wiesbaden: Ludwig Reichert, 302–17.

Bottéro, J. (1992) *Mesopotamia. Writing, Reasoning, and the Gods*, Chicago: University of Chicago Press.

——(2000) 'Religion and reasoning in Mesopotamia', in J. Bottéro, C. Herrenschmidt and J.-P. Vernant (eds) *Ancestor of the West. Writing, Reasoning, and*

Religion in Mesopotamia, Elam, and Greece, Chicago: University of Chicago Press, 1–66.

Bottéro, J., Herrenschmidt, C. and Vernant, J.-P. (eds) (2000) *Ancestor of the West. Writing, Reasoning, and Religion in Mesopotamia, Elam, and Greece*, Chicago: University of Chicago Press.

Braidwood, L. S. (1953) *Digging Beyond the Tigris: An American Woman Archeologist's Story of Life on a 'Dig' in the Kurdish Hills of Iraq*, New York: Henry Schuman.

Braidwood, L. S., Braidwood, R. J., Howe, B., Reed, C. A. and Watson, P. J. (eds) (1983) *Prehistoric Archeology along the Zagros Flanks* (Oriental Institute Publications 105) Chicago: Oriental Institute of the University of Chicago.

Braidwood, R. J. (1937) *Mounds in the Plain of Antioch* (Oriental Institute Publications 48) Chicago: University of Chicago Press.

Braidwood, R. J. and Howe, B. (1960) *Prehistoric Investigations in Iraqi Kurdistan* (Studies in Ancient Oriental Civilizations 31) Chicago: University of Chicago Press.

Brinkman, J. A. (1984) 'Settlement surveys and documentary evidence: Regional variation and secular trend in Mesopotamian demography', *Journal of Near Eastern Studies* 43: 169–80.

Britton, R. A. (1997) 'Stuck in the past: Historically oriented archaeology', *Archaeological Review from Cambridge* 14(2): 17–27.

Brusasco, P. (1999–2000) 'Family archives and the social use of space in Old Babylonian houses at Ur', *Mesopotamia* 34–5: 1–173.

Butzer, K. W. (1995) 'Environmental change in the Near East and human impact on the land', in J. M. Sasson (ed.) *Civilizations of the Ancient Near East*, New York: Scribner, 123–51.

Byrd, B. F. (2000) 'Households in transition: Neolithic social organization within Southwest Asia', in I. Kuijt (ed.) *Life in Neolithic Farming Communities: Social Organization, Identity, and Differentiation*, New York: Kluwer Academic/Plenum, 63–98.

Byrne, R. (1987) 'Climatic change and the origins of agriculture', in L. Manzanilla (ed.) *Studies in the Neolithic and Urban Revolutions. The V. Gordon Childe Colloquium, Mexico, 1986* (British Archaeological Reports International Series 349) Oxford: BAR, 21–34.

Cauvin, J. (2000a) *The Birth of the Gods and the Origins of Agriculture*, Cambridge: Cambridge University Press.

——(2000b) 'The symbolic foundations of the neolithic revolution in the Near East', in I. Kuijt (ed.) *Life in Neolithic Farming Communities. Social Organization, Identity, and Differentiation*, New York: Kluwer Academic/Plenum, 235–51.

——(2001) 'Ideology before economy', *Cambridge Archaeological Journal* 11: 106–7.

Charpin, D. (1995) 'The history of ancient Mesopotamia: An overview', in J. M. Sasson (ed.) *Civilizations of the Ancient Near East*, New York: Scribner, 807–29.

Childe, V. G. (1936) *Man Makes Himself*, London: Watts.

——(1952) *New Light on the Most Ancient East*, 4th edn, London: Routledge & Kegan Paul.

Christie, A. (1946) *Come, Tell Me How You Live*, London: The Bodley Head.

Chubb, M. (1957) *City in the Sand*, London: Geoffrey Bles (reissued 1999, London: Libri Publications).

Clutton-Brock, J. (1999) *A Natural History of Domesticated Mammals*, Cambridge: Cambridge University Press.

Cohen, M. N. (1977) *The Food Crisis in Prehistory*, New Haven: Yale University Press.

——(1989) *Health and the Rise of Civilization*, New Haven: Yale University Press.

Collins, P. (2000) *The Uruk Pheonomenon. The Role of Social Ideology in the Expansion of the Uruk Culture during the Fourth Millennium BC* (BAR International Series 900) Oxford: Archaeopress.

Collis, J. (1999) 'The nature of archaeological evidence', in G. Barker (ed.) *Companion Encyclopedia of Archaeology*, London: Routledge, 81–127.

Conrad, G. W. and Demarest, A. A. (1984) *Religion and Empire. The Dynamics of Aztec and Inca Expansionism*, Cambridge: Cambridge University Press.

Cowan, C. W. and Watson, P. J. (1992) 'Introduction', in C. W. Cowan and P. J. Watson (eds) *The Origins of Agriculture. An International Perspective*, Washington DC: Smithsonian Institution, 1–6.

Cowgill, G. L. (1975) 'On causes and consequences of ancient and modern population changes', *American Anthropologist* 77: 505–25.

Cribb, R. (1991a) *Nomads in Archaeology*, Cambridge: Cambridge University Press.

——(1991b) 'Mobile villagers: the structure and organisation of nomadic pastoral campsites in the Near East', in C. S. Gamble and W. A. Boismier (eds) *Ethnoarchaeological Approaches to Mobile Campsites. Hunter-gatherer and Pastoralist Case-studies*, Ann Arbor: International Monographs in Prehistory, 371–93.

Crowley, T. J. and North, G. R. (1991) *Paleoclimatology* (Oxford Monographs on Geology and Geophysics 18) Oxford: Oxford University Press.

Dalley, S. (ed.) (1998) *The Legacy of Mesopotamia*, Oxford: Oxford University Press.

D'Altroy, T. N. (2001a) 'A view of the plains from the mountains', in M. S. Rothman (ed.) *Uruk Mesopotamia and its Neighbors. Cross-Cultural Interactions in the Era of State Formation*, Santa Fe: School of American Research Press, 445–75.

——(2001b) 'Politics, resources, and blood in the Inka empire', in S. E. Alcock, T. N. D'Altroy, K. D. Morrison and C. M. Sinopoli (eds) *Empires. Perspectives from Archaeology and History*, Cambridge: Cambridge University Press, 201–26.

Dant, T. (1999) *Material Culture in the Social World*, Buckingham: Open University Press.

Davis, S. J. M. (1987) *The Archaeology of Animals*, London: Routledge.

Deagan, K. (2001) 'Dynamics of imperial adjustment in Spanish America: Ideology and social integration', in S. E. Alcock, T. N. D'Altroy, K. D. Morrison and C. M. Sinopoli (eds) *Empires. Perspectives from Archaeology and History*, Cambridge: Cambridge University Press, 179–94.

Dewar, R. (1991) 'Incorporating variation in occupation span into settlement-pattern analysis', *American Antiquity* 56: 604–20.

Dincauze, D. F. (2000) *Environmental Archaeology. Principles and Practice*, Cambridge: Cambridge University Press.

Dudgeon, A. G. (2000) *Hidden Victory. The Battle of Habbaniya, May 1941*, Stroud: Tempus.

Duistermaat, K. (2002) 'Two clay sealings', in A. Suleiman and O. Nieuwenhuyse (eds) *Tell Boueid II. A Late Neolithic Village on the Middle Khabur (Syria)* (Subartu XI) Turnhout: Brepols, 149–52.

During, B. (2001) 'Social dimensions in the architecture of Neolithic Çatalhöyük', *Anatolian Studies* 51: 1–18.

Earle, T. (1997) *How Chiefs Come to Power. The Political Economy in Prehistory*, Stanford: Stanford University Press.

Edwards, P. C. (1989) 'Revising the Broad Spectrum Revolution: and its role in the origins of Southwest Asian food production', *Antiquity* 63: 225–46.

Ellis, M. deJ. (1983) 'Correlation of archaeological and written evidence for the study of Mesopotamian institutions and chronology', *American Journal of Archaeology* 87: 497–507.

Emre, K. and Çınaroğlu, A. (1993) 'A group of metal Hittite vessels from Kınık-Kastamonu', in M. J. Mellink, E. Porada and T. Özgüç (eds) *Aspects of Art and Iconography: Anatolia and its Neighbours*, Ankara: Türk Tarih Kurumu, 675–717.

Englund, R. K. (1998) 'Texts from the Late Uruk period', in J. Bauer, R. K. Englund and M. Krebernik, *Mesopotamien. Späturuk-Zeit und Frühdynastische Zeit. Annäherungen 1* (Orbis Biblicus et Orientalis 160/1) Freiburg: Universitätsverlag Freiburg Schweiz, 15–233.

Faulkner, N. (2001/2) 'The Sedgeford project, Norfolk: An experiment in popular participation and dialectical method', *Archaeology International* 5: 16–20.

Feinman, G. M. (1998) 'Scale and social organization: perspectives on the archaic state', in G. M. Feinman and J. Marcus (eds) *Archaic States*, Santa Fe: School of American Research Press, 95–133.

Feinman, G. M. and Marcus, J. (eds) (1998) *Archaic States*, Santa Fe: School of American Research Press.

Finkbeiner, U. (1991) *Uruk Kampagne 35–37, 1982–1984. Die archäologische Oberflächenuntersuchung (Survey)* (Ausgrabungen in Uruk-Warka Endberichte 4) Mainz am Rhein: Philipp von Zabern.

Finkelstein, J. J. (1962) ' "Mesopotamia" ', *Journal of Near Eastern Studies* 21: 73–92.

Flannery, K. V. (1969) 'Origins and ecological effects of early domestication in Iran and the Near East', in P. J. Ucko and G. W. Dimbleby (eds) *The Domestication and Exploitation of Plants and Animals*, London: Duckworth: 73–100.

——(1972) 'The cultural evolution of civilizations', *Annual Review of Ecology and Systematics* 3: 399–426.

——(1998) 'The ground plans of archaic states', in G. M. Feinman and J. Marcus (eds) *Archaic States*, Santa Fe: School of American Research Press, 15–57.

Forest, J.-D. (1993) 'Çatal Hüyük et son décor: pour le déchiffrement d'un code symbolique', *Anatolica Antiqua* 2: 1–42.

——(1994) 'Towards an interpretation of the Çatal Höyük reliefs and paintings', in *1993 Yılı Anadolu Medeniyetleri Müzesi Konferansları*, Ankara: Anatolian Civilizations Museum, 118–36.

Forte, M. and Siliotti, A. (eds) (1997) *Virtual Archaeology*, London: Thames and Hudson.

Foster, B. R. (1993) 'Management and administration in the Sargonic period', in M. Liverani (ed.) *Akkad. The First World Empire* (History of the Ancient Near East Studies 5) Padua: Sargon srl, 25–39.

Frangipane, M. (2001) 'The transition between two opposing forms of power at Arslantepe (Malatya) at the beginning of the 3rd millennium', *Tüba-Ar. Turkish Academy of Sciences Journal of Archaeology* 4: 1–24.

French, D. (1973) *Aşvan 1968 – 1972. An Interim Report* (*Anatolian Studies* 23) London: British Institute of Archaeology at Ankara.

Gamble, C. (1999) *The Palaeolithic Societies of Europe*, Cambridge: Cambridge University Press.

——(2001) *Archaeology: The Basics*, London: Routledge.

Garrard, A., Colledge, S. and Martin, L. (1996) 'The emergence of crop cultivation and caprine herding in the "Marginal Zone" of the southern Levant', in D. R. Harris (ed.) *The Origins and Spread of Agriculture and Pastoralism in Eurasia*, London: UCL Press, 204–26.

Gates, M.-H. (1988) 'Dialogues between ancient Near Eastern texts and the archaeological record: Test cases from Bronze Age Syria', *Bulletin of the American Schools of Oriental Research* 270: 63–91.

Gellner, E. (1992) *Postmodernism, Reason and Religion*, London: Routledge.

Gibson, McG. (1972) *The City and Area of Kish*, Miami: Field Research Projects.

Gibson, McG. and McMahon, A. (1995) 'Investigation of the Early Dynastic-Akkadian transition: Report of the 18th and 19th seasons of excavation in Area WF, Nippur', *Iraq* 57: 1–39.

Giddens, A. (2001) *Sociology*, 4th edn, Cambridge: Polity Press.

George, A. R. (1997) 'Assyria and the Western World', in S. Parpola and R. M. Whiting (eds) *Assyria 1995*, Helsinki: The Neo-Assyrian Text Corpus Project, 69–75.

Goring-Morris, N. and Belfer-Cohen, A. (1997) 'The articulation of cultural processes and Late Quaternary environmental changes in Cisjordan', *Paléorient* 23(2): 71–93.

Green, A. (ed.) (1993) *The 6G Ash-Tip and its Contents: Cultic and Administrative Discard from the Temple?* (Abu Salabikh Excavations 4) London: British School of Archaeology in Iraq.

Grégoire, J.-P. (1999) 'Major units for the transformation of grain', in P. C. Anderson (ed.) *Prehistory of Agriculture. New Experimental and Ethnographic*

Approaches (Institute of Archaeology Monograph 40) Los Angeles: UCLA, Institute of Archaeology, 223–37.

Groube, L. (1996) 'The impact of diseases upon the emergence of agriculture', in D. R. Harris (ed.) *The Origins and Spread of Agriculture and Pastoralism in Eurasia*, London: UCL Press, 101–29.

Gurney, O. R. (1979) 'The Hittite empire', in M. T. Larsen (ed.) *Power and Propaganda. A Symposium on Ancient Empires* (Mesopotamia Copenhagen Studies in Assyriology 7) Copenhagen: Akademisk Forlag, 151–65.

Hamza, K. (2000) *Saddam's Bombmaker*, New York: Simon and Schuster.

Handcock, P. S. P. (1912) *Mesopotamian Archaeology. An Introduction to the Archaeology of Babylonia and Assyria*, London: Macmillan.

Hanson, J. (1998) *Decoding Homes and Houses*, Cambridge: Cambridge University Press.

Harris, D. R. (1996) 'Preface', in D. R. Harris (ed.) *The Origins and Spread of Agriculture and Pastoralism in Eurasia*, London: UCL Press, ix–xi.

Hassan, F. A. (1997) 'Beyond the surface: Comments on Hodder's "reflexive excavation methodology"', *Antiquity* 71: 1020–5.

Hauptmann, H. (1999) 'The Urfa region', in M. Özdoğan and N. Başgelen (eds) *Neolithic in Turkey. The Cradle of Civilization. New Discoveries*, Istanbul: Arkeoloji ve Sanat, 65–86.

Hayden, B. (1992) 'Models of domestication', in A. B. Gebauer and T. D. Price (eds) *Transitions to Agriculture in Prehistory* (Monographs in World Archaeology 4) Madison: Prehistory Press, 11–19.

——(1995) 'A new overview of domestication', in T. D. Price and A. B. Gebauer (eds) *Last Hunters – First Farmers. New Perspectives on the Prehistoric Transition to Agriculture*, Santa Fe: School of American Research Press, 273–99.

Heinz, M. (1997) 'How town plans reflect society', *Archaeological Review from Cambridge* 14(2): 23–44.

Helbaek, H. (1960) 'The palaeoethnobotany of the Near East and Europe', in R. J. Braidwood and B. Howe (eds) *Prehistoric Investigations in Iraqi Kurdistan* (Studies in Oriental Civilization 31) Chicago: University of Chicago Press, 99–118.

——(1969) 'Plant-collecting, dry-farming, and irrigation agriculture in prehistoric Deh Luran', in F. Hole, K. V. Flannery and J. A. Neely (eds) *Prehistory and Human Ecology of the Deh Luran Plain* (Museum of Anthropology Memoir 1) Ann Arbor: University of Michigan, 383–426.

Henrickson, E. F. (1981) 'Non-religious residential settlement patterning in the late Early Dynastic of the Diyala region', *Mesopotamia* 16: 43–140.

——(1982) 'Functional analysis of elite residences in the late Early Dynastic of the Diyala region', *Mesopotamia* 17: 5–33.

Henrickson, E. F. and Thuesen, I. (eds) (1989) *Upon this Foundation. The 'Ubaid Reconsidered*, Copenhagen: Museum Tusculanum Press.

Henry, D. O. (1989) *From Foraging to Agriculture. The Levant at the End of the Ice Age*, Philadelphia: University of Pennsylvania Press.

Herrenschmidt, C. (2000) 'Elamite civilization and writing', in J. Bottéro, C. Herrenschmidt and J.-P. Vernant (eds) *Ancestor of the West. Writing, Reasoning, and Religion in Mesopotamia, Elam, and Greece*, Chicago: University of Chicago Press, 69–89.

Hillier, B. and Hanson, J. (1984) *The Social Logic of Space*, Cambridge: Cambridge University Press.

Hillman, G. C. and Davies, M. S. (1999) 'Domestication rate in wild wheats and barley under primitive cultivation', in P. C. Anderson (ed.) *Prehistory of Agriculture. New Experimental and Ethnographic Approaches* (Institute of Archaeology Monograph 40) Los Angeles: University of California Press, 70–102.

Hillman, G. C. and Moulins, D. de (2000) 'The plant food economy of Abu Hureyra 1 and 2', in A. M. T. Moore, G. C. Hillman and A. J. Legge *Village on the Euphrates. From Foraging to Farming at Abu Hureyra*, Oxford: Oxford University Press: 327–422.

Hodder, I. (1990) *The Domestication of Europe. Structure and Contingency in Neolithic Societies*, Oxford: Blackwell.

——(1997) ' "Always momentary, fluid and flexible": Towards a reflexive excavation methodology', *Antiquity* 71: 691–700.

——(1998) 'Whose rationality? A response to Fekri Hassan', *Antiquity* 72: 213–17.

——(1999) *The Archaeological Process. An Introduction*, Oxford: Blackwell.

——(2001) 'Symbolism and the origins of agriculture in the Near East', *Cambridge Archaeological Journal* 11: 107–12.

Hodder, I. (ed.) (2000) *Towards Reflexive Methodology in Archaeology: The Example at Çatalhöyük*, Cambridge: McDonald Institute for Archaeological Research and British Institute of Archaeology at Ankara.

Hole, F. (1974) 'Tepe Tūlā'ī: An early campsite in Khuzistan, Iran', *Paléorient* 2: 219–42.

——(1979) 'Rediscovering the past in the present: Ethnoarchaeology in Luristan, Iran', in C. Kramer (ed.) *Ethnoarchaeology. Implications of Ethnography for Archaeology*, New York: Columbia University Press, 192–218.

——(1980) 'Archaeological survey in Southwest Asia', *Paléorient* 6(1): 21–44.

——(1995) 'Assessing the past through anthropological archaeology', in J. M. Sasson (ed.) *Civilizations of the Ancient Near East*, New York: Scribner, 2715–27.

——(1996) 'The context of caprine domestication in the Zagros region', in D. R. Harris (ed.) *The Origins and Spread of Agriculture and Pastoralism in Eurasia*, London: UCL Press, 263–81.

——(1999) 'Cultural anthropology in the Near East: Archaeological applications', in H. Kühne, R. Bernbeck and K. Bartl (eds) *Fluchtpunkt Uruk. Archäologische Einheit aus Methodischer Vielfalt. Schriften für Hans Jörg Nissen* (Internationale Archäologie Studia Honoria 6) Rahden: Verlag Marie Leidorf, 53–60.

Hourani, A. (1991) *A History of the Arab Peoples*, London: Faber and Faber.

Huot, J.-L. (1989) ''Ubaidian villages of lower Mesopotamia. Permanence and evolution from 'Ubaid 0 to 'Ubaid 4 as seen from Tell el'Ouelli', in E. F. Henrickson and I. Thuesen (eds) *Upon this Foundation. The 'Ubaid Reconsidered*, Copenhagen: Museum Tusculanum Press: 19–42.

Ingold, T. (1996) 'Growing plants and raising animals: An anthropological perspective on domestication', in D. R. Harris (ed.) *The Origins and Spread of Agriculture and Pastoralism in Eurasia*, London: UCL Press, 12–24.

Invernizzi, A. (2000) 'Discovering Babylon with Pietro Della Valle', in P. Matthiae, A. Enea, L. Peyronel and F. Pinnock (eds) *Proceedings of the First International Congress on the Archaeology of the Ancient Near East*, Rome: Università degli Studi di Roma 'La Sapienza', 643–9.

Jacobsen, T. (1995) 'Searching for Sumer and Akkad', in J. M. Sasson (ed.) *Civilizations of the Ancient Near East*, New York: Scribner, 2743–52.

Janssen, C. (1996) 'When the house is on fire and the children are gone', in K. R. Veenhof (ed.) *Houses and Households in Ancient Mesopotamia* (papers read at the 40e Rencontre Assyriologique Internationale Leiden, 5–8 July 1993) Leiden: Nederlands Historisch-Archaeologisch Instituut te Istanbul, 237–46.

Johnson, G. A. (1972) 'A test of the utility of central place theory in archaeology', in P. J. Ucko, R. Tringham and G. W. Dimbleby (eds) *Man, Settlement and Urbanism*, London: Duckworth, 769–85.

——(1975) 'Locational analysis and the investigation of Uruk local exchange systems', in J. A. Sabloff and C. C. Lamberg-Karlovsky (eds) *Ancient Civilization and Trade*, Albuquerque: University of New Mexico Press, 285–339.

Kepinski-Lecomte, C. (1996) 'Spatial occupation of a new town Haradum (Iraqi Middle Euphrates, 11th–17th centuries BC)', in K. R. Veenhof (ed.) *Houses and Households in Ancient Mesopotamia* (papers read at the 40e Rencontre Assyriologique Internationale Leiden, 5–8 July 1993) Leiden: Nederlands Historisch-Archaeologisch Instituut te Istanbul, 191–6.

Kessler, K. (1997) ' "Royal roads" and other questions of the Neo-Assyrian communication system', in S. Parpola and R. M. Whiting (eds) *Assyria 1995*, Helsinki: The Neo-Assyrian Text Corpus Project, 129–36.

Kirkbride, D. (1982) 'Umm Dabaghiyah', in J. E. Curtis (ed.) *Fifty Years of Mesopotamian Discovery*, London: British School of Archaeology in Iraq, 11–21.

Kletter, R. and De-Groot, A. (2001) 'Excavating to excess? Implications of the last decade of archaeology in Israel', *Journal of Mediterranean Archaeology* 14: 76–85.

Kohl, P. L. (1975) 'The archaeology of trade', *Dialectical Anthropology* 1: 43–50.

——(1989) 'The material culture of the modern era in the ancient Orient: Suggestions for future work', in D. Miller, M. Rowlands and C. Tilley (eds) *Domination and Resistance* (One World Archaeology 3) London: Unwin Hyman, 240–5.

Kohlmeyer, K. (1981) ' "Wovon man nicht sprechen kann" – Grenzen der Interpretation von bei Oberflächenforschungen gewonnenen archäologischen Informationen', *Mitteilungen der Deutschen Orient-Gesellschaft zu Berlin* 113: 53–79.

——(1996) 'Houses in Habuba Kabira-South. Spatial organisation and planning of Late Uruk residential architecture', in K. R. Veenhof (ed.) *Houses and Households in Ancient Mesopotamia* (papers read at the 40e Rencontre Assyriologique Internationale Leiden, 5–8 July 1993) Leiden: Nederlands Historisch-Archaeologisch Instituut te Istanbul, 89–103.

Koldewey, R. (1914) *The Excavations at Babylon*, London: Macmillan.

Kose, A. (2000) 'Das "Palas" auf Tell A von Girsu – Wohnstätte eines hellenistisch-parthischen Sammlers von Gudeastatuen?', *Baghdader Mitteilungen* 31: 377–431.

Kuhrt, A. (2001) 'The Achaemenid Persian empire (*c*.550–*c*.330 BCE): Continuities, adaptations, transformations', in S. E. Alcock, T. N. D'Altroy, K. D. Morrison and C. M. Sinopoli (eds) *Empires. Perspectives from Archaeology and History*, Cambridge: Cambridge University Press, 93–123.

Lamberg-Karlovsky, C. C. (1996) 'The archaeological evidence for international commerce: Public and/or private enterprise in Mesopotamia?', in M. Hudson and B. A. Levine (eds) *Privatization in the Ancient Near East and Classical World* (Peabody Museum Bulletin 5) Cambridge MA: Peabody Museum of Archaeology and Ethnology, Harvard University, 73–108.

——(1999) 'Households, land tenure, and communication systems in the 6th–4th millennia of Greater Mesopotamia', in M. Hudson and B. A. Levine (eds) *Urbanization and Land Ownership in the Ancient Near East* (Peabody Museum Bulletin 7) Cambridge MA: Peabody Museum of Archaeology and Ethnology, Harvard University: 167–201.

Lampl, P. (1968) *Cities and Planning in the Ancient Near East*, London: Studio Vista.

Larsen, M. T. (1979) 'The tradition of empire in Mesopotamia', in M. T. Larsen (ed.) *Power and Propaganda. A Symposium on Ancient Empires* (Mesopotamia Copenhagen Studies in Assyriology 7) Copenhagen: Akademisk Forlag: 75–103.

——(1989) 'Orientalism and Near Eastern archaeology', in D. Miller, M. Rowlands and C. Tilley (eds) *Domination and Resistance* (One World Archaeology 3) London: Unwin Hyman, 229–39.

——(1996) *The Conquest of Assyria: Excavations in an Antique Land, 1840–1860*, New York: Routledge.

Lebeau, M. (1996) 'Les maisons de Melebiya. Approche fonctionelle de l'habitat privé au IIIe millénaire av. notre ère en Haute Mésopotamie', in K. R. Veenhof (ed.) *Houses and Households in Ancient Mesopotamia* (papers read at the 40e Rencontre Assyriologique Internationale Leiden, 5–8 July 1993) Leiden: Nederlands Historisch-Archaeologisch Instituut te Istanbul, 129–36.

Lees, S. H. and Bates, D. G. (1974) 'The origins of specialized nomadic pastoralism: A systemic model', *American Antiquity* 39: 187–93.

Legge, A. J. (1996) 'The beginning of caprine domestication in Southwest Asia', in D. R. Harris (ed.) *The Origins and Spread of Agriculture and Pastoralism in Eurasia*, London: UCL Press, 238–62.

Legge, A. J. and Rowley-Conwy, P. A. (2000) 'The exploitation of animals', in A. M. T. Moore, G. C. Hillman and A. J. Legge (eds) *Village on the Euphrates. From Foraging to Farming at Abu Hureyra*, Oxford: Oxford University Press: 423–71.

Lightfoot, K. G. and Martinez, A. (1995) 'Frontiers and boundaries in archaeological perspective', *Annual Review of Anthropology* 24: 471–92.

Liverani, M. (1973) 'Memorandum on the approach to historiographic texts', *Orientalia* 42: 178–94.

——(1979) 'The ideology of the Assyrian empire', in M. T. Larsen (ed.) *Power and Propaganda. A Symposium on Ancient Empires* (Mesopotamia Copenhagen Studies in Assyriology 7) Copenhagen: Akademisk Forlag, 297–317.

——(1988) *Antico Oriente. Storia Società Economia*, Rome: Editori Laterza.

——(1993) 'Akkad: An introduction', in M. Liverani (ed.) *Akkad. The First World Empire* (History of the Ancient Near East Studies 5) Padua: Sargon srl, 1–10.

——(1996) '2084: Ancient propaganda and historical criticism', in J. S. Cooper and G. M. Schwartz (eds) *The Study of the Ancient Near East in the 21st Century*, Winona Lake: Eisenbrauns, 283–9.

——(1997) 'Ancient Near Eastern cities and modern ideologies', in G. Wilhelm (ed.) *Die Orientalische Stadt: Kontinuität, Wandel, Bruch*, Saarbrücken: Saarbrücker Druckerei und Verlag, 85–107.

——(1999) 'History and archaeology in the ancient Near East: 150 years of a difficult relationship', in H. Kühne, R. Bernbeck and K. Bartl (eds) *Fluchtpunkt Uruk. Archäologische Einheit aus Methodischer Vielfalt. Schriften für Hans Jörg Nissen* (Internationale Archäologie Studia Honoria 6) Rahden: Verlag Marie Leidorf, 1–11.

——(2001) 'The fall of the Assyrian empire: Ancient and modern interpretations', in S. E. Alcock, T. N. D'Altroy, K. D. Morrison and C. M. Sinopoli (eds.) *Empires. Perspectives from Archaeology and History*, Cambridge: Cambridge University Press, 374–91.

Lloyd, S. (1938) 'Some ancient sites in the Sinjar district', *Iraq* 5: 123–42.

——(1947) *Foundations in the Dust*, Harmondsworth: Penguin (reissued 1980, London: Thames and Hudson).

——(1956) *Early Anatolia*, Harmondsworth: Penguin.

——(1963) *Mounds of the Near East*, Edinburgh: Edinburgh University Press.

——(1969) 'Back to Ingharra. Some further thoughts on the excavations at East Kish', *Iraq* 31: 40–8.

——(1978) *The Archaeology of Mesopotamia from the Old Stone Age to the Persian Conquest*, London: Thames and Hudson.

——(1986) *The Interval. A Life in Near Eastern Archaeology*, Faringdon: Lloyd Collon.

Lucas, G. (2001a) 'Destruction and the rhetoric of excavation', *Norwegian Archaeological Review* 34: 35–46.

——(2001b) *Critical Approaches to Fieldwork. Contemporary and Historical Archaeological Practice*, London: Routledge.

Lumsden, S. (2000) 'On Sennacherib's Nineveh', in P. Matthiae, A. Enea, L. Peyronel and F. Pinnock (eds.) *Proceedings of the First International Congress on the Archaeology of the Ancient Near East*, Rome: Università degli Studi di Roma 'La Sapienza', 815–34.

——(2001) 'Power and identity in the Neo-Assyrian world', in I. Nielsen (ed.) *The Royal Palace Institution in the First Millennium BC* (Monographs of the Danish Institute at Athens 4) Aarhus: Aarhus University Press, 33–51.

Lyman, R. L., O'Brien, M. J. and Dunnell, R. C. (1997) *The Rise and Fall of Culture History*, New York: Plenum Press.

McCorriston, J. (2001) 'Comments on G. Algaze, "Initial social complexity in Southwestern Asia. The Mesopotamian advantage" ', *Current Anthropology* 42: 221–2.

McCorriston, J. and Hole, F. (1991) 'The ecology of seasonal stress and the origins of agriculture in the Near East', *American Anthropologist* 93: 46–69.

McGuire, R. H. (1983) 'Breaking down cultural complexity: Inequality and heterogeneity', in M. B. Schiffer (ed.) *Advances in Archaeological Method and Theory Volume 6*, New York: Academic Press, 91–142.

McNab, A. (1993) *Bravo Two Zero*, London: Bantam Press.

Mahdi, M. (1964) *Ibn Khaldûn's Philosophy of History*, Chicago: University of Chicago Press.

Mallowan, M. E. L. (1936) 'The excavations at Tall Chagar Bazar and an archaeological survey of the Habur region, 1934–5', *Iraq* 3: 1–86.

Malville, N. J. (2001) 'Long-distance transport of bulk goods in the pre-Hispanic American Southwest', *Journal of Anthropological Archaeology* 20: 230–43.

Mann, M. (1986) *The Sources of Social Power*, Cambridge: Cambridge University Press.

Marcus, J. (1998) 'The peaks and valleys of ancient states: An extension of the dynamic model', in G. M. Feinman and J. Marcus (eds) *Archaic States*, Santa Fe: School of American Research Press, 59–94.

Marcus, J. and Feinman, G. M. (1998) 'Introduction', in G. M. Feinman and J. Marcus (eds) *Archaic States*, Santa Fe: School of American Research Press, 3–13.

Masry, A. H. (1981) 'Traditions of archaeological research in the Near East', *World Archaeology* 13: 222–39.

Matheson, S. (1961) *Time off to Dig. Archaeology and Adventure in Remote Afghanistan*, London: Odhams Press.

Matthews, R. J. (1993) *Cities, Seals and Writing: Archaic Seal Impressions from Jemdet Nasr and Ur* (Materialien zu den frühen Schriftzeugnissen des Vorderen Orients 2) Berlin: Gebr. Mann.

——(1994) 'Imperial catastrophe or local incident? An Akkadian hoard from Tell Brak, Syria', *Cambridge Archaeological Journal* 4: 290–302.

——(1996a) 'Systematic surface collection', in I. Hodder (ed.) *On the Surface: Çatalhöyük 1993–95*, Cambridge: McDonald Institute for Archaeological Research and British Institute of Archaeology at Ankara, 73–7.

——(1996b) 'Surface scraping and planning', in I. Hodder (ed.) *On the Surface: Çatalhöyük 1993–95*, Cambridge: McDonald Institute for Archaeological Research and British Institute of Archaeology at Ankara, 79–99.

——(1999/2000) 'Hittites and "barbarians" in the late Bronze Age: Regional survey in northern Turkey', *Archaeology International* 3: 32–5.

——(2000a) *The Early Prehistory of Mesopotamia, 500,000 to 4,500 BC* (Subartu V) Turnhout: Brepols.

——(2000b) 'Time with the past in Paphlagonia', in P. Matthiae, A. Enea, L. Peyronel and F. Pinnock (eds) *Proceedings of the First International Congress on the Archaeology of the Ancient Near East*, Rome: Università degli Studi di Roma 'La Sapienza', 1013–27.

——(2002) *Secrets of the Dark Mound. Excavations at Jemdet Nasr 1926–1928* (Iraq Archaeological Reports 6) London: British School of Archaeology in Iraq.

——(in press) *Exploring a Regional Centre in Upper Mesopotamia, 1994–1996* (Excavations at Tell Brak 4) Cambridge: McDonald Institute and British School of Archaeology in Iraq.

Matthews, R. J. and Postgate, J. N. (1987) 'Excavations at Abu Salabikh, 1985–86', *Iraq* 49: 91–119.

Matthews, W. and Postgate, J. N. (1994) 'The imprint of living in an early Mesopotamian city: Questions and answers', in R. Luff and P. Rowley-Conwy (eds) *Whither Environmental Archaeology?* (Oxbow Monograph 38) Oxford: Oxbow, 171–212.

Matthews, W., French, C. A. I., Lawrence, T., Cutler, D. F. and Jones, M. K. (1997) 'Microstratigraphic traces of site formation processes and human activities: High definition archaeology', *World Archaeology* 29(2): 281–308.

Meadow, R. H. and Zeder, M. A. (eds) (1978) *Approaches to Faunal Analysis in the Middle East* (Peabody Museum Bulletin 2) Cambridge MA: Peabody Museum of Archaeology and Ethnology, Harvard University.

Mellaart, J. (1967) *Çatal Hüyük. A Neolithic Town in Anatolia*, London: Thames and Hudson.

Michalowski, P. (1991) 'Charisma and control: On continuity and change in early Mesopotamian bureaucratic systems', in McG. Gibson and R. D. Biggs (eds) *The Organization of Power. Aspects of Bureaucracy in the Ancient Near East* (Studies in Ancient Oriental Civilization 46) 2nd edn, Chicago: University of Chicago Press, 45–57.

——(1993) 'Memory and deed: The historiography of the political expansion of the Akkad state', in M. Liverani (ed.) *Akkad. The First World Empire* (History of the Ancient Near East Studies 5) Padua: Sargon srl, 69–90.

Miller, N. F. (1992) 'The origins of plant cultivation in the Near East', in C. W. Cowan and P. J. Watson (eds) *The Origins of Agriculture. An International Perspective*, Washington DC: Smithsonian Institution: 39–58.

Miller, N. F. and Smart, T. L. (1984) 'Intentional burning of dung as fuel: A mechanism for the incorporation of charred seeds into the archeological record', *Journal of Ethnobiology* 4: 15–28.

Molleson, T. I. (2000) 'The people of Abu Hureyra', in A. M. T. Moore, G. C. Hillman and A J. Legge (eds) *Village on the Euphrates. From Foraging to Farming at Abu Hureyra*, Oxford: Oxford University Press, 301–24.

Moore, A. M. T. and Hillman, G. C. (1992) 'The Pleistocene to Holocene transition and human economy in Southwest Asia: The impact of the Younger Dryas', *American Antiquity* 57: 482–94.

Moore, A. M. T., Hillman, G. C. and Legge, A. J. (eds) (2000) *Village on the Euphrates. From Foraging to Farming at Abu Hureyra*, Oxford: Oxford University Press.

Moorey, P. R. S. (1980) *Cemeteries of the First Millennium BC at Deve Höyük* (BAR International Series 87) Oxford: British Archaeological Reports.

——(1994) *Ancient Mesopotamian Materials and Industries. The Archaeological Evidence*, Oxford: Clarendon Press.

Moreland, J. (2001) *Archaeology and Text*, London: Duckworth.

Morris, I. (1997) 'Archaeology as cultural history', *Archaeological Review from Cambridge* 14(1): 3–16.

——(2000) *Archaeology as Cultural History: Words and Things in Iron Age Greece*, Oxford: Blackwell.

Muscarella, O. W. (1998) 'Relations between Phrygia and Assyria in the 8th century BC', in H. Erkanal, V. Donbaz and A. Uğuroğlu (eds) *XXXIV. International Assyriology Congress*, Ankara: Türk Tarih Kurumu, 149–57.

Nemet-Nejat, K. R. (1998) *Daily Life in Ancient Mesopotamia*, Westport: Greenwood Press.

Niknami, K. A. (2000) *Methodological Aspects of Iranian Archaeology: Past and Present* (British Archaeological Reports International Series 852) Oxford: Archaeopress.

Nissen, H. J. (1988) *The Early History of the Ancient Near East 9000–2000 BC*, Chicago: University of Chicago Press.

——(1993) 'Settlement patterns and material culture of the Akkadian period: Continuity and discontinuity', in M. Liverani (ed.) *Akkad. The First World Empire* (History of the Ancient Near East Studies 5) Padua: Sargon srl, 91–106.

——(1995) 'Ancient Western Asia before the age of empires', in J. M. Sasson (ed.) *Civilizations of the Ancient Near East*, New York: Scribner, 791–806.

——(2001) 'Cultural and political networks in the ancient Near East during the fourth and third millennia BC', in M. S. Rothman (ed.) *Uruk Mesopotamia and its Neighbors. Cross-Cultural Interactions in the Era of State Formation*, Santa Fe: School of American Research Press, 149–79.

Northedge, A. (1997) 'Samarra: Islamic period', in E. M. Meyers (ed.) *The Oxford Encyclopedia of Archaeology in the Near East 4*, Oxford: Oxford University Press: 473–6.

Oakes, L. (1994) *Teaching the Assyrians at Key Stage 2*, London: The Historical Association.

——(2001) *Step into…Ancient Mesopotamia*, London: Lorenz Books.

Oppenheim, A. L. (1977) *Ancient Mesopotamia. Portrait of a Dead Civilization*, revised edn, Chicago: University of Chicago Press.

Özdoğan, M. (1998) 'Ideology and archaeology in Turkey', in L. Meskell (ed.) *Archaeology Under Fire. Nationalism, Politics and Heritage in the Eastern Mediterranean and Middle East*, London: Routledge, 111–23.

Özgüç, T. (1978) *Excavations at Maşat Höyük and Investigations in its Vicinity*, Ankara: Türk Tarih Kurumu.

Pallis, S. A. (1956) *The Antiquity of Iraq*, Copenhagen: Ejnar Munksgaard.

Parker, B. J. (1997) 'The northern frontier of Assyria: An archaeological perspective', in S. Parpola and R. M. Whiting (eds) *Assyria 1995*, Helsinki: The Neo-Assyrian Text Corpus Project, 217–44.

Parpola, S. (2000) 'The Mesopotamian soul of Western culture', *Bulletin of the Canadian Society for Mesopotamian Studies* 35: 29–34.

Parrot, A. (1946) *Archéologie mésopotamienne. Les étapes*, Paris: Albin Michel.

——(1953) *Archéologie mésopotamienne. Technique et problèmes*, Paris: Albin Michel.

Peebles, C. S. and Kus, S. M. (1977) 'Some archaeological correlates of ranked societies', *American Antiquity* 42: 421–48.

Peltenburg, E. (2000) 'From nucleation to dispersal. Late third millennium BC settlement pattern transformations in the Near East and Aegean', in O. Rouault and M. Wäfler (eds) *La Djéziré et l'Euphrate Syriens de la protohistoire à la fin du IIe millénaire av. JC* (Subartu VII) Turnhout: Brepols, 183–206.

Perkins, A. (1949) *The Comparative Archeology of Early Mesopotamia* (Studies in Ancient Oriental Civilization 25) Chicago: University of Chicago Press.

Peters, J., Helmer, D., von den Driesch, A. and Saña Segui, M. (1999) 'Early animal husbandry in the northern Levant', *Paléorient* 25(2): 27–47.

Pfälzner, P. (1996) 'Activity areas and the social organisation of third millennium BC households', in K. R. Veenhof (ed.) *Houses and Households in Ancient Mesopotamia* (papers read at the 40e Rencontre Assyriologique Internationale Leiden, 5–8 July 1993) Leiden: Nederlands Historisch-Archaeologisch Instituut te Istanbul, 117–27.

Pittman, H. (2001) 'Mesopotamian intraregional relations reflected through glyptic evidence in the Late Chalcolithic 1–5 periods', in M. S. Rothman (ed.) *Uruk Mesopotamia and its Neighbors. Cross-Cultural Interactions in the Era of State Formation*, Santa Fe: School of American Research Press, 403–43.

Pollock, S. (1983) 'Style and information: An analysis of Susiana ceramics', *Journal of Anthropological Archaeology* 2: 354–90.

——(1992) 'Bureaucrats and managers, peasants and pastoralists, imperialists and traders: Research on the Uruk and Jemdet Nasr periods in Mesopotamia', *Journal of World Prehistory* 6: 297–336.

——(1999) *Ancient Mesopotamia*, Cambridge: Cambridge University Press.

——(2001) 'The Uruk period in southern Mesopotamia', in M. S. Rothman (ed.) *Uruk Mesopotamia and its Neighbors. Cross-Cultural Interactions in the Era of State Formation*, Santa Fe: School of American Research Press, 181–231.

Pollock, S. and Lutz, C. (1994) 'Archaeology deployed for the Gulf War', *Critique of Anthropology* 14: 263–84.

Postgate, J. N. (1979) 'The economic structure of the Assyrian empire', in M. T. Larsen (ed.) *Power and Propaganda. A Symposium on Ancient Empires* (Mesopotamia Copenhagen Studies in Assyriology 7) Copenhagen: Akademisk Forlag, 193–221.

——(1982) 'Abu Salabikh', in J. Curtis (ed.) *Fifty Years of Mesopotamian Discovery*, London: British School of Archaeology in Iraq, 48–61.

——(1986) 'The transition from Uruk to Early Dynastic: Continuities and discontinuities in the record of settlement', in U. Finkbeiner and W. Röllig (eds) *Ǧamdat Nasr: Period or Regional Style?* (Beihefte zum Tübinger Atlas des Vorderen Orients B62) Wiesbaden: Ludwig Reichert, 90–106.

——(1990a) 'Archaeology and the texts – bridging the gap', *Zeitschrift für Assyriologie und Vorderasiatische Archäologie* 80: 228–40.

——(1990b) 'Excavations at Abu Salabikh, 1988–89', *Iraq* 52: 95–106.

——(1992) *Early Mesopotamia. Society and Economy at the Dawn of History*, London: Routledge.

——(1992–93) 'A Sumerian city: Town and country in the 3rd millennium BC', *Scienze dell'Antichità Storia Archaeologia Antropologia* 6–7: 409–35.

——(1994a) 'In search of the first empires', *Bulletin of the American Schools of Oriental Research* 293: 1–13.

——(1994b) 'How many Sumerians per hectare? – Probing the anatomy of an early city', *Cambridge Archaeological Journal* 4: 47–65.

Postgate, J. N. and Payne, S. (1975) 'Some Old Babylonian shepherds and their flocks', *Journal of Semitic Studies* 20: 1–21.

Postgate, J. N. and Powell, M. (eds) (1988) *Irrigation and Cultivation in Mesopotamia Part I (Bulletin on Sumerian Agriculture* 4) Cambridge: Sumerian Agriculture Group.

Postgate, J. N., Wang, T. and Wilkinson, T. (1995) 'The evidence for early writing: Utilitarian or ceremonial?', *Antiquity* 69: 459–80.

Potts, D. T. (1997) *Mesopotamian Civilization. The Material Foundations*, Ithaca NY: Cornell University Press.

Price, T. D. and Gebauer, A. B. (1995) 'New perspectives on the transition to agriculture', in T. D. Price and A. B. Gebauer (eds) *Last Hunters – First Farmers. New Perspectives on the Prehistoric Transition to Agriculture*, Santa Fe: School of American Research Press, 3–19.

Pumpelly, R. (1908) *Explorations in Turkestan. Expedition of 1904. Prehistoric Civilizations of Anau*, Washington DC: Carnegie Institution.

Reade, J. (1979) 'Ideology and propaganda in Assyrian art', in M. T. Larsen (ed.) *Power and Propaganda. A Symposium on Ancient Empires* (Mesopotamia Copenhagen Studies in Assyriology 7) Copenhagen: Akademisk Forlag, 329–43.

——(1993) 'Hormuzd Rassam and his discoveries', *Iraq* 55: 39–62.

Redman, C. L. (1978) *The Rise of Civilization. From Early Farmers to Urban Society in the Ancient Near East*, San Francisco: W. H. Freeman.

——(1982) 'Archaeological survey and the study of Mesopotamian urban systems', *Journal of Field Archaeology* 9: 375–82.

Reitz, E. J. and Wing, E. S. (1999) *Zooarchaeology* (Cambridge Manuals in Archaeology) Cambridge: Cambridge University Press.

Renfrew, C. and Bahn, P. (2000) *Archaeology. Theories, Methods and Practice*, 3rd edn, London: Thames and Hudson.

Richardson, P. J., Boyd, R. and Bettinger, R. L. (2001) 'Was agriculture impossible during the Pleistocene but mandatory during the Holocene? A climate change hypothesis', *American Antiquity* 66: 387–411.

Rindos, D. (1980) 'Symbiosis, instability, and the origins and spread of agriculture: A new model', *Current Anthropology* 21: 751–72.

Roaf, M. (1989) 'Social organization and social activities at Tell Madhhur', in E. F. Henrickson and I. Thuesen (eds) *Upon this Foundation – the 'Ubaid Reconsidered*, Copenhagen: Museum Tusculanum Press, 91–146.

——(1990) *Cultural Atlas of Mesopotamia and the Ancient Near East*, Oxford: Facts on File.

Roaf, M. and Killick, R. (1987) 'A mysterious affair of styles: The Ninevite 5 pottery of northern Mesopotamia', *Iraq* 49: 199–230.

Roberts, N. (1998) *The Holocene. An Environmental History*, Oxford: Blackwell.

Roberts, N., Boyer, P. and Parish, R. (1996) 'Preliminary results of geoarchaeological investigations at Çatalhöyük', in I. Hodder (ed.) *On the Surface: Çatalhöyük 1993–95*, Cambridge: McDonald Institute for Archaeological Research and British Institute of Archaeology at Ankara, 19–40.

Rosenberg, M. (1999) 'Hallan Çemi', in M. Özdoğan and N. Başgelen (eds) *Neolithic in Turkey. The Cradle of Civilization. New Discoveries*, Istanbul: Arkeoloji ve Sanat, 25–33.

Rosenberg, M. and Redding, R. W. (2000) 'Hallan Çemi and early village organization in eastern Anatolia', in I. Kuijt (ed.) *Life in Neolithic Farming Communities. Social Organization, Identity, and Differentiation*, New York: Kluwer Academic/Plenum, 39–61.

Rosenberg, M., Nesbitt, R., Redding, R. W. and Peasnall, B. (1998) 'Hallan Çemi, pig husbandry, and post-Pleistocene adaptations along the Taurus-Zagros arc (Turkey)', *Paléorient* 24(1): 25–41.

Rosenberg, M., Nesbitt, R. M., Redding, R. W. and Strasser, T. F. (1995) 'Hallan Çemi Tepesi: Some preliminary observations concerning Early Neolithic subsistence behaviors in eastern Anatolia', *Anatolica* 21: 1–12.

Rosenthal, F. (1968) *A History of Muslim Historiography*, Leiden: E. J. Brill.

Roskams, S. (2001) *Excavation*, Cambridge: Cambridge University Press.

Rothman, M. S. (1994) 'Introduction part I. Evolutionary typologies and cultural complexity', in G. Stein and M. S. Rothman (eds) *Chiefdoms and Early States in the Near East. The Organizational Dynamics of Complexity* (Monographs in World Archaeology 18) Madison: Prehistory Press, 1–10.

——(ed.) (2001a) *Uruk Mesopotamia and its Neighbors. Cross-Cultural Interactions in the Era of State Formation*, Santa Fe: School of American Research Press.

——(2001b) 'The Tigris piedmont, eastern Jazira, and highland western Iran in the fourth millennium BC', in M. S. Rothman (ed.) *Uruk Mesopotamia and its Neighbors. Cross-Cultural Interactions in the Era of State Formation*, Santa Fe: School of American Research Press, 349–401.

Rowton, M. B. (1973) 'Urban autonomy in a nomadic environment', *Journal of Near Eastern Studies* 32: 201–15.

——(1981) 'Economic and political factors in ancient nomadism', in J. S. Castillo (ed.) *Nomads and Sedentary Peoples* (30th International Congress of Human Sciences in Asia and North Africa) Mexico: El Colegio de Mexico, 25–36.

Safar, F., Mustafa, M. A. and Lloyd, S. (1981) *Eridu*, Baghdad: State Organization of Antquities and Heritage.

Said, E. (1978) *Orientalism. Western Conceptions of the Orient*, London: Routledge & Kegan Paul.

Sasson, J. M. (1984) 'Thoughts of Zimri-Lim', *Biblical Archaeologist* 47: 110–20.

Schmidt, J. (1974) 'Zwei Tempel der Obed-Zeit in Uruk', *Baghdader Mitteilungen* 7: 173–87.

Schmidt, K. (2000) 'Göbekli Tepe, southeastern Turkey. A preliminary report on the 1995–1999 excavations', *Paléorient* 26(1): 45–54.

Schreiber, K. (2001) 'The Wari empire of Middle Horizon Peru: The epistemological challenge of documenting an empire without documentary evidence', in S. E. Alcock, T. N. D'Altroy, K. D. Morrison and C. M. Sinopoli (eds) *Empires. Perspectives from Archaeology and History*, Cambridge: Cambridge University Press, 70–92.

Schwartz, G. M. (1994) 'Rural economic specialization and early urbanization in the Khabur Valley, Syria', in G. M. Schwartz and S. E. Falconer (eds) *Archaeological Views from the Countryside. Village Communities in Early Complex Societies*, Washington DC: Smithsonian Institution Press, 19–36.

——(1995) 'Pastoral nomadism in ancient Western Asia', in J. M. Sasson (ed.) *Civilizations of the Ancient Near East*, New York: Scribner, 249–58.

——(2001) 'Syria and the Uruk expansion', in M. S. Rothman (ed.) *Uruk Mesopotamia and its Neighbors. Cross-Cultural Interactions in the Era of State Formation*, Santa Fe: School of American Research Press, 233–64.

Schwartz, G. M. and Falconer, S. E. (1994) 'Rural approaches to social complexity', in G. M. Schwartz and S. E. Falconer (eds) *Archaeological Views from the Countryside. Village Communities in Early Complex Societies*, Washington DC: Smithsonian Institution Press, 1–9.

Service, E. R. (1975) *Origins of the State and Civilization: The Process of Cultural Evolution*, New York: Norton.

Shanks, M. and Tilley, C. (1987) *Social Theory and Archaeology*, Oxford: Polity Press.

Shell, C. A. (1996) 'Magnetometric survey at Çatalhöyük East', in I. Hodder (ed.) *On the Surface: Çatalhöyük 1993–95*, Cambridge: McDonald Institute for Archaeological Research and British Institute of Archaeology at Ankara, 101–13.

Shennan, S. (2001) 'Demography and cultural innovation: A model and its implications for the emergence of modern human culture', *Cambridge Archaeological Journal* 11: 5–16.

Sinopoli, C. M. (1994) 'The archaeology of empires', *Annual Review of Anthropology* 23: 159–80.

Smith, M. E. (2001) 'The Aztec empire and the Mesoamerican world system', in S. E. Alcock, T. N. D'Altroy, K. D. Morrison and C. M. Sinopoli (eds) *Empires. Perspectives from Archaeology and History*, Cambridge: Cambridge University Press, 128–54.

Smith, M. E. and Montiel, L. (2001) 'The archaeological study of empires and imperialism in pre-Hispanic central Mexico', *Journal of Anthropological Archaeology* 20: 245–84.

Smith, P. E. L. and Young Jr, T. C. (1983) 'The force of numbers: Population pressure in the central western Zagros 12,000–4500 BC', in T. C. Young Jr, P. E. L. Smith and P. Mortensen (eds) *The Hilly Flanks. Essays on the Prehistory of Southwestern Asia Presented to Robert J. Braidwood* (Studies in Ancient Oriental

Civilization 36) Chicago: Oriental Institute of the University of Chicago, 141–61.

Snell, D. C. (1997) *Life in the Ancient Near East 3100–332 BCE*, New Haven: Yale University Press.

Stein, G. (1994a) 'Introduction part II. The organizational dynamics of complexity in Greater Mesopotamia', in G. Stein and M. S. Rothman (eds) *Chiefdoms and Early States in the Near East. The Organizational Dynamics of Complexity* (Monographs in World Archaeology 18) Madison: Prehistory Press, 11–22.

——(1994b) 'Economy, ritual, and power in 'Ubaid Mesopotamia', in G. Stein and M. S. Rothman (eds) *Chiefdoms and Early States in the Near East. The Organizational Dynamics of Complexity* (Monographs in World Archaeology 18) Madison: Prehistory Press, 35–46.

——(1994c) 'Segmentary states and organizational variation in early complex societies: A rural perspective', in G. M. Schwartz and S. E. Falconer (eds) *Archaeological Views from the Countryside. Village Communities in Early Complex Societies*, Washington DC: Smithsonian Institution Press, 10–18.

——(1996) 'Producers, patrons, and prestige: Craft specialists and emergent elites in Mesopotamia from 5500–3100 BC', in B. Wailes (ed.) *Craft Specialization and Social Evolution: In Memory of V. Gordon Childe* (University Museum Monograph 93. University Museum Symposium Series VI) Philadelphia: University of Pennsylvania Museum: 25–38.

——(1998) 'Heterogeneity, power, and political economy: Some current research issues in the archaeology of Old World complex societies', *Journal of Archaeological Research* 6: 1–44.

——(1999b) *Rethinking World Systems. Diasporas, Colonies, and Interaction in Uruk Mesopotamia*, Tuscon: University of Arizona Press.

——(2001) 'Indigenous social complexity at Hacınebi (Turkey) and the organization of Uruk colonial contact', in M. S. Rothman (ed.) *Uruk Mesopotamia and its Neighbors. Cross-Cultural Interactions in the Era of State Formation*, Santa Fe: School of American Research Press, 265–305.

Stein, G. (ed.) (1999a) 'The Uruk expansion: Northern perspectives from Hacınebi, Hassek Höyük and Gawra', *Paléorient* 25(1).

Stein, G. and Blackman, M. J. (1993) 'The organizational context of specialized craft production in early Mesopotamian states', *Research in Economic Anthropology* 14: 29–59.

Stein, G. and Rothman, M. S. (eds) (1994) *Chiefdoms and Early States in the Near East. The Organizational Dynamics of Complexity* (Monographs in World Archaeology 18) Madison: Prehistory Press.

Steinkeller, P. (1991) 'The administrative and economic organization of the Ur III state: The core and the periphery', in McG. Gibson and R. D. Biggs (eds) *The Organization of Power. Aspects of Bureaucracy in the Ancient Near East* (Studies in Ancient Oriental Civilization 46) 2nd edn, Chicago: University of Chicago Press, 15–33.

——(1993) 'Settlement patterns and material culture of the Akkadian period: Continuity and discontinuity', in M. Liverani (ed.) *Akkad, the First World*

Empire: Structure, Ideology, Traditions (History of the Ancient Near East Studies 5) Padua:Sargon srl, 91–129.

——(2002) 'Archaic city seals and the question of early Babylonian unity', in T. Abusch (ed.) *Riches Hidden in Secret Places. Ancient Near Eastern Studies in Memory of Thorkild Jacobsen*, Winona Lake: Eisenbrauns, 249–57.

Stol, M. (1995) 'Private life in ancient Mesopotamia', in J. M. Sasson (ed.) *Civilizations of the Ancient Near East*, New York: Scribner, 485–501.

Stone, E. C. (1981) 'Texts, architecture and ethnographic analogy: Patterns of residence in Old Babylonian Nippur', *Iraq* 43: 19–33.

——(1987) *Nippur Neighborhoods* (Studies in Ancient Oriental Civilization 44) Chicago: Oriental Institute of the University of Chicago.

——(1994) 'The anatomy of a Mesopotamian city: The Mashkan-shapir project', *Bulletin of the Canadian Society for Mesopotamian Studies* 27: 15–24.

——(1997) 'City-states and their centers. The Mesopotamian example', in D. L. Nichols and T. H. Charlton (eds) *The Archaeology of City-States. Cross-Cultural Approaches*, Washington DC: Smithsonian Institution Press, 15–26.

——(1999) 'The constraints on state and urban form in ancient Mesopotamia', in M. Hudson and B. A. Levine (eds) *Urbanization and Land Ownership in the Ancient Near East* (Peabody Museum Bulletin 7) Cambridge: Peabody Museum of Archaeology and Ethnology, Harvard University, 203–27.

Stone, E. C. and Zimansky, P. (1992) 'Mashkan-shapir and the anatomy of an Old Babylonian city', *Biblical Archaeologist* 55: 212–18.

——(1994) 'The Tell Abu Duwari Project, 1988–1990', *Journal of Field Archaeology* 21: 437–55.

Strika, V. (2000) 'The perception of the past in the Near East. Two case-studies: Iraq and Saudi Arabia', in P. Matthiae, A. Enea, L. Peyronel and F. Pinnock (eds) *Proceedings of the First International Congress on the Archaeology of the Ancient Near East*, Rome: Università degli Studi di Roma 'La Sapienza': 1579–86.

Stronach, D. (1997) 'Notes on the fall of Nineveh', in S. Parpola and R. M. Whiting (eds) *Assyria 1995*, Helsinki: The Neo-Assyrian Text Corpus Project, 307–24.

Taagepera, R. (1978a) 'Size and duration of empires: Systematics of size', *Social Science Research* 7: 108–27.

——(1978b) 'Size and duration of empires. Growth-decline curves, 3000–600 BC', *Social Science Research* 7: 180–96.

Tainter, J. A. (1988) *The Collapse of Complex Societies*, Cambridge: Cambridge University Press.

Talbert, R. J. A. (2000) *Barrington Atlas of the Greek and Roman World*, Princeton: Princeton University Press.

Thomas, R. (2000) *Herodotus in Context*, Cambridge: Cambridge University Press.

Tobler, A. J. (1950) *Excavations at Tepe Gawra. Volume II Levels IX–XX*, Philadelphia: University of Pennsylvania Press.

Trigger, B. G. (1989) *A History of Archaeological Thought*, Cambridge: Cambridge University Press.

Tringham, R. (1995) 'Archaeological houses, households, housework and the home', in D. N. Benjamin (ed.) *The Home: Words, Interpretations, Meanings, and Environments*, Aldershot: Avebury, 79–107.

Uerpmann, H.-P. (1996) 'Animal domestication – accident or intention?', in D. R. Harris (ed.) *The Origins and Spread of Agriculture and Pastoralism in Eurasia*, London: UCL Press, 227–37.

Van De Mieroop, M. (1997a) 'On writing a history of the ancient Near East', *Bibliotheca Orientalis* 54: 285–305.

——(1997b) *The Ancient Mesopotamian City*, Oxford: Oxford University Press.

——(1999a) *Cuneiform Texts and the Writing of History*, London: Routledge.

——(1999b) 'Thoughts on urban real estate in ancient Mesopotamia', in M. Hudson and B. A. Levine (eds) *Urbanization and Land Ownership in the Ancient Near East* (Peabody Museum Bulletin 7) Cambridge: Peabody Museum of Archaeology and Ethnology, Harvard University, 253–87.

van Driel, G. (2001) 'On villages', in W. H. van Soldt (ed.) *Veenhof Anniversary Volume. Studies Presented to Klaas R. Veenhof on the Occasion of his Sixty-fifth Birthday*, Leiden: Nederlands Instituut voor het Nabije Oosten, 103–18.

van Zeist, W. and Bottema, S. (1977) 'Palynological investigations in western Iran', *Palaeohistoria* 19: 19–85.

van Zeist, W. and de Roller, G. J. (1991–2) 'The plant husbandry of aceramic Çayönü, SE Turkey', *Palaeohistoria* 33/34: 65–96.

Veenhof, K. R. (1995) 'Kanesh: An Assyrian colony in Anatolia', in J. M. Sasson (ed.) *Civilizations of the Ancient Near East*, New York: Scribner, 859–71.

Veenhof, K. R. (ed.) (1996) *Houses and Households in Ancient Mesopotamia* (papers read at the 40e Rencontre Assyriologique Internationale Leiden, 5–8 July 1993) Leiden: Nederlands Historisch-Archaeologisch Instituut te Istanbul.

Verhoeven, K. and Daels, L. (1994) 'Remote sensing and geographical information systems (GIS) for archaeological research (applied in Mesopotamia)', in H. Gasche, M. Tanret, C. Janssen and A. Degraeve (eds) *Cinquante-deux réflexions sur le Proche-Orient ancien offertes en homage à Léon De Meyer* (Mesopotamian History and Environment Occasional Publications II) Leuven: Peeters, 519–39.

Vermeule, E. (1996) 'Archaeology and philology: The Dirt and the Word', *Transactions of the American Philological Association* 126: 1–10.

von Dassow, E. (1999) 'On writing the history of southern Mesopotamia', *Zeitschrift für Assyriologie und Vorderasiatische Archäologie* 89: 227–46.

Watson, P. J. (1980) 'The theory and practice of ethnoarchaeology with special reference to the Near East', *Paléorient* 6(1): 55–64.

——(1991) 'Origins of food production in Western Asia and Eastern North America: A consideration of interdisciplinary research in anthropology and archaeology', in L. C. K. Shane and E. J. Cushing (eds) *Quaternary Landscapes*, Minneapolis: University of Minnesota Press, 1–37.

Watson, P. J. and LeBlanc, S. A. (1990) *Girikihacıyan. A Halafian Site in Southeastern Turkey* (Monograph 33) Los Angeles: Institute of Archaeology, University of California, Los Angeles.

Wattenmaker, P. (1994) 'State formation and the organization of domestic craft production at third-millennium BC Kurban Höyük, southeast Turkey', in G. M. Schwartz and S. E. Falconer (eds) *Archaeological Views from the Countryside. Village Communities in Early Complex Societies*, Washington DC: Smithsonian Institution Press, 109–20.

——(1998) *Household and State in Upper Mesopotamia. Specialized Economy and the Social Uses of Goods in an Early Complex Society*, Washington DC: Smithsonian Institution Press.

Weiss, H. (1977) 'Periodization, population, and early state formation in Khuzistan', in L. Levine and T. Cuyler Young (eds) *Mountains and Lowlands: Essays in the Archaeology of Greater Mesopotamia*, Malibu: Undena, 347–70.

——(2000) 'Beyond the Younger Dryas. Collapse as adaptation to abrupt climate change in ancient West Asia and the Eastern Mediterranean', in G. Bawden and R. M. Reycraft (eds) *Environmental Disaster and the Archaeology of Human Response* (Maxwell Museum of Anthropology Anthropological Papers 7) Albuquerque: University of New Mexico, 75–98.

Weiss, H. and Bradley, R. S. (2001) 'What drives societal collapse?', *Science* 291: 609–10.

Weiss, H. and Courty, M.-A. (1993) 'The genesis and collapse of the Akkadian empire: The accidental refraction of historical law', in M. Liverani (ed.) *Akkad. The First World Empire* (History of the Ancient Near East Studies 5) Padua: Sargon srl, 131–55.

Wenke, R. J. (1981) 'Explaining the evolution of cultural complexity: A review', in M. B. Schiffer (ed.) *Advances in Archaeological Method and Theory, Volume 4*, New York: Academic Press: 79–127.

Westenholz, A. (1979) 'The Old Akkadian empire in contemporary opinion', in M. T. Larsen (ed.) *Power and Propaganda. A Symposium on Ancient Empires* (Mesopotamia Copenhagen Studies in Assyriology 7) Copenhagen: Akademisk Forlag, 107–24.

Westenholz, J. G. (1998) 'Relations between Mesopotamia and Anatolia in the age of the Sargonic kings', in H. Erkanal, V. Donbaz and A. Uğuroğlu (eds) *XXXIV. International Assyriology Congress*, Ankara: Türk Tarih Kurumu, 5–22.

Wheeler, Margaret (1956) *Walls of Jericho*, London: Chatto and Windus.

Wheeler, Mortimer (1956) *Still Digging. Interleaves from an Antiquary's Notebook*, London: Michael Joseph.

Whittle, A. (1996) *Europe in the Neolithic. The Creation of New Worlds*, Cambridge: Cambridge University Press.

Wilkinson, T. J. (1999) 'Demographic trends from archaeological survey: Case studies from the Levant and Near East', in J. Bintliff and K. Sbonias (eds) *Reconstructing Past Population Trends in Mediterranean Europe (3000 BC–AD 1800)*, Oxford: Oxbow Books, 45–64.

——(2000) 'Regional approaches to Mesopotamian archaeology: The contribution of archaeological surveys', *Journal of Archaeological Research* 8: 219–67.

Winter, I. J. (1997) 'Art *in* empire: The royal image and the visual dimensions of Assyrian ideology', in S. Parpola and R. M. Whiting (eds) *Assyria 1995*, Helsinki: The Neo-Assyrian Text Corpus Project, 359–81.

——(2000) 'Babylonian archaeologists of the(ir) Mesopotamian past', in P. Matthiae, A. Enea, L. Peyronel and F. Pinnock (eds) *Proceedings of the First International Congress on the Archaeology of the Ancient Near East*, Rome: Università degli Studi di Roma 'La Sapienza', 1785–800.

Woolley, L. (1938) *Ur of the Chaldees*, Harmondsworth: Penguin.

Woolley, L. and Mallowan, M. (1976) *Ur Excavations Volume VII. The Old Babylonian Period*, London: British Museum Publications.

Woolley, L. and Moorey, P. R. S. (1982) *Ur 'of the Chaldees'*, London: Herbert Press.

Wright, H. T. (1969) *The Administration of Rural Production in an Early Mesopotamian Town* (Museum of Anthropology, University of Michigan, Anthropological Papers 38) Ann Arbor: University of Michigan.

——(1977) 'Recent research on the origin of the state', *Annual Review of Anthropology* 6: 379–97.

——(1978) 'Toward an explanation of the origin of the state', in R. Cohen and E. R. Service (eds) *Origins of the State. The Anthropology of Political Evolution*, Philadelphia: Institute for the Study of Human Issues, 49–68.

——(1981) 'The southern margins of Sumer: Archaeological survey of the area of Eridu and Ur', in R. McC. Adams (ed.) *Heartland of Cities. Surveys of Ancient Settlement and Land Use on the Central Floodplain of the Euphrates*, Chicago: University of Chicago Press, 295–345.

——(1998) 'Uruk states in southwestern Iran', in G. M. Feinman and J. Marcus (eds) *Archaic States*, Santa Fe: School of American Research Press, 173–97.

——(2001) 'Cultural action in the Uruk world', in M. S. Rothman (ed.) *Uruk Mesopotamia and its Neighbors. Cross-Cultural Interactions in the Era of State Formation*, Santa Fe: School of American Research Press, 123–47.

Wright, H. T. and Johnson, G. A. (1975) 'Population, exchange, and early state formation in southwestern Iran', *American Anthropologist* 77: 267–89.

Wright, H. T. and Rupley, E. S. A. (2001) 'Calibrated radiocarbon age determinations of Uruk-related assemblages', in M. S. Rothman (ed.) *Uruk Mesopotamia and its Neighbors. Cross-Cultural Interactions in the Era of State Formation*, Santa Fe: School of American Research Press, 85–122.

Wright Jr, H. E. (1993) 'Environmental determinism in Near Eastern prehistory', *Current Anthropology* 34: 458–69.

Wylie, A. (1985) 'The reaction against analogy', in M. B. Schiffer (ed.) *Advances in Archaeological Method and Theory Volume 8*, Orlando: Academic Press, 63–111.

Yoffee, N. (1979) 'The decline and rise of Mesopotamian civilization: An ethnoarchaeological perspective on the evolution of social complexity', *American Antiquity* 44: 5–35.

——(1988) 'The collapse of ancient Mesopotamian states and civilization', in N. Yoffee and G. L. Cowgill (eds) *The Collapse of Ancient States and Civilizations*, Tuscon: University of Arizona Press, 44–68.

——(1995) 'Political economy in early Mesopotamian states', *Annual Review of Anthropology* 24: 281–311.

——(1999) 'Robert McCormick Adams', in T. Murray (ed.) *Encyclopedia of Archaeology. The Great Archaeologists*, Santa Barbara: ABC-Clio, 791–810.

Zabbal, F. (2000) 'Foreword', in J. Bottéro, C. Herrenschmidt and J.-P. Vernant, *Ancestor of the West. Writing, Reasoning, and Religion in Mesopotamia, Elam, and Greece*, Chicago: University of Chicago Press, vii–xi.

Zeder, M. A. (1991) *Feeding Cities. Specialized Animal Economy in the Ancient Near East*, Washington DC: Smithsonian Institution Press.

——(1994) 'Of kings and shepherds: Specialized animal economy in Ur III Mesopotamia', in G. Stein and M. S. Rothman (eds) *Chiefdoms and Early States in the Near East. The Organizational Dynamics of Complexity* (Monographs in World Archaeology 18) Madison: Prehistory Press, 175–91.

——(1999) 'Animal domestication in the Zagros: A review of past and current research', *Paléorient* 25(2): 11–25.

Zettler, R. L. (1987) 'Administration of the temple of Inanna at Nippur under the Third Dynasty of Ur: Archaeological and documentary evidence', in McG. Gibson and R. D. Biggs (eds) *The Organization of Power. Aspects of Bureaucracy in the Ancient Near East* (Studies in Ancient Oriental Civilization 46) Chicago: Oriental Institute of the University of Chicago, 101–14.

——(1992) *The Ur III Temple of Inanna at Nippur. The Operation and Organization of Urban Religious Institutions in Mesopotamia in the Late Third Millennium BC* (Berliner Beiträge zum Vorderen Orient 11) Berlin: Dietrich Reimer.

——(1996) 'Written documents as excavated artifacts and the holistic interpretation of the Mesopotamian archaeological record', in J. S. Cooper and G. M. Schwartz (eds) *The Study of the Ancient Near East in the 21st Century*, Winona Lake: Eisenbrauns, 81–101.

Zeuner, F. E. (1963) *A History of Domesticated Animals*, London: Hutchinson.

Zimansky, P. E. (1985) *Ecology and Empire: The Structure of the Urartian State* (Studies in Ancient Oriental Civilization 41) Chicago: Oriental Institute of the University of Chicago.

Zohary, D. (1989) 'Domestication of the Southwest Asian Neolithic crop assemblage of cereals, pulses, and flax: The evidence from the living plants', in D. R. Harris and G. C. Hillman (eds) *Foraging and Farming: The Evolution of plant Exploitation*, London: Unwin Hyman, 358–73.

——(1999) 'Domestication of the Neolithic Near Eastern crop assemblage', in P. C. Anderson (ed.) *Prehistory of Agriculture. New Experimental and Ethnographic Approaches* (Institute of Archaeology Monograph 40) Los Angeles: University of California, Los Angeles: 42–50.

Zohary, D. and Hopf, M. (1993) *Domestication of Plants in the Old World*, Oxford: Clarendon Press.

Index

abandonment: categories of artefact assemblages 180
Abbasids 135, 139
Abraham 15
Abu Duwari (ancient Maškan-šapir) 160–3
Abu Hureyra **2**, 71, 75, 77–8, 80, 82, 85–6; large mammal bones from **85**
Abu Salabikh: burial in Early Dynastic house 176, **177**; city plan 165, **165**; investigations of small Sumerian city 17, 159, 163–7, 172–6, **173**, 182–3, 185, 198; on map of Mesopotamian sites **2**; plan of mounds **164**
Achaemenid empire 148, 152, 193
Adab *see* Bismaya
Adams, Robert 17, 143, 145, 148; integrated approach 64, 65; on need for specifically archaeological approaches 153–4; on significance of texts 131; survey of Diyala region 50–3, 54; Uruk-Warka research 53–4, 113, 114, 115; views on complex societies 98–9, 117; work on rise and development of cities 158; work as stimulus to others 54–5, 160
administration: building at Abu Salabikh 166; and collapse of empires 144, 150; in early states and complex societies 98–9, 110, 113–14, 123, 148–9; Wright's study of Sakheri Sughir 183
adult education: British Museum events 196–7

Adumatu 200
aerial photography: Adams' survey work 50; of Daur in 1918 **203**; Hole's ideas for archaeology of pastoralism 187; investigation of Abu Salabikh 163; investigations of Abu Duwari 160; of Najaf **112**
Africa: early European colonialism 124
agriculture *see* farming
Akkad region 50, 133, 198
Akkadian empire 65, 127, 133, 145, 146, 149, 150, 152–3
Akkadian language 120
Aleppo 9, 10, 172
Alexander the Great 5
Algaze, Guillermo: Uruk expansion model 114, 114–18, 121, 122, 123–5
alluvium and alluviation: Lower Mesopotamian 15, 102, 114, 115, 116, 117, 198; problems 39, 52, 53, 55, 187
American archaeologists 11, 14, 15, 16, 17
American Schools of Oriental Research 163
Americas 81, 150, *see also* Mexico; New World; North America; Peru
Amnānum 158
Amuq 49
analogy: archaeological interpretation by 123–5, 166; Roaf's list of everyday activities 170
Anatolia 45, 67, 82, 108; core and periphery interaction in complex

3

626 Index

societies 114, 115, 117, 119, 120; evidence for Akkadian imperial presence 145; in Western study of history 193, *see also* under place-names and regions

Anau: Pumpelly's excavations 22–3

ancient Greece 8; in Western study of history 193

ancient history 193, 200–1

Anderson, Patricia 78

Andrae, Walter: excavation of Aššur 12, **13**

animal bones: Abu Duwari 162; Abu Hureyra **85**, 86; evidence for diet and environment 45; evidence for food production patterns 178; of pigs at Hallan Çemi 82–4; Pumpelly's excavations in Anau 22–3; study of in social context 181; Umm Dabaghiyah 86–8; Zeder's approach in study of urban/rural interactions 186; zooarchaeology 80, *see also* faunal remains

animal husbandry: development of 68–9, 76; evidence in Ur imperial texts 138–9; pigs at Hallan Çemi 82–5; practices of common people 156, *see also* domestication

animals: pastoral herding of nomads 186–7; and shift to sedentary farming 70, 79–89

Anšan *see* Tal-e Malyan

Al Ansary, A.-R.T. 200

anthropological archaeology 16, 19, 22–5, 26, 57, 79; approaches to atextual periods 58; approaches to empires 132, 133–4; approaches to everyday life 155; approaches to social complexity 95–6, 96–100, 113; significance of texts 131; Wright's study of Sakheri Sughir 183

Antioch 24, 49

antiquities laws: late 1930s 16

Anu Ziggurat/White Temple complex 110, 114, 116

AQA (Assessment and Qualifications Alliance) 196

'Aqar Quf 16

Arab archaeologists 200

Arabia: European campaign during First World War 14

Arabian Gulf: imperial trade with 146

Arabic literature: Western ignorance 3–4

archaeo-historical approach 52, 61, 99–100

archaeological record 31–2, 34–5, 56; attestation of complex societies 93, 94–6, 124; Byrd's study of early Neolithic households 180; of dominated peripheries in imperial context 144; and excavation 43, 160; importance of material culture 179; non-textual evidence of everyday life 156, 178; textual and non-textual archaeology 58, 60–1, 156; Uruk phenomenon 108, 125

archaeology: academic discourse and future discourses 190–3; adult education events concerning Near East 196–7; contrast of history in Auden's view 31; development of theory 19–20; as discipline practised in Southwest Asia 27, 198–9; example of Tell Abu Duwari/Maškan-šapir 162–3; focusing on ordinary people 155; hand-in-hand with epigraphy 60–1; interpretation by analogy 123–4; National Curriculum 194–5; professionalisation of 190; study of at author's university 200–1; TV programmes 195–6; in upper secondary education 196, *see also* under different types of archaeology

archaic states 100

architecture: Abu Duwari site 162; Anu Ziggurat/White Temple complex 110, 114; core/periphery interactions in imperial context 143–4; in culture history approach

23; Eridu temples 102, **103**; evidence for hunting at Umm Dabaghiyah 86; evidence in Uruk Mesopotamia 119, 121; factual accounts 190; megaliths at Göbekli Tepe 90; plans recovered from Uruk-period sites 108; reconstruction in depictions of ancient buildings 193; Stone's insights into Nippur 62–3; study of by Mesopotamian archaeologists 58; 'tholoi' 21; Tringham's approach to study of households 179–80

archives *see* textual sources; written texts

Arpachiyah **2**, 16, 65

Arslantepe **2**, 118, 123, 150

art: at Çatalhöyük site 37, 46; Cauvin's study of early Neolithic 91; study of by archaeologists 58; use of in imperial centres 139–41, 146

artefacts: Byrd's study of early Neolithic households 180; contextual study of material culture 181–2; and cultural expectations 60; movement of between imperial entities 146; sampling for recovery of 43; typology of 65; written documents as 61, 131

Asia: and use of Orient as term 6, *see also* East Asia; Southwest Asia; Western Asia

Asia Minor: Roman and Persian roads 143, *see also* Anatolia

Assos 12

Aššur (god) 149

Aššur (place) **2**, 120, 134, 135, 136, 139, 157–8; early excavations 9, 12, **13**; threat of flooding 135, 202–4

Assyria 198; early archaeology 6–7, 8, 9; in education 193, 197, *see also* under place-names and regions

Assyrian empire 133, 135, 143, 144, 145, 146, 147, 149; as history option in National Curriculum 194, 195; palaces 135, 136, 141, 146

Assyriology and Assyriologists 15, 56–7, 59–60, 185

Auden, W.H. 31

Aztecs 194

Babylon **2**, 157–8; ancient excavations 5; as centre of empire 134, 135; nineteenth-century explorations 3, 8–9, 12; seventeenth-century excavations 1; Tower of **3**; in Western study of history 193

Babylonia 5, 50, 116, 198, *see also* Old Babylonian period

backhoe sectioning 55

Baghdad 9, 10, 11, 14, 16, 135, 172

Baghouz 123

Bahrani, Zainab 5–6, 7, 8, 25

Balawat 9

Banahilk 16

Banks, Edgar 14

Barda Balka 16, 68

Barker, A.J. 197, 198

Bar-Yosef, O. 68, 71

beer: brewing of 105

Behistun *see* Bisitun

Beijing 6

Bell, Gertrude 7, 14

Bender, Barbara 90

Benin 194, 195

Benjamin of Tudela, Rabbi 1

Berman, Judith: work on Ubaid pottery 107–8

Bey, Hamdi 11

Beydar **2**, 158, 198

Bible and biblical connections: depriviuleging of in education 197; and evolution of Mesopotamian archaeology 18–19, 57; Noah and the Flood 9, 15; Western historical tradition 7, 201

Binford, Lewis R. 22, 72–3

Bisitun 3

Bismaya (ancient Adab) 14

Blackman, M.J. 145

Blanton, Richard 99

Bogucki, P. 68

bones 25, 174, *see also* animal bones;
    skeletal remains
Borsippa 1, **3**, 8, 9, 12
botanical remains *see* plant remains
Botta, Paul Emile 3, 6–7, 8, 9, 136, 137
Bottéro, Jean 8, 27–8, 56, 59–60, 64
Bouqras 17, 35
Braidwood, Linda 192
Braidwood, Robert 16, 24–5, 28, 55,
    70, 76, 155
Brak **2**, 16, 118, 150, 158; hoard of
    precious items 151, **151**; recent
    and ongoing excavations 33, **34**,
    35, 198
bread: baking of 105
Brinkman, J.A. 51, 58, 152
Britain: archaeology and history in
    upper secondary education 196;
    relations and interactions with
    Iraq 14, 197–8, *see also* Institute of
    Archaeology, London
British archaeologists: and British
    control of Iraq 14; diggers 44, 45;
    early loot-grabbing in
    Mesopotamia 6–7; excavations
    throughout 1920s 14–15; work at
    Abu Salabikh 163; work under
    Mallowan 16, 16–17
British Museum 6, 9, 11, 14, 194–5,
    196, 196–7
Bronze Age 102, 120, 146, 189
Brusasco, Paolo: study of Old
    Babylonian houses 176–8
Budge, Wallis 11
buildings: exposed in entirety at
    Çatalhöyük 45–6; reconstructing
    in depictions 193; studies of in
    social contexts 179, 180, 181–2, *see
    also* houses; monumental
    constructions; palaces; temples
bullae 98
Bulletin on Sumerian Agriculture 185
burial goods and gifts 31, 107, 162
burial practices: Abu Duwari 162;
    core/periphery interactions in
    imperial context 144; Early
    Dynastic households 167, 176,
    177; need to investigate at Dur-

Šarrukin 139; research at
    Çatalhöyük 37, 46
Byrd, Brian 180
Byrne, Roger 72
Byzantium 193

Cairo 172
camp-sites: hunter-gatherers 68–9
canals 160, 186
carnelian 104, 105, 113, **151**
Çatalhöyük: current programme of
    research 35–42; During's study of
    urban context 179; illustration of
    building **36**; on map of
    Mesopotamian sites **2**; plan of
    surface architecture **42**
Cauvin, Jacques 68, 91, 92
cave sites: excavations by Garrod 15,
    see also Shanidar
Çayönü 76
CD-ROM 193
cemeteries 14–15, 160–2
ceramics *see* pottery
cereals 71–2, 75, 76–7, 78, 84, 90
Chagar Bazar 16
Charpin, Dominique 57
Chicago University 15, 16
chiefdoms 94, 95, 101, 107
Childe, Gordon 7, 69, 70–1, 72, 82
China 193
Choga Mami 17
Christie, Agatha 192
chronology: and archaeological
    stratigraphy 12; by assemblage of
    material culture 20–1, 65;
    construction of Mesopotamian
    past 64–6; episodes of occupation
    at Abu Hureyra 77; factual
    accounts 190; framework for Early
    Dynastic period 15; Henrickson's
    study of Early Dynastic
    households 167–8; possible future
    work at Abu Duwari 160; and
    pottery analysis 106; Taagepera's
    patterns of empire 132–3
Chubb, Mary 192
cities 157–8, 182; centres of empire
    134, 136–7, 141; innovative

archaeological approaches
159–67; key role of households
170; list of names from Jemdet
Nasr 115–16; major structures of
Uruk-Warka **111**; reconstruction
of in depictions 193; significance
of Eridu 103; structure of smaller
settlements 168; studies of urban
layout 166–7, 168, *see also*
urban/rural flux and interaction;
urbanism and urbanisation
city-states 115, 116, 157, 163
civil engineering projects 117, 135, 189
civilisation: theories 7, 29
Cizre 5
classical texts: archaeology's shift
away from 57; Western historical
tradition 7, 201
clay objects: bullae 98; key concerns
during excavations 44, 45; Ur III
temple of Inanna 63, *see also*
pottery
clay tablets 15, 31, 108, 111, 115
climate: effect on settlement of Uruk-
Warka 110; plant evidence 76;
potential role in history of states
101; and shift to sedentary
farming and animal-rearing 70–2,
74, 81, 82
clothing and dress: interactions in
imperial context 143–4, 145
Cohen, Mark: *The Food Crisis in
Prehistory* 73, 82
colonialism: Western 1, 4, 199
colonisation: of Uruk peripheral
settlements 118, 120, 123
commodities: core/periphery
exchange in imperial context 135,
145; exchange of between
households 169; urban/rural
interaction 182, 183–4, *see also*
high-status commodities
common people 156–7; archaeology
focusing on 155, 157, 162, 163,
179, 180–1, 188; Van De
Mieroop's views 156–7, 190–1
communications 48, 150; core/

periphery relations in imperial
context 143, 146
complex societies: addressing issues
93–4; approaches to study of
96–102; archaeological correlates
95–6; development of public
interaction 91; early development
of 24, 54; significance of the
household 169–70; Ubaid period
102–8; urbanocentric approaches
185; Uruk phenomenon 108–26,
148, *see also* social complexity
computing technologies:
reconstruction and visualisation
192–3
Constantinople 6
consumption: Wattenmaker's study of
households 178–9
contextual archaeology *see*
interpretive or contextual
archaeology
core–periphery interactions: complex
societies 115, 117–20, 122;
imperial context 142
cosmopolitanism: Late-Ubaid
societies 104
countryside *see* rural areas; urban/
rural flux and interaction
Courty, M.-A. 149
Cowan, C.W. 74
craft activities 138, 162; specialisation
in complex societies 14, 96, 107,
113, 114
Crawford, Vaughn 50
Crimean War 9
Crusades 1
cult and ritual 90; in complex societies
95, 98–110; concerns of common
people 156; need to investigate at
Dur-Sarrukin 139; structures in
Ubaid period 102, **103**, 105;
theories of role of Uruk-Warka
103–4, 114, 115, 168
cultural development: Eurocentric
image of Mesopotamia 7;
evidence of Ubaid pottery 107;
late Palaeolithic 73; progress in
understanding of 198

cultural ecology 158
cultural evolution: beginning of
sedentism 72
cultural identity 131
culture: continuity in city of Eridu
103–4; factual accounts 190;
Giddens on aspects of 29–30;
household activities 169; Western
bias towards Greek civilisation
193, see also culture history;
material culture; science of culture
culture history: approaches to analysis
of pottery 106; periods 16, 50–1;
Sumerian question 15; as
theoretical context 19, 20–2, 23–4,
25, 26
cuneiform: archive documents from
Mašat Höyük 147; early
nineteenth-century attempts to
decipher 3; inscriptions discovered
in seventeenth century 1; property
texts found at Nippur 62–3; tablets
from Abu Duwari 162; tablets
from Abu Salabikh 163, 166;
tablets in Ur III temple of Inanna
63; as testimony and
archaeological record 31, 58, 132;
traders' records in Assyrian
Akkadian language 120, see also
proto-cuneiform
Cutha 9
Cuzco 134
cylinder seals 111, 114, 119, 121, 149,
160, 162

Daily Telegraph 9
Dalley, Stephanie 8
D'Altroy, Terence 121
dam construction 17, 34, 109, 135,
189, 202–4
Damascus 172
Danish archaeologists: excavations at
Shimshara 17
Dant, Tim 30, 169
Dassow, E. von see von Dassow, E.
data analysis: Çatahöyük 47;
geoarchaeological methods 39;
statistical approaches 23, 48

dating: development of scientific
methods 66; difficulties in study of
nomads 187; of sediments 39, 71
Daur **203**
Davies, M.S. 68
death see burial practices
death-life axis: Forest's study of
Çatahöyük art 37, 46
deep stratigraphic sounding: Andrae's
method 12
Deh Luran 76
Della Valle, Pietro see Pietro della
Valle
Delougaz, Pinhas 15
demography see population
deposits: Abu Salabikh 174–6, 175;
construction of stratigraphic
sequence 65; investigation and
analysis 40–1, 43–4, 45, 70–1,
75–6
diaries: online narratives 192
diet 45, 76, 139, 162
Dilmun 146
disease: and shift to sedentism 73–4, 89
Diyala region 15, 49–50, 50–3, 54,
167–8
Diyala river 17
dog: as first domesticated animal 79
dolomite: production of objects at
Uruk-Warka 113
domestic household 99, 155, 168;
Abu Salabikh 166, 172, 176; in
feminist archaeology 25–6; studies
and approaches to 167–8, 169–82;
Ubaid period 105, 107, see also
houses
domestication: animals 80–9; origins
of 29, 70, 71, 72, 79, 91, see also
animal husbandry; plants:
domestication of
dress see clothing and dress
Dudgeon, A.G. 198
Dur-Šarrukin 136–9
During, Bleda 179
Durkheim, Emile 30

Eanna 114
Earle, Tim 94, 100, 113, 121

Early Dynastic period 15, 16, 65; burial of the dead 176, **177**; dating of Abu Salabikh site 163, 166; Henrickson's study of households 167–8; rural sites 183, 185; Uruk-Warka 53, 54

East Asia: animal domestication 81

East India Company 3

Ebla **2**, 150, 158

ecological archaeology: approaches 58, 96, 186

economic archaeology: approaches 16, 19–20, 58, 79, 155

economic development: importance of household 170

economic life 29; and collapse of empires 150; development of at Uruk-Warka 113–14; evidence at Abu Duwari 162; factors in nomadism 188; need to investigate at Dur-Šarrukin 139; Ubaid-period complex societies 104–5, 105–6, 108; Wattenmaker's study of Kurban Höyük 176–8, *see also* political economy

educational system: Mesopotamia's standing in 193–7

Egypt: development of ceramic typology 12; in education and study 193, 194, 196, 197; empires 133; online reconstructions of ancient monuments 192–3; Wheeler's tour of excavations 32

L'Egypte restituée (Aufrère et al) 193

Elam: development of writing 121

elites: at Abu Salabikh 166; at Uruk-Warka 114, 114–15; bias towards in study of urban complexity 178; and grand construction schemes 110–11; ideologies 121, 180; in imperial context 134, 136, 144, 145; main contexts of written evidence 156; Pollock's study of Ubaid-period pottery 108; Stein's study of complex societies 100, 107, *see also* kings and kingship

empires 93, 94, 101, 127–8;

characteristics and correlates 128–31; core–periphery relations 142–6; expansion, consolidation and collapse 147–54; imperial core 134–42; Taagepera's comparative study 127, 132–3, 143, 147–9, 193; and their borders 146–7, *see also* imperialism

England: Mesopotamia's standing in educational system 193–7; Victorian attitudes 8, 9

Enki (god) 102

environmental evidence 43, 45, 76, 77–8, 101

Epic of Gilgamesh 9

epigraphy 56, 58–9, 183; combined with archaeology 60–1, *see also* Assyriology; written texts

Epipalaeolithic period 69, 77

Erech *see* Uruk-Warka

Eresh 163

Eridu **2**, 14, 16, 102; Ubaid-period temples 102–3, **103**, 104–5

erosion 39, 41, 53, 187

Ešnunna 157–8

ethnic conflicts: in modern times 202

ethnicity: continuity of in city of Eridu 103–4; groupings in imperial centres 138

ethnoarchaeology: approaches 124, 172, 183, 187

ethnography: Adams' use of 52, 64; approaches to study of household 170, 171–2, 176–8, 179; and socio-cultural typologies 97; studies of nomads 188; use of analogy 62, 166, 170

Euphrates, River 5, 6, 117, 118; Adams' survey of central floodplain 54; dam construction and irrigation projects 17, 109; Heinz's study of settlements on 168; in Liverani's AD 2084 vision 189; tracing of probable old beds of 160, 163–4, *see also* Abu Hureyra

Eurocentric tradition: achievements 8; concept of cultural development

7; ignorance of Arabic achievements 3–4; use of geographical terms 6

Europe: recent archaeological approaches to Neolithic 179; tradition of culture history 19, 20; tradition of science and history 4

everyday life: archaeology focusing on 155, 191; informed by Abu Salabikh excavations 176; National Curriculum for history 194; studies of households 167, 170, 177, 180

evolution: and domestication for animals 79

evolutionary archaeology: approaches to social complexity 96, 97

excavation 27; development of highly targeted retrieval methods 55; example of project of Çatalhöyük site 41–7, 56; of imperial centres 142; incompetent or unsuitable methods 14, 15, 61, 135; issues of progress 33; lacking specific research programme 27–8; of mass graves from modern conflicts 202; multi-scalar approaches 181–2; Parrot's suggestions for staff 33; techniques at Abu Duwari 160; Wheeler's comments on Near East operations 32

excavations: mounted in ancient Babylonia 5

exchange: between Uruk and enclave at Hacınebi 119–20; core/periphery interactions in imperial context 145; urban/rural interactions 182–3, 186

families: in studies of households 167–8, 176–8, 180

Fara 12, 15, 163

farming: core/periphery subsistence patterns 144; origins and development of 24, 28, 29, 69; pastoral nomads 186–7; practices of common people 156; study of Abu Hurerya 77–8; transmutation

from hunting and gathering 28–9, 68–9, 70–92; Wright's study of rural production 183, see also animal husbandry; cereals; pulses

Faulkner, N. 27

faunal remains 23, 85, 174, 175, 185, see also animal bones

feasting: complex hunter-gatherer communities 90, 91

Feinman, G.M. 94, 100, 143

feminist archaeology 25–6

Fertile Crescent 70, 71, 76

fieldwork 55, 201; current debates 34–5; mid-twentieth-century books by women 192; moratorium on projects in Iraq 180, 189–90, 198; need for involvement of local communities 199, 204; Parrot's suggestions for staffing 33

Finkelstein, J.J. 5

First World War 12, 14, 197, 198, 202; military trenches of Ottoman forces **203**

Flannery, Kent V. 69, 73, 95, 97–8

flint 45, 113, 174

Flood: 'Deluge Tablet' 9; evidence at Ur 15, see also Noah

flooding: threat to Aššur 135, 202–4

food: crisis in prehistory 73; importance of rural areas 182; and pottery use in Ubaid period 108; practices of common people 156; processing equipment in Eridu temples 104–5; production at Uruk-Warka 110, 113; in studies of households 167, 178; supplies in imperial centres 137–8, 145, see also cereals; pulses

footwear: suitable for excavating in Southwest Asia 44

Forest, Jean-Daniel: study of Çatalhöyük site 37, 46

French archaeologists: early loot-grabbing 6–7; explorations in 1851 8–9; incompetent excavations 14; long-term excavations at Telloh 10–11, 15

French educational system: exclusion of study of Mesopotamia 196
funding: problems for rescue projects 28
futures: Liverani's vision of the year 2084 189; transcending history 198–204

Gallipoli 14, 202
Gamble, Clive 28–9
Garrod, Dorothy 15
Gates, M.-H. 64
Gawra **2**, 16, 102; Ubaid-period temples 103–4, 104–5, **104**, 105
gazelles: domestication of 80, 82, 85–6
Gebauer, A.B. 68
gender *see* feminist archaeology; male-female axis
genetic studies: showing population in Pleistocene period 73
geoarchaeology: approaches at Çatalhöyük site 39–40
geographical analysis: Adams' use of new approaches 53–4, *see also* GIS (Geographical Information Systems)
geographical boundaries *see* spatial boundaries
geographical terms: definition of 5–6; during Akkadian empire 145
geomorphological techniques 52, 160
German archaeologists 12, 13, 15
German Oriental Society 12
Gibson, McG. 50
Giddens, Anthony 29–30, 68, 155, 169
gift-giving: complex hunter-gatherer communities 90, 91
Gilgamesh 53, 149, *see also Epic of Gilgamesh*
Gird Ali Agha 16
Girikihacıyan **2**, 23
GIS (Geographical Information Systems) 55, 192–3
glyptic styles 111, 120
goats: domestication of 80, 82, 85–6; herding strategies gleaned from texts 185; hunting of 84

Göbekli Höyuk 93
Göbekli Tepe **2**, 90–1, 91, 92, 102
Godin Tepe **2**, 118, 122
gods: significance of to imperial kings 149; and temples 168
graves: Abu Salabikh 176; of those slaughtered in modern conflicts 202
Greater Mesopotamia: use of term 5
Greece 55, *see also* ancient Greece
Greek civilisation: bias of Western study of history 193
Grotefend, George Frederick 3
Groube, L. 73, 74, 89
Gudea 5
Gulf War 198, 202

Habuba Karira **2**, 109, 118, 168
Habur region 49
Habur river 5, 6, 9
Hacınebi Tepe **2**, 109, 119–20, 121, 182
Haditha region 17
Halaf: culture historical period 16, 20–1, 23, 65, 123
Hall, H.R. 14
Hallan Çemi: complexity of settlements 93; domestication of the pig 80, 82–5; early Holocene pre-agricultural sedentism 89–90; evidence for feasting as social development 91, 92; on map of Mesopotamian sites **2**; plan of early settlement **83**
Hammurabi of Babylon 12, 160
Hamrin region 17, 102, 170
Hamza, K. 202
Haradum 168
Harran 144
Harris, D.R. 67
Harris matrix 43
Hassek Höyük 109, 118
Hassuna: culture historical period 16, 65
Hatra 18
Hattusa 147
Hayden, Brian 73, 91
Haynes, J.H. 11
Hazar Merd 15

Heinz, Marlies 168
Helbaek, Hans 76
Henrickson, Elizabeth: study of Early
    Dynastic period households 167–8
herding: early Neolithic communities
    of Southwest Asia 88–9; pastoral
    nomadism 185, 186–7
Herodotus 20
Herrenschmidt, Clarisse 121
Hertzfeld, E. 14
al-Hiba 12
hierarchy see settlement hierarchy
high-status commodities: Abu Duwari
    162; in imperial contexts 144, 145,
    146, 151, see also metals; precious
    and semi-precious stones
Hillman, G.C. 68, 71
Hilprecht, H.V. 11
historians 99–100, 191, 199
historical models: analogies used by
    Algaze and Stein 124–5
historical narratives 4, 8, 57, see also
    narrative
historical trajectories: complex
    societies 95, 124
historiography: lack of narrative
    sources 190–1
history: Adams' consideration of 53,
    54, 64; Auden's view 31; 'from
    above' 142, 191; 'from below'
    156–7; study of in secondary
    education 194–5, 196; text-aided
    27; transcending 198–204, see also
    ancient history; archaeo-historical
    approach
Hittites: empire 133, 146–7, 149, 152
hoarding: and collapse of empires
    151–2; items at Tell Brak **151**
Hodder, Ian 29, 36, 37, 38, 46–7,
    91–2, 124
Hole, Frank 48, 55, 71, 186–7
holistic approaches: study of empires
    132, 136, 142; urban/rural/
    nomadic interactions 183–4
Holocene period 39, 69; boundary
    with Pleistocene period 72; climate
    changes 70, 71, 82; early social
    relations and complexity 91, 93;

plant changes and adaptation 74;
    population estimates 73–4; pre-
    agricultural sedentism 90
hominids: early forms 29, 68
horses 145
host countries: need to involve in
    future work 199–202
Hourani, A. 4
House of Commons 197
houses: Abu Duwari 162; Abu
    Salabikh 165, **165**, 166, 172–6,
    173; Brusacso's study of Old
    Babylonian Ur 176–8; Habuba
    Karira 168; Koldewey's
    discoveries at Babylon 12; neglect
    of excavations of 157; recent and
    future archaelogical approaches
    179–82; Roaf's study at Tell
    Madhhur 170–1, **171**, 181, see also
    domestic household
Howe, B. 24
höyük (mound) 40
human development: 'big questions'
    29, 67; Braidwood's work 24, 28;
    Cauvin's view of Neolithic
    revolution 91; most momentous
    change 67–8
hunting: continued importance of in
    Neolithic period 86, 88–9;
    evidence at Göbekli Tepe 90
hunting and gathering: transmutation
    to sedentary farming 28, 68–9,
    70–92, 198
Hyksos 193

Ibn al-Biruni 4
Ibn Battuta 4
Ibn Khaldun 4, 29, 182, 186
Ice Age: last 69, 71, 79
iconography 92, 111, 114, see also art;
    symbolism
'idea archaeology' 25
ideologies: concerns of common
    people 156, 180, 181;
    development of at Uruk
    settlements 113–14, 121; imperial
    context 139–42, 143–4, 149, 150
illicit digging 18, 34

images: and future of archaeological interpretation 190, 192–3
Imperial Ottoman Museum (Istanbul) 4, 11
imperialism: British control of Iraq 198; creation of new states after First World War 14; and Eurocentric image of Mesopotamia 7, 8; need for archaeologists to consider 199; 'prehistory of' 115, see also empires
Inanna (god) 115
Incas 127, 134
index fossils: defining Adams' historical periods 50–1
India 193
Indus Valley 146, 194, 195
Industrial Revolution: Western Europe 1
Ingharra see Kish
Institute of Archaeology, London 32
interdisciplinary approaches: origins of farming 92; studies of Nippur 63–4; to mundane aspects of living 155, 163; to study of empire 139, 153
interpretive or contextual archaeology 20, 30, 142, 179–80, 181–2
Iran: core and periphery interaction in complex societies 115, 117; culture history 20; domesticaton of plants 76; fieldwork and publications influenced by Adams 54; Hole's experience of Luri pastoral nomads 187; and Mesopotamia as term 5; pristine states in fourth millennium BC 98; proto-Elamite culture 116; revolution of 1979 18; Uruk phenomenon 108, see also under place-names and regions
Iran–Iraq War 202
Iraq: Akkadian material still lying underneath 153; Braidwood's Iraq-Jarmo project 24, 28; civil engineering projects 17; discovery of Sumerian presence in 15; domesticaton of plants 76;

importance of Diyala region project 50; innovative approaches to archaeological projects 159; invasion of Kuwait (1990) 18, 198; laws limiting export of finds from 16; looting of palaces by Western powers 6–7; low level of public awareness of relation to Mesopotamia 197–8; and Mesopotamia as term 5, 6; moratorium on Western fieldwork 180, 189–90, 198; recent field projects 35; regions surveyed **48**; relations and interactions with Britain 14, 197–8; remote regions 17; return of research projects in 1980s 18; study of houses and households 180, see also under place-names and regions
Iraq Museum (Baghdad) 14
Iraqi archaeologists 16, 17, 199, 204
Iraqi people 202
Ireland: archaeology and history in upper secondary education 196
irrigation: and complex societies 105, 117; decline of systems 4–5; programmes 17, 109; use of backhoe sectioning 55
Islam: in Middle Ages 4; modern manifestation of Mesopotamian region 6
Islamic era: first surveys of sites 14; need for greater sensitivity to 201; urban residence patterns 172; work by Iraqi archaeologists 16
Israel 33
Istanbul see Imperial Ottoman Museum
Ištar Temple (Aššur) 12
Italy 55, 193

Jacobsen, Thorkild 17, 49–50, 50, 55
Janssen, C. 61
Jarmo **2**, 16, 24
Jazirah 17, 198
Jebel Aruda 109, 118
Jemdet Nasr **2**, 15, 18, 61, 115;

culture historical period 16, 65, 115, 116
jewellery 14–15, 162, 176
Johnson, Gregory 98
Jones, Felix 35
Jordan: European campaign during First World War 14

Karim Shahir 16
Karun, River 5
Kassites 16
Khafajah **2**, 15, 167–8
al-Khan 16
Khorsabad 9, 15, 134, 136–9; on map of Mesopotamian sites **2**; plan of city **137**; Sargon's palace 136, **138**
Khuzistan *see* Tula'i
Killick, Robert 66
kings and kingship 103, 111, 113, 114, 149, 190; ideology 136, 141
Kınık-Kastamonu 152
kinship: Forest's study of Çatahöyük art 37; tensions with institution 172
Kish 8–9, 14, 15, 18
Kohl, Philip L. 117, 201
Koldewey, Robert 12
Konya plain *see* Çatalhöyük
Kültepe-Kaneš **2**, 120, 158
Kurban Höyük **2**, 118; Wattenmaker's study of households 178–9
Kus, S.M. 95
Kut al-Amara 202
Kuwait: Iraqi invasion (1990) 18, 198
Kuyunjik mound 35

labour: activities of common people 156, 169; division of in complex societies 106; gender division of in Abu Hureyra 78; lack of knowledge about in imperial centres 138; urban life at Abu Salabikh 182–3; in Uruk cities 113, 114, 118
Lagaš 10, 11
Lake Huleh 71
Lake Van (Turkey) 9

lakes: dating of recovered sediments 39
Lamberg-Karlovsky, C.C. 169
land use: Adams' survey of Diyala region 51–3; ancient and modern 48; in imperial context 137–8, 144
landscape: Adams' survey work 64; control of by Hittites 146–7; problem of alluvium deposition 52; and reconstruction in depictions 193; study of Abu Hureyra 77–8; survey 39, 48, 55
languages: need for Western archaeologists to learn 200–1; in textual archives of imperial cities 142
lapis lazuli 104, 105, 145, **151**
Larsa 5, 8, 102, 115
Larsen, M.T. 127, 149–50
Law, Bonar 197
Layard, Austen Henry 3, 6–7, 8, 9, 10, 14–15, 137
Lebanon 32
LeBlanc, Stephen 23
Legge, A.J. 85–6
Leiden: archaeological conference 16
Lesbos 12
Levant 67, 76, 82, 180, *see also* under place-names and regions
lineages: Forest's study of Çatahöyük art 37
literacy 61, 113, 157, 158
lithics: study of 65
Liverani, Mario 10, 17, 57; on cities of Mesopotamia 157–8; on empires 132, 136, 141–2, 145, 150, 152; vision of the year 2084 189, 204
Lloyd, Seton 3–4, 7, 15, 16, 36, 44, 50, 136; survey of Sinjar region 49, 51, 55
local communities: need for involvement of 199–200, 201–2, 204
Loftus, W.K. 8
London *see* Institute of Archaeology
looting 6–7, 11
Louvre 6
Lower Mesopotamia: Adams' survey

work 50–5, 115; alluvium 15, 114,
    115; core and periphery
    interactions of complex societies
    115, 117–20; survey projects in
    1960s 17
Lugalbanda 149
luminescence dating 39
Luri: pastoral nomads 187
Lutz, C. 198

McCorriston, Joy 71, 169
MacNeice, Louis 123
Madhhur **2**; Ubaid-period house
    170–1, **171**, 181
Magan 146
Maghzaliya 17
male-female axis: Forest's study of
    Çatahöyük art 37, 46
Mallowan, Max 16, 16–17, 49, 50, 55
Malville, Nancy 143
Mansur: Round City 135
manufacturing: traces of at Abu
    Duwari site 162
maps: Hole's work on pastoralism
    187; surface features of Abu
    Duwari site 160; used by Adams in
    Diyala survey 50, 52
Marcus, Joyce 94, 100–1
Mari **2**, 157–8, 158, 191
marriage: core–periphery alliances
    119–20
Martineau, Harriet 169
Marx, Karl 91
Maşat Höyük 147
Maškan-šapir: city plan **161**; on map
    of Mesopotamian sites **2**; Stone's
    work 159–63, 172
Massignon, L. 14
al-Mas'udi 4
Māt Bīrītim 5
Matarrah 16
material culture 30–1, 59, 114;
    Akkadian 152–3; approaches to
    study of households 179–80, 183;
    assemblage excavated from Abu
    Salabikh 166; and construction of
    chronology 20–1, 65; contextual
    study of 181–2; evidence of

common people 156; Halaf period
    123; in imperial context 139,
    144–5; issues regarding smaller
    settlements 55; Palaeolothic
    lifeways 69; research at
    Çatalhöyük 36, 37; Ubaid period
    106, 108; Uruk core and
    peripheral settlements 118, 119,
    120, 121
Matheson, Sylvia 192
Matthews, Roger 33
Matthews, Wendy 163, 174, 175–6
Maya 194, 196
Meadow, R.H. 71
Medes: empire 148
Meet the Ancestors (TV programme)
    195–6
megaliths: Göbekli Tepe 90
Mellaart, James 36–7, 40
Meluhha 146
Mesopotamia: archaeological record
    31, 60–1; culture history and
    anthropological archaeology
    19–26; as currently out of
    fieldwork bounds 27; development
    of writing 121; Eurocentric and
    imperial image of 7–8; European
    campaign during First World War
    14; as geographical term 5–6, 67;
    in Liverani's AD 2084 vision 189;
    low level of public awareness
    197–8; main issues of research 29;
    map of archaeological sites **2**;
    Marcus's model of state
    development 100–1, **101**; modern
    lands of 198; openness and
    accessibility of 149–50; progress in
    understanding of cultural
    developments 198; in Western
    study of history 193, *see also* under
    place-names and regions
Mesopotamian archaeology: accounts
    of development 6–8; achievements
    of Islamic intellectuals 4;
    approaches of anthropological
    archaeology 22–5, 57; Arabic
    achievements 3–4; chronological
    sequence 12; current practice and

approaches 27, 183, 198–9; emergence of modern discipline 10; European tradition of culture history 20–2; evolution into modern discipline 18–19; historical events 1–3; inadequate treatment of common everyday life 155; involvement of Western political powers 1, 5; in Liverani's AD 2084 vision 189, 204; mid-twentieth-century books by women 192; need for non-invasive techniques 40–1; need to involve host countries 199–202; nineteenth-century pioneers 7–8; possible future directions 189–90, 199–204; technique of survey 47; tendency to neglect non-textual archaeology 58; transformation by German achievements 12

Mesopotamian past: and archaeological record 32, 56; at time of Western engagement 4–5; 'big questions' of human development 67; chronology 64–6; Eurocentric achievements 8; kidnapping of in early decades of archaeology 7; modern study 1, 27; need to redefine 8; prominence of pottery 106; scope for new technology in reconstructing 192–3; standing of in English educational system 193–7; Stone's aim to reconstruct 159–60, 162; urbanocentric approaches 184–5; and Western biblico-classical tradition 201

metallurgy 113, 162
metals 31, 118, 119, 145
Mexico: Tula empire 127
micro-analyses 166–7
micromorphology: analysis of deposits 45, 76, 175–6
microstratigraphy: deposits from Abu Salabikh house 174; Tringham's approach to study of households 180

Middle Ages 1, 4, 6

Middle East 5, 193, 201, 202, see also under countries and regions
Mieroop, Marc van de see Van de Mieroop, Marc
military: cantonments at Samarra 139; concerns of common people 156; domination of peripheries in imperial context 146; imperial art showing 139–41; interactions at borders of empire 146–7, 152; trenches of Ottoman forces in 1918 **203**

Mitanni 133
M'lefaat 89–90, 198
modernity: origins of 29
Mohammed 'Arab **18**, 66
Molleson, Theya 78
Montiel, L. 127, 132, 134
monumental constructions: at imperial centres 135, 139; complex societies 96, 110–11; online reconstructions of ancient Egypt 192–3

Moore, Andrew M.T. 70, 71, 77
Moorey, P.R.S. 106
Moreland, John 30–1, 58, 157
Morris, Ian 22, 60
Moslawi 9
mosques: building of in modern Turkey 111; complexes at Samarra 139

Mosul 10, 16, 17
mounds: Abu Duwari 160; Abu Salabikh 164–5, **164**; Çatalhöyük 40–1; composition of 175; Hassuna 16; Kuyunjik 35; survey and excavation methods 44, 49, 50–1; Umm Dabaghiyah 86

Mozan 198
mud-brick: early inability to discern and excavate structures 137; excavated buildings in Nippur **11**; excavations by Sherqatis 12; and formation of mound 40; houses at city of Abu Salabikh 165, 174; houses at site of Çatalhöyük 36–7, **36**, 41, 45; Koldewey's tracing of 12; platforms for Eridu temples

10; single context planning for excavation 43; tracing at Diyala sites 15

multi-period sites: Adams' survey of Diyala region 51, 52–3

murals *see* wall-paintings

museums: claiming of early archaeological finds 6–7

Nabonidus (king) 5

Nabopolassar (king) 5

Nagar 158

Najaf 111, **112**

Naram-Sin 141, 151

narrative: method of archaeological interpretation 190–2; Tringham's approach to study of households 179–80, *see also* historical narratives

National Curriculum 194–5

Neandertals 17, 68, 69

Near East: Braidwood's concerns 24; environmental and cultural history 72; Liverani's general survey 57; Nissen's survey 49; Orientalist conception 201; origin of term 6; possible future directions of archaeology 189–90; standing of in English educational system 193–7; Wheeler's tour of excavations 32

Nebuchadrezzar 12

neighbourhoods: recent archaeological approaches 179; Stone's insights 162, 172

Nemet-Nejat, Karen 156

Nemrik 89–90, 198

Neo-Assyrian period 184

Neolithic period: campsites of pastoral nomads 187; Halaf phenomenon 20–1, 23; 'Neolithic revolution' 69, 70, 89–92; new relationships between animals and humans 79, 82–9; plants and new subsistence strategies 74, 76–8; recent archaeological approaches 179–80; site of Çatalhöyük 35, 36,

39–41, **42**; transition to Bronze Age 102; Zagros foothills 16

Nepal: research on movement and portage by foot 143

Nergal (god) 160

neutron activation analysis 107

Nevalı Çori 92, 102

New Archaeology 20, 22, 47, 96

New World: empires 127, 133–4

Niebuhr, Carsten 1–3

Niknami, K.A. 20

Nimrud: as centre of empire 134, 136; early archaeological explorations 3, 9, 10, 137; on map of Mesopotamian sites **2**; online reconstructions of Northwest Palace 192; twentieth-century research excavations 17, 18

Nineveh: Algaze's theory of Uruk settlement 118; as centre of empire 134, 135, 136, 139, 151; early archaeological explorations 3, 7, 9, 10, 137; incompetent British excavations 14; Kuyunjik mound 35; on map of Mesopotamian sites **2**; research excavations in 1980s 18; work under Mallowan in 1930s 16

Ninevite 5 period 66, 116

Nippur 115, 157–8, 158, 159; American long-term commitment to 11, 17; excavated mud-brick buildings **11**; ground-plans of excavated buildings **62**; Layard's excavations 8; on map of Mesopotamian sites **2**; Stone's insights into 62–3, 172

Nissen, Hans: on chronological systems 66; ideas about Ubaid period 106, 123; refinement of survey techniques 53; on settlement patterns 49; on Uruk-Warka findings 109–10, 110, 116, 123

Noah 9

nomads 187–8, *see also* pastoral nomadism

North America: approaches to study of New World empires 134; input of anthropological archaeology 19, 22, 57, *see also* American archaeologists

oasis theory 70, 72
objects: construction of histories of 65, 66; of daily life 167; Giddens on culture 29–30; and texts 58, *see also* things
obsidian 45, 123
Old Babylonian period: Brusacso's study of houses at Ur 176–8; chronology established at Ur 65; cities of Mesopotamia 157–8; Stone's insights into Nippur 62–3; Woolley's excavations of Ur 61
onagers: domestication of at Umm Dabaghiyah 80, 86–8; remains found at Abu Hureyra 85–6
Oppenheim, A.L. 59
Orient: as term 6
Orientalism: attitudes 7, 198, 201
Orwell, George: *1984* 189
Ottoman Empire 4, 10, 14, 198, 201, 202
Oxford: archaeological team from 15

palaces: of imperial elite 134, 135, 136, 139, 146; Koldewey's discoveries at Babylon 12; Layard's discoveries 3, 6–7, 10; online reconstructions of Nimrud building 192; Reade's study of Assyrian art 141
palaeoethnobotany 75–6, 79
Palaeolithic period: early archaeology of 15; emphasis on 'society' in study of 94; hunter-gatherer camps 69; major discoveries by Soleckis 17; processes influencing origins of farming 73, 92
Palegawra 16, 69
Paléorient 119
Palestine: Wheeler's tour of excavations 32
Paphlagonia, Project **56**
Parpola, Simo 8

Parrot, André 16, 32–3; long-term excavations at Telloh **10**, 33
Parthian empire 124
pastoral nomadism: Hole's work 186–7; urban/rural interaction 183–4, **184**
peace: idea of building bridges through archaeology 202
Peebles, C.S. 95
Pennsylvania, University of 14
Perkins, Anne: *The Comparative Archaeology of Early Mesopotamia* 21–2, 23
Persia: Achaimenid 193
Persian empire 148
Peru: Wari empire 127
Peters, J. 11, 84–5
Petrie, Flinders 12
Phoenicians 195
photography 43, *see also* aerial photography
Phrygian empire 146
phytoliths 76, 78
Pietro della Valle 1
pig: domestication of at Hallan Çemi 80, 82–5
pithoi 162
Pittman, Holly 120
Place, Victor 9, 137
plant remains: analysis of Abu Salabikh house 174, 175; anthropological approaches 22–3; key concerns during excavation 43, 44, 45; Moore's study of Abu Hurerya 77; palaeoethnobotany 75–6; Umm Dabaghiyah 86; urban/rural concerns 185, *see also* phytoliths; pollen; seeds
plants: broader food base in late Pleistocene 73; domestication of 70, 71–2, 74–5, 76–7, 78–9, 81–2; and shift to sedentary farming 70, 74–9
Pleistocene period 69, 71, 72, 73, 82
political economy: Algaze's approach to Uruk phenomenon 114–18
political entities: empires as 128–31, 147, *see also* socio-political entities
political identity 131

political theory 183
politics: factors in nomadism 188; relationships during First World War 14; and use of Mesopotamia as term 6; Western interest in Middle East 5
pollen: within lake-bed deposits 39, 70–1
Pollock, Susan 19, 25–6, 104, 108, 110, 181, 185, 198, 201
population 48; Adams' studies 51–2, 53, 54–5; Postgate's findings at Abu Salabikh 167; settlement at Uruk-Warka 110; and shift to sedentary farming 70, 72–4, 78–9, 82
post-colonial stances 141–2, 199
Postgate, J.N. 63, 125, 131; chart of city/village interactions in Neo-Assyrian period 184, **184**; investigations at Abu Salabikh 159, 163–7, 172–4, 182–3
post-processual archaeology 179–80
potsherds 45, 49, 50, 51, 160, 160–2
pottery: Abu Salabikh deposits 174; Adams' work on quantification of 54; Akkadian 152; and construction of chronological framework 65, 66; culture historical periods 16, 23; dating of sites on Konya plain 39; early period in Abu Hureyra 77; factual accounts 190; Halaf period 123; Lloyd's illustrations from Sinjar survey 49; painted 21, 22, 102, 106–7, 108; production at Tell Leilan 145; production in neighbourhoods 162, 166; significance of ceramic typology 12; study of in social contexts 178, 181, 182; Ubaid period 104, 105–6, 106–8, 170; Uruk period 108, 110, 114, 119, 121, 182
Potts, Dan T.: *Mesopotamian Civilization* 64, 185
power: in complex societies 94, 100, 101, 107, 113–14, 116; core/ periphery interactions in imperial context 144; imperial 127, 135–6;

and shaping of social interaction 180
precious and semi-precious stones 31, 104, 105, 118
prehistoric sites 15, 16, 17
prehistory 73, 116; empires 94, 127–8, 152–3; evolution of complex societies 24–5, 93–4; 'of imperialism' 115; precursors to Uruk phenomenon 122–3; significance of Barda Balka 68
Preusser, C. 14
Price, T.D. 68
priestly residences 37, 40, 96
Processual Archaeology *see* New Archaeology
production: complex societies 95, 107, 114, 117; of high-status commodities 145, 146; peripheries in imperial context 144, 144–5; Postgate's chart of city/village interactions **184**; Wattenmaker's study of domestic households 178–9; Wright's study of Sakheri Sughir 183
propinquity theory *see* oasis theory
proto-archaeology 5
proto-cuneiform 15, 61, 111
pulses: domestication of 75, 76
Pumpelly, Raphael 22–3, 70, 72, 82
push and pull theories 72, 82, 91

Qala'at Sherqat 12
Qermez Dere **2**, 89–90, 198
Qurna 9

racecourse: Samarra 139, **140**
radiocarbon dating 39, 66, 71
RAF (Royal Air Force) 198
Rashid 'Ali 16
Rassam, Hormuzd 9–10
raw materials: import and exchange of 135, 145, 149
Rawlinson, Henry Creswicke 3, 8
Reade, Julian 9, 10, 141
Redman, Charles 199
reflexive methodology: approach to Çatalhöyük site 37, 46–7

regional approaches: need for basis
    55; survey 17, 39, 183
relief sculptures: Çatalhöyük 37;
    looted from Assyrian palaces 6–7;
    in palace of Sargon II 136
religious creed and practice: anti-
    establishment cities 111; evidence
    at Uruk-Warka 114; Ubaid-period
    temples 103–4, 105
religious ideologies 121, 144
religious organisations: role in
    development of complexity 98–9
religious quarters: Abu Duwari 160
remote sensing 41
rescue or salvage archaeology 17, **18**,
    28, 34, 35, 135, 189, 204
research programmes: 1960s and
    1970s 17; essential areas of
    concern 27–9; example of
    Çatalhöyük 35–42; excavations in
    1980s 18; investigation of ideas
    and things 29–31; rescue and
    salvage contexts 35, *see also*
    fieldwork
resources: of complex societies 94;
    exploitation of Mesopotamia in
    Liverani's AD 2084 vision 189;
    imbalance between Lower
    Mesopotamian heartlands and
    outside world 149–50; Postgate's
    chart of city/village interactions
    184; poverty of Uruk heartland
    114; urban/rural interaction 183
Rich, Claudius 3
Rindos, David 74
ritual *see* cult and ritual
Riyadh 200
roads: Roman and Persian 143
Roaf, Michael 66, 170–1, 181
Roman empire 134, 194; and
    Mesopotamia as term 5, 6; study of
    in upper secondary education 196
Romano-Byzantines 41
Rosenberg, Michael 84
Rothman, Mitchell 99, 121
Rowley-Conwy, P.A. 85–6
Rowton, Michael 186, 188
royal inscriptions 141

rural areas: archaeologists' neglect of
    158; and development of complex
    societies 100; Liverani's vision of
    the year 2084 189; new
    appreciation of significance of
    185, *see also* urban/rural flux and
    interaction; villages

Sabi Abyad 98
Safar, Fuad 16
Said, Edward 7
Sakheri Sughir 183
salvage archaeology *see* rescue or
    salvage archaeology
Samarra 16, 65, 123; imperial
    racecourse 139, **140**; on map of
    Mesopotamian sites **2**
sampling 43, 54–5
Samsat 5
Sargon II 136
Sarzec, Ernest de: long-term
    excavations at Telloh 10–11, **10**
SAS (Special Air Service) 198
Sasanian period: Diyala region 52
Sasson, Jack 191
satellite imagery 54, 55, 160
satrapies: of Median and Persian
    empires 148
Sawwan **2**, 17, 65
Schmidt, K. 90
schools *see* educational system
science of culture 4, 20
sciences: development of 29
sculpture: Uruk-Warka 111, *see also*
    relief sculptures
seals and sealings 65, 66, 98, 119,
    149, 162, 166; recovered from
    Uruk-period sites 108, 110,
    113–14, 115, *see also* cylinder seals
seasonality: increase in due to climate
    changes 71–2; rural/urban
    concerns 185, 186; study of Abu
    Hurerya 77; transmutation to
    sedentism 28
Second World War 16, 197, 198, 202
sedentism: cult and ritual as element
    of 90–1; first settlements in early
    Holocene 93; occupants of Hallan

Çemi 82; prior to development of agriculture 89–90; shift to 28, 72, 73–4, 78–9, 89, 198
sediments: analysis of 39, 70–1, 175
seeds 25, 77
Seleucia 18
Seleucid empire 124
Sennacherib 134
settlement archaeology 48–9
settlement hierarchy 95, 96, 110, 111, 113, 137–8
settlement patterns: Adams' work 51–2, 53–4, 54–5, 64; Algaze's theory 117–18; anthropological archaeology 57; Çatalhöyük site 38–40; culture history method 21; early Holocene pre-agricultural sedentism 89–90; in imperial context 144, 150–1, 152; smaller settlements 168; surveying for 48–9; urban residence 172
Shanidar **2**, 17
Shanks, M. 202
Shatt al-'Arab 9
sheep: domestication of 80, 82, 85–6; herding strategies gleaned from texts 185; hunting of 84
Sheikh Hamad 9
shell: deposits 174
Sherqatis 12
Shimshara 17
shrines 179
Sin-iddinam of Larsa 160
single context planning system 43
Sinjar region 49, 51
Sinopoli, Carla M. 128, 134
Sippar 5, 9, 157–8, 158
skeletal remains 17, 78, 156, *see also* animal bones
slaves 118, 145
Smith, George 9
Smith, M.E. 127, 132, 134
Snell, Daniel 170
social actors 179
social anthropology: Postgate's perspective 163
social changes: and domestication of plants 78–9; early Neolithic 92; and rise of complex societies 100, 117
social complexity 94–6; approaches to study of 96–102, 178, 185; Ubaid period 102–8; Uruk phenomenon 108–26, *see also* complex societies
social facts 30
social identity: Wattenmaker's study of domestic households 178–9
social relations and interactions: asymmetry 122, 141; construction from physical culture 30, 31; elements affecting food production and sedentism 90; evidence of Ubaid pottery 107; practices at Abu Duwari site 162; recent approaches to urban context 179, 180
social reproduction: feminist archaeology 25–6
social stratification 95, 106, 108, 138
societies: archaeological interpretation by analogy 124; Giddens' observations 29–30, 155; increasing emphasis on role of 94; role of material culture 179–80; and study of household 169, *see also* complex societies
sociology: research on material culture 30
socio-political entities 93–4, *see also* political entities
socio-political organisation: pottery as evidence 107, 108
soil samples 43
Solecki, Ralph and Rose 17
al-Soof, Behnam Abu 17
Sotto 17
Southwest Asia: Binford's theory of post-Pleistocene population 72–3; change from hunting and gathering to farming 68–9, 76–7, 89–92; chronological sequence of animal domestication 80–1; current practice of archaeology 27, 35; need for consolidation of survey data 55; need to involve host countries in future work 199–202; origins of seasonal

climate 72; specialisation in archaeology of 190; use of term 6, *see also* under place-names and regions
Soviet archaeologists: work on Jazirah 17
Spanish empire 150
spatial boundaries: method of culture history 20–1
spatial patterns: Abu Salabikh 166–7, 172, 175–6; reconstruction of social space 193; studies of houses and households 167–8, 176, 179, 180
spices 145
stamp seals 21, 104
the state: development of 29, 198; and the tribe 186
states: Algaze's Uruk expansion model 115–16; development of 93, 94, 95, 100–1, **101**, 102; newly created after First World War 14; study of 97, 100, 131; Uruk period 108–9
statistics: and data analysis 23, 48, 66, 183
statues 5, 11
Stein, Gil: approach to complexity 99, 100, 101, 123, 123–5; attempt to repudiate Algaze's theory 121–2; on ideologies and material culture 59, 120; study of production at Tell Leilan 145; study of Ubaid-period temples 105, 107; work at Hacınebi Tepe 119–20, 122
Steinkeller, Piotr 115, 116, 121, 125, 150
Stela of the Vultures 11
Steward, Julian 96–7
Stol, Marten 156
Stone, Elizabeth 61–3, 168, 172; work at Maškan-šapir 159–63, 172
stone reliefs *see* relief sculptures
stratification 32, 65, 66
stratigraphy 23, 65, *see also* deep stratigraphic sounding
Strika, Vincenzo 4
Sumer 115, 197, 198; in National Curriculum for history 194, 194–5, 195
Sumerian sites: early archaeological

work 12, 14–15; 'Sumerian question' 15, *see also* under place-names and regions
surface planning 40–1; Abu Duwari site 160; Abu Salabikh 164; Çatalhöyük site 41–2, **42**
Surghul 12
Šuruppak 12, 163
survey 27, 47–55; Algaze's work in southeast Anatolia 114; considerations for future 55; map of regions **48**; programmes at Uruk-Warka 110, 111–12, 114; projects on Lower Mesopotamian plains 17, 50–5, 115; regional work 39, 183; rigorous work conducted in Turkey 55, **56**; time-depth of periods 51
Susa **2**, 102, 107, 134, 135, 146
Susiana plain 107, 108, 115, 123, 148–9
symbolic structure: Hodder's study of early agriculture 91–2
symbolism: Cauvin's study of early Neolithic 91; research at Çatahöyük 37, 46
Syria: archaeologists in 1930s 16; civil engineering projects 17; domestication of plants 76; Heinz's study of settlements 168; and Mesopotamia as term 5; Rassam's excavations 9; recent projects 34, 35, 198; regions surveyed **48**; survey and rescue work in 1980s 18; Wheeler's tour of excavations 32, *see also* under place-names and regions

Taagepera, Rein: comparative study of empires 127, 132–3, 143, 147–9, 193
al-Tabari 4
tablets 11, 61, 115, 116, 118–19, *see also* clay tablets; cuneiform tablets
Tal-e Malyan (ancient Ansan) 186
Taylor J.E. 8
teaching *see* educational system
technological innovation: imperial contexts 138, 148–9

technologies: complex societies 105–6, 117
television programmes: on archaeology 195–6
tell (mound) 40, 49, 189
Tell Abada 102
Tell Agrab 15
Tell Asmar 15, 151, 167–8
Tell Boueid 98
Tell Harmal l68
Tell Leilan 145, 198
Tell el-'Oueili 102, 198
Tell Sheikh Hassan 109, 118
Tell Sifr 8
Tell Taya 151
Tell al-Ubaid 14, 102
Tell Uqair 16
Telloh **2**, 5, 9, 12; French long-term excavations 10–11, **10**, 15, 33
Telul eth-Thalathat 17
temples: complex societies 96, 102; cultural material from Abu Salabikh 166; German finds at Uruk-Warka 15; imperial cities 134, 135, 136; Koldewey's discoveries at Babylon 12; similarity of houses at Habuba Kabira 168; Ubaid period 102–5, **103**, **104**, *see also* Anu Ziggurat/White Temple complex
Tepe Gawra *see* Gawra
Tepe Sialk 118
Tepecik 118
textiles 104–5, 145, 178, 182
textual sources: as archaeological record 31–2, 171; and defining social complexity 94, 101; evidence found in Old Babylonian houses 178; small amounts from domestic contexts 158–9; strategies of pastoral nomads 186; studies in absence of 171–2; and study of empire 127, 128, 134, 138–9, 145, 153; urban/rural interaction 183; used to reconstruct 'history from above' 191, *see also* Assyriology; written texts

things: archaeological 30–1, *see also* objects
Thompson, Campbell 14
Tigris, River 4, 5, **18**, 66, 117, 118; dam construction and irrigation projects 17, 109; flood threat from dam to Aššur 135, 202–4; in Liverani's AD 2084 vision 189
Tilley, C. 202
Time Team (TV programme) 195–6
tombs 96, 105
tools: necessary for mud-brick excavations 44; stone 78, 88; study of in social context 178, 181
topographic archaeology: Adams' research 50, 52; Hole's maps in work on pastoralism 187
Toprakkale 9
trade: concerns of common people 156; practices at Abu Duwari site 162; Uruk societies 114, 115, 118, 119, 120; within complex hunter-gatherer communities 91
trade diasporas: Stein's models 122, 125
Tringham, Ruth 20, 179–80, 190
Tula empire (central Mexico) 127
Tula'i (Khuzistan) 187
Turkestan *see* Anau
Turkey: area of Hittite empire 146; civil engineering projects 17; domestication of plants 76; and Mesopotamia as term 5; modern mosque-building 111; programme of diachronic study 204; Rassam's excavations 9, 10; recent field projects 34, 35; regions surveyed **48**; rigorous surveys currently conducted 55, **56**; survey and rescue work in 1980s 18, *see also* under place-names and regions
Turkish Directorate General of Monuments and Museums 33–4
typology: ceramic 12; and construction of chronological framework 65, 66, 106; of human society (step typology) 97

Ubaid period 16, 65, 101, 102–8, 122–3, 170–1, 181
Uerpmann, Hans-Peter 80
Umm Dabaghiyah **2**, 17, 35; domestication of onagers 80, 86–8; plan of levels 3–4 **87**; wall-painting **87**
United Kingdom (UK): funding of research 28; state of education about Near East 197, *see also* British archaeologists; British Museum
United Nations (UN) 202
United States of America *see* American archaeologists; North America
universities: lack of students with knowledge of Near East 197
Ur **2**, 157–8, 158, 183; ancient excavations 5; archaeological investigations from mid-nineteenth century 8; Brusacso's study of Old Babylonian houses 176–8; as centre of empire 134, 135, 144; as cultic centre 115; establishment of chronological sequence 65; ideology of Ur III kings 141; later Ubaid period 102; of the Chaldees 14–15, 24; Old Babylonian 61; Postgate's work on urban space 166; seventeenth-century excavations 1; soundings by Thompson 14; trade with Arabian Gulf 146; Ur III empire 138–9, 145, 146, 149, 150, 186; Ur III temple of Inanna at Nippur 63
Urartu: empire 147
urban settlement and development: Adams' work 52, 53–4, 114
urban/rural flux and interaction 48, 138, 172, 182–8
urbanism and urbanisation 29, 99, 157, 182, 198, *see also* cities
urbanocentrism: approaches to Mesopotamian past 184–5
Uruk period 16, 65, 66, 99, 101, 102, 108, 115, 116, 146, 157, 163, 182

Uruk 'phenomenon' 104, 108–26, 132, 148, 148–9, 149, 150, 168
Uruk-Warka (biblical Erech) **2**, 15, 103–4, 122, 182; Adams' research 53–4, 113, 114; city structures **111**; and 'Uruk phenonemon' 109–26, 149

Van 9, 10
Van de Mieroop, Marc 57, 59, 60, 100, 142, 156, 156–7, 176, 190–1
Vikings 194
villages: Braidwood's work on origins and development of 24, 28; issues of material culture 55; Wright's study of Sakheri Sughir 183, *see also* rural areas
virtual reality: tours round ancient buildings 193
von Dassow, E. 575

Wahida, Ghanim 17
wall-paintings 37, 86, **87**, 136
Wallerstein, I. 117
walls: city of Abu Duwari 160; city at Abu Salabikh 164, **164**, 166; city of Dur-Sarrukin 136, 139; defence of empire 146; enclosure 48
Wari empire (Peru) 127
Warka: archaeological investigations from mid-nineteenth century 8, *see also* Uruk-Warka
wars *see* ethnic conflicts; First World War; Gulf War; Second World War
Wasit: work of Iraqi archaeologists 16
water transport: development of social complexity 117
waterways: traces 160
Watson, Patty Jo 23, 74, 123
Wattenmaker, Patricia 169–70, 178–9
wealth: attested by Gawra tombs 105; hoarding of 151–2
Weber, Max 91
websites 192, 193, 194, 195, 196
Weiss, H. 149, 153
Western archaeology and archaeologists: early loot-grabbing

6–7; ignorance of Arabic achievements 3–4; intentions of nineteenth-century pioneers 7–8; need to involve host country communities 199–202; scientific tradition 47, 199

Western Asia: Arabic achievements 3–4; modern nomads 188; use of term 6

Western attitudes: bias against Middle East in education 193; towards Iraq's archaeological heritage 198

Western education *see* educational system

Western powers: involvement with Mesopotamia 1, 5

wetland sites: recovery of organic materials 31

Wheeler, Margaret 192

Wheeler, Mortimer 32, 33, 47, 192

White, Leslie 96–7

White Temple complex *see* Anu Ziggurat/White Temple complex

Whittle, Alasdair 91

Winter, Irene 5

women: Neolithic gender division of labour at Abu Hureyra 78; writing on fieldwork in mid-twentieth century 192

Woolley, Leonard 14–15, 16, 61

world systems theory 117–18, 121–2, 125

worship: activities at Abu Duwari site 162

Wright, H.E. 71–2

Wright, Henry 29, 93, 98, 126, 183

writing: early development in Mesopotamia and Elam 121; evidence at Uruk-Warka 113, 114, 116; pictographic 118; Proto-Elamite 148–9

written texts: as artefacts 61, 131; and cultural expectations 60; imperial contexts 142, 152–3, 156; and neglect of non-textual archaeology 58; recovered from Uruk-Warka 113; unreliability of 158–9; used by Zettler in Ur II temple study 63, *see also* Assyriology; epigraphy; textual sources

Wylie, Alison 124

Yarim Tepe 17

Yoffee, N. 50, 115, 141

Younger Dryas: changes in climate 71–2, 77

Zabbal, F. 200

Zagros mountains 15, 16, 28, 69, 70, 73, 82, 187

Zarzi 15, 69

Zawi Chemi Shanidar 89–90

Zeder, Melinda 81–2, 186

Zeribar, Lake 71

Zettler, Richard: study of Ur III temple of Inanna 63, 64

Zeuner, Frederik 81

ziggurats 12, 136, *see also* Anu Ziggurat/White Temple complex

zooarchaeology 79–80, 89, 186